The Common Millionaire

Robert Heller

**'It's no trick to make a lot of money, if
all you want is to make a lot of money'
- Mr Bernstein in *Citizen Kane***

CORONET BOOKS
Hodder and Stoughton

Printed and bound in Great Britain
for Coronet Books
Hodder and Stoughton, London
By C. Nicholls & Company Ltd
The Philips Park Press, Manchester

ISBN 0 340 20802 3

FOREWORD

This book sprang from an obsession, not with wealth as such, but with the contrast between its public and private faces. Journalism led me to the desks, sometimes into the homes, of men whose fame rested less on their achievements, which varied from the great to the disgraceful, than on the results of those deeds — the accumulation of either wealth or the appearance of wealth. Riches had changed all these men in different ways, some for the better, some for the worse. But their careers and behaviour, as they strutted their stages, the more I studied them, seemed to conform to some unwritten body of economic laws: and these laws are my subject.

Like other legal systems, this one has been modified by time: today's rich are different from yesterday's. But their names are often the same, and the sources of their fortunes similar, to those of the past. The first act in this theatre of wealth describes the inheritance, protection and preservation of such fortunes, including those of the aristocracy of money. The second act introduces shadier characters, because its theme is illusion: the practice of deceit, honest and otherwise. Whatever origins wealth has, however, big money tends to breed more millions still — and the theme of the third act is how the rich get richer.

The fourth act stresses the vital importance, in creating a lasting cornucopia, of waiting for it: of letting time get on your side. The fifth deals with the phenomenon which is usually only recognized in one form — the incidence of pure luck: but chance is not the only benefactor who thrusts wealth on the deserving and undeserving alike: there is, for instance, the government, any government. The final book includes many of my favourite millionaires — men who have persevered with the one genuine talent which marks them out from the rest of the world, and from which that world truly benefits.

There are four entr'actes or intermissions: cautionary tales. One describes the perilous divide between excessive conservatism and over-zealous change: the second the penalties of lack

7

of concentration: another the meaning of minginess and the hazard of uncontrol: a fourth the dangers of gluttony. It is often only when the rich man has been incautious that the private and public images suddenly coincide and the reality emerges. That reality is that riches and true human achievement bear only a tenuous relationship to each other: but that, if only you are rich enough, nobody will ever notice the truth.

I owe a special debt of gratitude to Felicity Krish, an invaluable assistant in every way; to Jeanne Bernkopf for her admirable editing; to Ross Claiborne (also of Delacorte) and Hilary Rubinstein for unfailing support and ideas; others who have helped me directly and indirectly, including my excellent colleagues on *Management Today*; Simon Dally at Weidenfeld & Nicolson; John Thackray; and the authors of the works quoted in the bibliography. Anthony Bambridge and John Davis of *The Observer* have both enlightened me and published my articles, some of whose material is incorporated in these pages. But this book is above all dedicated to my children, for making it all worthwhile.

The Rich are Different

Containing as much of the secrets of making money as is
necessary or proper to acquaint the reader with at the
beginning of this history of the Common Millionaire.

Making a million is easier than it used to be; and it never was
very hard – which is why the trick has been managed down the
ages by so many entrants extracted from the ranks of the
untalented, the uninspired, and the forgettable. In this age,
however, thanks to the blessings of inflation, the points total
for winning players, while seemingly the same, is far lower. It's
as if, in the game of financial football, the goal had been
widened almost to the full extent of the pitch.

To match a million in the dollars of 1914, when a world war
ended the golden age of plutocracy, would require $4.8 million
today. A million in 1928, before a cataclysmic depression
robbed some silver age plutocrats of their riches, is the
equivalent nowadays of $3.2 million. A million in 1948, when
the rebuilders of the post-war economy began to reap their
rewards, equals $2.2 million in the currency of the early 1970s
– a time-stop which is deep in a new era, the Age of the
Common Millionaire.

To look at the inflationary process the other way round, a
1970s million in pounds represents only £378,000 in 1948
money, £210,000 in 1928 and a little nest-egg of £117,000 in
1914. If the counting is in dollars, the true score in 1914
currency becomes smaller still (a dollar millionaire in 1973
was roughly 60% poorer than one of the sterling variety and
used to be 80% nearer to poverty). Inflation has not only
belittled the score, it has made scoring easier. The apparent or
monetary value of assets has steadily risen, so that a man
buying any treasure, from a cider press to a car plant, has an
overwhelming chance of reselling at a profit, which is the basic
activity of every Croesus who ever cashed a cheque.

The rackets of the rich cover a range of real-life fairy tales that even Scheherazade, given another thousand and one nights, could not exhaust. Ballpoint pens, ball-bearings, demolition, construction, shipbuilding, shipowning, broking, breaking, farming, not farming, molybdenum, milling, holes in the ground, filling holes in the ground, stealing, borrowing, lending, foreclosing, carpets, convertibles, soup, soupcans, pictures of soupcans, salad oil, non-existent salad oil, betting, taking bets, extortion, exemption, Chinese money, Chinese food – the catalogue rolls on endlessly and with as much variation as the names and backgrounds of the blessed.

It's not exactly a roll of honour; nearer, somewhat, to a roll of dishonour, since, in a significant bevy of cases the basic wealth-creating activity has been augmented, if not by fraud, by tricks, devices, stratagems; all variants of the conjurer's game of doing it with mirrors. The basic activity, however, never changes. The millionaire earns his title by selling, or being able to sell, some property, some product, some service, some idea, for more than cost. The wider the gulf between cost and realized value, the more rapidly the player gets to his ultimate reward. There have always been the two invariable extremes of technique. The player can choose between selling to a myriad customers at low profits (ten million customers at a dime apiece) or to a select clientèle at high profits (ten suckers at $100,000 a throw). But in the golden and silver ages, the resultant wealth was measured certifiably in cash, negotiable gilt-edged securities, and real property, all of which took time to accumulate.

That measure was only natural in a time of low or no taxes, of minimal inheritance tax, and of a political dispensation which enshrined inequality. The truly kingly fortunes all stem from this golden age – the Rockefellers (put at five US billions today), and the Rothschilds (weighed in collectively at a hundred billion): the Du Ponts (worth over seven and a half billion in the mid 1960s), and the Mellons (supposedly neck-and-neck with the Rockies, thanks to heavy holdings in the Mellon National Bank, Gulf Oil, Alcoa, *et al*).

No calculations have been made of the proportion of the world's wealth which, right here and now, is held by the three hundred richest families. Their share is plainly that of a particularly voracious lion. The combined total of the outstanding US nest-eggs mentioned in this chapter alone –

Mellons, Du Ponts, Rockefellers, Getty, Rosenwald, Land, Hughes, Mayer — must handsomely exceed $20,000 million. That is equal to about the total end-1972 market worth of General Motors — and there is, of course, always the chance that these mighty aggregations, which are only the chapter headings, so to speak, in the golden book of international wealth, are under, not over-estimated. In most cases, if the concept of a man's wealth is widened to include all assets which he can enjoy exclusively, all business interests which he can influence while holding only a proportion (or none) of the shares, he emerges as richer by far than even an expert optimist can guess.

Land probably still constitutes or lies behind and beneath many of the greatest fortunes — although aristocrats, because of their touching faith in primogeniture and distrust of new-fangled financial devices, have often frittered away their wealth in estate taxes. The Duke of Westminster, who died in 1953, bequeathed a tax liability of from £15 million to £20 million. That this bill could be met, without touching 270 acres in two fashionable little villages, Belgravia and Mayfair, is some measure of the mighty iceberg of aristocratic fortunes.

The predominance of such imperial old-line families led one careful researcher, Ferdinand Lundberg, to conclude that "there is less and less room for new millionaires". But an old-new billionaire contradicted him. "Large fortunes will be made," wrote J. P. Getty, "in the next two decades by men who are beginners today." As usual in money matters the thinker was wrong, the Midas right.

In 1973 a minor British retailer of Iraqi extraction, one Albert Gubay, created a headline sensation by skipping the country with the proceeds from selling shares in his discount grocery chain. Gubay, while cashing in £7.4 million worth only recently, had sworn solemnly to keep his remaining £4 million stake as a long-term investment; in fact, he off-loaded the latter shares on the quiet, making a total cash take of possibly £14 million from all his sales. He had only been in business for a decade. He operated only thirty-eight stores around Wales and its borders. Had Gubay never existed, neither the GNP nor the general welfare would have been affected one whit. Yet this one small grocer's snatch leaves any salary in the world limping.

Very few men, no matter how distinguished, powerful or valuable, earn £100,000 a year. To match the egregious Gubay, even before tax, they would have to labour for 140 years, or more than three working lifetimes. To match his joys after tax, the figures should probably be doubled, and that takes no account of the interest on Gubay's dollop of dubious reward – and the annual interest would also handily exceed £100,000.

The aristo-plutocrats – Astors (now in the seventh generation), Mellons, Rockefellers, Thyssens, Agnellis – may stay atop some lofty, reserved Olympus. But on the lower slopes (and not so much further down) a new and different breed has been climbing fast, propelled in part by the natural force of mass. The millionaire gets rich by creaming off part of the general pool of wealth. The deeper and wider the pool, the smaller the amount of skimming required to fill the same size money pot.

Thanks to the sheer abundance of natural resources and stupendously lax political control, the USA has spawned the bulk of the world's millionaires, from the gold and silver kings to the stock-option fat-cats of today. Between 1914 and 1972 the gross national product of the USA – the annual stream of real wealth – has multiplied nearly four and three-quarter times. With no benefit of inflation, in real terms, $100 million in 1914 currency was 0.2% of the US GNP, whereas in 1972, measured in 1914 dollars, it was only 0.04%. Despite all the supposed efforts of politicians to curb and spread the wealth, the share of property and income held by the few has, according to several studies, remained more or less constant. Possibly there is some natural law, like that of water finding its own level, which constantly forces a given ratio of the national income into the hands of those who already have more than their *per capita* share or are burning to do so.

But the simple, mathematical growth of the pool of wealth is only the start of the story. Equally important has been the discovery of the modern philosopher's stone, the authentic way of creating thick wealth out of thin air.

An heir to many millions and creator of a fair few himself once observed that in talking about modern fortunes, people "confused wealth and money". He was, it turns out, distinguishing between the wealths of the mint and of the mind, but his remark holds the key to the Age of the Common

12

Millionaire. For the Common Millionaire has succeeded in divorcing real wealth – property, the creation of new resources – from money.

In the first Rockefeller's day, to create money, you had to create an equivalent amount of assets. True, Wall Street in those days had no hesitation about multiplying such real objects by unreal accretions of paper, a pastime known agriculturally as "watering the stock". J. Pierpont Morgan in 1901 poured forth "securities" (an interesting euphemism in the circumstances) to a face-value of over a billion dollars in launching US Steel on a gullible world. On the official count he printed $726.8 million more in paper than the company, in visible material form, was worth. In 1929 and by similar zealous work at the printing press Goldman Sachs issued one quarter of a billion in securities in a mere month. Even today, the most ambitious and hot-handed financier in Manhattan would blanch at this Everest of paper.

But the day of the old pirate has gone; now is the time of the new piranha. His sharp-toothed discovery is that the wealth represented by real assets, or by no assets at all, can still be transmogrified by the paper multiplier, only with perfect legality.

The new open sesame to Aladdin's cave is the phrase "discounting of growth". The Common Millionaire sells, not what he owns, but what (God willing) he *will* own one fine day. The buyers purchase, not today, but a tomorrow that sometimes never comes. The cardinal invention of capitalism, the joint stock company, was carried in the 1960s to what may be its final form, an engine for the creation of endless wealth unsupported by any concrete foundation.

Under this newest of dispensations, the company promoter doesn't have to water stock: the public dilutes it for him. Suiting the technique to the times, the piranha promoter doesn't issue vastly excessive quantities of the same paper but instead issues shares which are not shares (warrants, convertibles, letter stocks, etc.) in the promise that by the time they become real live equity, the real values will have caught up.

The Age of the Common Millionaire made possible, with perfect honesty, a trick of which J. P. Morgan himself would have been proud. In the more extreme cases, a man could sell an overjoyed public a fraction of his shares for a price which, on a traditional basis of valuation, would purchase the entire

13

caboose. He would retain total control of the company through paper, valued at several times the cash fortune now safely in his pocket, which could be used as currency to purchase more assets, to which a similar multiplier could be applied, and so on, not quite *ad infinitum*.

In actuality, such operations reverse the historic process of capitalism. Instead of the equity holder taking all the risk, and consequently all the rewards, he now partly off-loads his risk for the highest price the market will bear and takes his reward in advance.

Bear traps a-plenty lie along such paths. But the essential truth remains unchanged. The market capitalization of major companies has risen to such unthinkably large sums that possession of a tithe of a tithe of the stock equals a monumental fortune, even by Morgan standards. At the end of 1972 there were 161 US companies, ranging from IBM ($468 million) to Merrill Lynch, where a 1% holding was worth $10 million, and 339 more, from Dun and Bradstreet ($9.9 million) to McCormick, where a similar stake produced a clear $3.3 million.

Market capitalization, however, is an entirely hypothetical figure obtained by multiplying the number of shares in issue, only a small proportion of which are actually on the loose, by the market price of the day; that, of course, would drop like a quarry full of stones if even a quarter of the shares came on offer.

But 1% of Shell Transport and Trading in early 1973 was still notionally worth some £18 million: and the Samuel family, heirs to the founder who spotted that selling kerosene was a better deal than flogging sea-shells, presumably have many of those percentage points. The family holding of Julius Rosenwald, the clever merchant who made Sears Roebuck the world's richest retailer, was put at $12\frac{1}{2}\%$: if still intact at the end of 1972, years after Rosenwald's death, that modest-sounding stake was in theory worth over two billions as the 1970s unfolded.

The rich today can thus achieve via the stock market the condition which their predecessors contrived by paying no tax: the combination of massive real assets with maximum personal liquidity. To put it crudely, you can't take your cash out in income, because the government grabs it: so you take the booty in stock, which the government touches either lightly

14

or not at all. It's a sweet paradox. The efforts of governments to restore equality by soaking the rich have led directly to the development of methods which have created far more rich — and efforts to inundate these with taxes will probably make still more millionaires.

And the rich today *are* different. Not just because (as Hemingway correctly argued against Scott Fitzgerald) they have more money: but because they are a different breed of furry cat. The millionaires and billionaires of the golden age were would-be princes. Deprived by fate of royal stature, they out-spent those who had it. In the mid-1960s it was noted with astonishment that one spectacularly successful Texas oilman, Algur H. Meadows, with $55 million to his name, had shelled out only half a million on his dream-house, less than the first Rockefeller, most parsimonious of all the millionaires, spent in a single year on the upkeep of one family estate, his $30 million, 7,000 acre Tarrytown pad.

The Common Millionaire lives in the same way as the good bourgeois citizen, only more so — and even the Common Billionaire may do much the same. J. P. Getty bought his splendid mansion, Sutton Place, from the third Duke of Sutherland for a supposed half-million in sterling. A Vanderbilt would have regarded that kind of money as a decorator's bill (Cornelius spent $5 million on a Newport cottage which he only used for ten weeks a year). Almost the only lavish similarity between the ultra-rich of the golden and silver ages is the passion for paying great prices for art: even then, demand for a greatly diminished supply of Old Masters waned so markedly that it took over a generation before the Duveen prices charged to the earlier merchant princes were seen again — and that was in depreciated money. *The Mall in St James's Park* by Gainsborough cost Frick $300,000: the same artist's *Mr and Mrs Andrews*, at 1973 exchange rates fetched only $357,000.

Mostly, today's new millionaires come from the amorphous mass of the middle classes and bear the stamp of their origin. Even the titled exceptions start about their millions in a down-to-earth or déclassé way. Baron Marcel Bich, for example, is a French aristo whose cash in hand of over $40 million was accumulated on the humble base of the disposable ballpoint pen. Bich launched this after the war on $1,000. From sales of 1,500 million Bic pens a year, the good Baron in

1971 gleaned $10 million of profit (which comes to .0066666 cents per Bic and is thus a perfect example of the multitudinous small profit approach).

The foresight of the rich is their prime justification. Although nearly all owners of big, middling and small money owe much of it to multiplication by mirrors, many derived their riches originally from some flash of true inspiration, the equivalent in the material world of Nijinsky's leap, Picasso's Cubism, Proust's memory; Land's instant camera, Getty's Kuwait oil, even Bich's ballpoints represent breakthroughs from which millions of people have had real benefit, and from which, therefore, millions in currency have naturally flowed.

The breakthrough, the searing stroke of genius, lies in spotting a demand, latent or blatant, and simultaneously noting how that demand can be satisfied at the necessary premium over the cost of supply. Characters like David Sarnoff, the genius of RCA, are in this sense great philosophers and artists: and very few artists or thinkers in other spheres can boast a dramatic series of achievements to excel Sarnoff's treble.

In 1916, almost alone in his faith, Sarnoff wrote, "I have in mind a plan of development which would make radio a household utility": in 1922–25 sales of his "radio music boxes" came to $83 million. In 1923, he wrote "I believe that television ... will come to pass in due course", a belief that cost him $50 million before a pay-off of incalculable size. He then pumped another $130 million into his final bonanza, colour TV. Although Sarnoff laid one large egg — correctly seeing that computers would boom, but incorrectly assessing RCA's chances in this unfamiliar, booby-trapped market — verily he earned his reward.

Whether the return is proportionate to the contribution is another matter. In the overpowering majority of cases, there can't be any argument. The balance between capital and income has been tilted grossly in favour of capital: and the capital gains of the cut-price variety of capitalist often bear only the slightest relation to the social or even economic value of their work.

In the Age of the Common Millionaire, the possession of fifty millions as opposed to five hundred of them has a primarily social connotation. The billionaire is an uncrowned monarch: the multimillionaire is a global potentate: even the

Common Millionaire is a welcome, highly-placed courtier (like Bebe Rebozo at the court of Richard Nixon), and a potential folk-hero. At each of these three levels, there is a common denominator: the affirmation by the rich that money means nothing to them. They are telling the truth and lying in their Sulka socks at one and the same time, because the possession of money bestows the ineffable power to make more money still; and power, for most of the rich, is the name of their game.

All wealth equates with power, which has as many forms as there are Rolls-Royces. To Andrew Carnegie, once he was through with giving steel rivals and steelworkers hell, wealth equated with the power to establish free public libraries: to George Armstrong, a Southern millionaire, wealth meant the ability to offer a staggering sum to a small military college in Mississippi if, in its curriculum, it stressed the racial superiority of the white man (the college, to its undying credit, refused): to a legion of rich men, it means the power, free of any fear of the sack, boot, or axe, to dominate the corporations which they have created.

Antony Jay, the management writer, once asked a tycoon wherein lay his own contribution, given all the brilliant and forceful men in his employ. "I'll tell you" said the Croesus, "I own 67.5%."

But for the mass of millionaires, the loot is a by-product of achieving some other end, although the objective and its results get mysteriously intertwined. That doesn't matter: the clue is still that the budding Baruch or Bluhdorn has to decide what he wants. That is the first step along the yellow-brick road, and most businessmen – 9,999 out of 10,000 – never get even that far. But lack of focused intention, of truly moving motivation, is only part of the story. While nearly everybody vaguely "wants" a million, few are prepared to work for it. Lack of knack is equally crippling. Tall Texan stories abound of the brilliant men who drilled on land known to be stiff with oil, but found nothing but dry holes.

There are hundreds of millionaires who have only one gift – making money. In this they resemble the master chess player who is good at nothing else. Making money resembles chess in other ways, not least in its cosy relationship with mathematics, still more in its abundance of traps, ploys, gambits, stratagems, variations, even its recognized offensive and defensive openings. As in chess, the money maker gains more through his opponent's mistakes than through his own immaculate brilliance: and for every winner there must be at least one loser.

The First Law of Millions states that "every millionaire creates his wealth at somebody else's expense", and it is this law which the new techniques for divorcing capital from income and taxes have exploited to such wondrous effect. The sale of shares to the public to guard against estate taxes or whatever, has almost inadvertently created a new dimension of wealth: it has enlarged the number of those whose finances can be tapped by the resourceful few.

As long ago as 1968, the Internal Revenue Service calculated that the total of US millionaires, having risen by 150% in a decade, had passed a hundred thousand. One downy investment banker, sitting on nest-eggs belonging to some of the choicest US clients, remarked that, for all his experience, he was constantly amazed by the number of unknown, substantial private fortunes: lump sums that lie forever protected in the giant investment portfolios of the banks (Morgan Guaranty, the champion in this arena, looks after $27,000 million, not counting real estate): great lumps which often lie, silently sleeping and fructifying in their sleep, behind the anonymous nameplates in which banks rejoice.

Trusts and nominee (or dummy) companies are two of the more obvious ways in which the wealthy can squirrel their wealth away from view (and sometimes from their nearest and dearest). There are doubtless banks in the USA still storing cash – reportedly a million belonging to the bank-hating W. C. Fields, under names like Mahata Kane Jeeves and Otis Criblecoblis. Fields had hundreds of bank books and once claimed to have $50,000 in wartime Germany "in case that little bastard wins". For the same reason, many of the war rich put their money in Switzerland: and here, too, some of the famous numbered accounts doubtless contain wealth whose identification has passed into the grave.

Many of these rich, old or *nouveau*, have no more knowledge of three-dimensional monetary chess than the novice player – although the moves may be played for them brilliantly by some well-rewarded functionary. The novice, however, must make the moves himself, and knowledge of them is not enough to turn the graduate into a grandmaster. He needs, like a supreme player of real chess, an extra and indefinable quality

18

which, in making money, manifests itself in different forms: as luck, as timing, as genius, as ruthlessness, as insight, as opportunism, as stubbornness. But increasingly, in the Age of the Common Millionaire, that star distinction has achieved a more common form: common craft. Which means that, even for assiduous evaders of millions, knowledge of the rules and the gambits is essential, not for self-enrichment, but for self-protection.

On the Permanence of Money
or
You Can Take it With You

SCENE 1

THE VIRTUES OF INHERITANCE

or

Nothing Licks a Silver Spoon

A fortunate accident which befell Mellons, Du Ponts, Rockefellers, Gettys, Hughes and countless others at the moment of birth. The eccentric behaviour of Sir Winston Churchill, with some proper animadversions on compound interest.

In the USA the lone eagle Howard Hughes and the flock of Du Ponts represent two styles of inherited wealth as different in their ways as Greta Garbo and the Marx Brothers were in theirs. In Europe the financial powers cluster in tidy family groups: Peugeot and Michelin in France: Agnelli and Pirelli in Italy: Thyssen and Flick in Germany: Cowdray and Vestey in Britain: Rothschilds all over Europe (twenty-nine of fifty-eight weddings of the founding fathers' descendants united first cousins, which at least kept the money in the family): these are only odd summits of the vast, glistening mountain range of inherited wealth and power.

It's the simplest path to a million: inheriting the goods. Even in this age of people's capitalism, that is how most millionaires achieved their particular financial paradises – with the help of time and the magic of compound interest.

It works this way. By dint of luck, labour and loose laws, an ancestor in some mid-West Bible belt, or Midlands oasis, put together a million in 1920 when a dollar was a dollar, a pound was a pound and a mark was a bad joke. It has never been especially difficult to achieve 7% growth tax-free, which doubles your money every ten years, quadruples it every twenty, octuples it every thirty, multiplies it by sixteen in forty years, and in half a century turns that million into thirty-two millions. You have to be especially inspired in your choice of investment or adviser (and remember with a million you can afford advice) to do worse, although it's not impossible.

Sir Winston Churchill seems to have managed this discouraging feat. His Boer War escapades, journalism and American lectures netted him £10,000 in his very early manhood. The young Churchill, who had a shrewder eye for the main chance than for money, entrusted the lot to Sir Ernest Cassel, an old family friend. That was his first mistake. The fact that somebody was on dining, golfing or even advising terms with your parents is no qualification for employing him to mind your own money or (as Churchill put it in his instructions to Cassel) to "feed my sheep". Churchill himself ruefully admits that in a few years all the sheep had been roasted and devoured. Had the capital been preserved intact and grown by only 8% per annum, Churchill would have died worth £1.3 million from that single source.

To revert to the lucky scion of a 1920s millionaire: if he survived his parent for fifty years, secured his 7% growth and spent only the income – he would then, from a starting point of a nice, steady rich income in the Roaring Twenties, now be pulling down 7,000 pounds or dollars a day for doing precisely nothing and he would be in a position to make thirty-two further millionaires out of his lucky heirs. This story glosses over painful subjects like the Great Depression, inheritance taxes and tax in general. But if the million was safely locked up in a sound private business with good marketing connections and tolerable growth (as many, many family millions were), the scenario is perfectly credible.

Some sagas far exceed this fictional rendering in their true fantasy. Clarence B. Mott, for instance, was a successful wheel and axle manufacturer in the days long before the motor industry had spawned its mega-millions. He sold his business to the infant General Motors for a parcel of shares in 1913. While Mott continued to labour sagely and well in the vineyard of the great corporation, the shares worked for him to so gratifying an extent – their total reached two and a half million – that the Mott fortune, in the old man's nineties (he died at ninety-seven in 1973), was valued at some $800 million.

Great Depression or no, GM shares have fructified in a way which is characteristic of the huge concerns born in the age of affluence before the First World War. A few years back, a

London stockjobber sold, to his pride, a £1.5 million line of shares in Shell Transport for a Scottish broker. Later he met the Scot, who told him their origin. Back in 1910, a canny father had left his sons £10,000. The jobber had just off-loaded the holding of one son.

Many sizeable fortunes have turned into great piles of shining gold by the same partly mathematical trick. Even a half-wit can reasonably hope to achieve the 7% magic. But suppose the lad is actually bright, or, still better, lucky. Merely doubling the compound growth rate to 14% turns a million into $32 million in only twenty-five years. In just forty years the family fortunes will stand at $250 million, a quarter of a billion.

No matter what happens to the value of money in the next four decades, no matter how intensively the family breeds, that sum will still spell great riches. It will yield, with no trouble at all, an income of $12½ million a year, and will grow at no less than $35 million annually. That mathematics explains how, despite heroic philanthropy, even on a Rockefeller scale, the surviving fortune is still enough to keep a large family in regal condition.

It also explains how vital philanthropy is simply to prevent the mushrooming of great private fortunes from undermining the economic foundations of the State. Indeed, the US government felt obliged to bring suit against one wealthy, dead eccentric, who left his fortune in perpetual trust: there his bread was to do nothing save breed compound interest, which would be ploughed back to breed still more interest, compounding in its turn: within a perfectly foreseeable period, the trust would have cornered all the liquid wealth in the USA ($100 million compounding at 10% ends up after a century at over $2,000,000 million, or roughly double today's American GNP). This lunatic scheme was not so far-out: in 1906 it was calculated that if John D. Rockefeller's wealth simply grew at the current rate of interest, he would own $90,000,000 million by 1936. The would-be mini-Rockefeller's trust was duly overthrown by the courts. But, more intelligently applied, geometric progression keeps personal fortunes marching on, seemingly forever.

There are, of course, several catches in this beneficent process. Fortunes can dissipate rapidly in the second generation, let alone the third and fourth, as family members (and the

25

proportion of incompetents and wastrels) also multiply geometrically. It can be taken almost for granted that the money won't be thrown away in some hare-brained manner, like actually paying the full inheritance taxes which the law lays down. But, for compounding to work its magic, reasonable time is required in the early stages. If the money has been made in business, and is still invested there, it is dangerous for the scions to abandon all interests save their own enjoyment.

In some cases, the managers of the good old family firm would gladly pay their heir a million a year to keep clear of the office. No doubt, the satraps minding the A & P (the Great Atlantic and Pacific Tea Company) supermarkets for all Huntington Hartford and the other heirs were worth, were delighted to see Hunt engaged in losing millions at a safe distance on wild projects for establishing Shangri-La on Hog Island or, single-handed, reversing the remorseless flood of modern art with a fretwork museum (since abandoned) on Columbus Circle in New York.

But A & P hasn't benefited in any obvious way from Hunt Hartford's abstinence. The greatness has fled, even if the Atlantic and Pacific remain. In the 1961–71 decade, the company's earnings per share declined by 9.4% *per annum*, a lapse which was entirely owed to its own incompetence. If the family owns a store, or a thousand stores, somebody in the family should mind it.

The management mafia at Du Pont likes to point out that Du Ponts play hardly any part in the company's affairs. Yet in 1973 there were three members of the family in the best observation place of all – the summit. Irenee Du Pont was a senior vice president, and a solid, dominating phalanx of Du Ponts sat on the finance committee, which is where they keep the money. (Apart from backsliders like Lammot du Pont Copeland Jr., who ran up one of the USA's bonanza bankruptcies, keeping the money is something at which Du Ponts have usually been good.)

Compounding, for this family, has taken $36,000, the cost of their original gunpowder plant on the Brandywine in 1802, to the estimated seven billions-plus of today. Even with a few hundred descendants putting their fingers in the pie – 632 of them sat down to celebrate the 150th anniversary – that leaves plenty of succulent slices all round. As a mathematical curiosity, $36,000 to the magic $7,000 million in 170 years is a compound growth of 7% a year, which accurately rubs in the truth that time is money.

The inheritor has alternatives to watching his pile from a close vantage point. He can manage the fortune directly himself: as, in one way or another, most heirs tend to do. Their fathers, powerful and puritanical about money (especially their own), inflict the work ethic on their children, imbue them in the business from early days and persuade them, without much difficulty, that, if you want to reach the top, the easiest way is to start there.

Wealthy descendants like the grocer Sainsburys or retailer Simon Marks in Britain, Hughes and Getty in the USA, or the Philips heirs in the Netherlands have developed their inheritances beyond the imaginative powers even of the family begetters. Yet folklore still has it that the rosiest path to managerial ruin is nepotism: that with each successive management generation the original impetus and talent gets progressively weaker, until it disappears, usually in disaster.

This theory is hard to square with the facts of companies like Sainsbury, led by one sound Sainsbury after another, or Pilkingtons, which led the world in the invention (on the premises) and exploitation of float glass, despite the handicap of having half-a-dozen other Pilkingtons on the premises; or S. C. Johnson, still literally waxing strong in Racine, Wisconsin on a dose of fourth generation management. When a British toy firm called Lines, once worth £17 million to its ruling family, dissolved into a worthless puddle, *The Guardian* newspaper observed smugly in the received manner that "second and third generation managements are not usually the best", and in truth it's hard not to sneer when somebody called Raymond C. Firestone is made chairman in a rubber company founded by somebody called Harvey S. Firestone – even if the press dutifully points out that Firestone Jr. "started work with the company in 1933 as a gas station attendant".

But such sneers are too facile, reminiscent of the cracks which Harold Wilson made at "the fourteenth Earl of Home" when the latter was elevated to Prime Minister: as Home reasonably replied, there was presumably a fourteenth Mr. Wilson. Everybody is second or third generation. The fact that pa or grandpa was a business genius doesn't mean that son or grandson must turn the former's silk purses into sow's ears.

In his *Up The Organisation* the arch anti-nepot Robert

Townsend points out that "Gerry Eskow succeeded his father as president of Yale Express in 1960. Five years later the company went bankrupt." This merely proves, not that son should never follow dad, but that Gerry Eskow should never have followed his progenitor. Non-family managements are just as capable of allowing events to drench their balance sheets.

For every weakness of family management there is an almost exact balance of strengths. Genetics is a bad management selection system, true; but you have to find managers somewhere – and the family does provide an immediate pool of men who should be deeply versed in, and deeply committed to, the business from birth. True, a non-family man of real talent will doubtless shy away from a company where his way to the top is barred or narrowed by birth; but the family provides a built-in focus of loyalty and continuity which can make even non-family managers work above their natural level.

True, the family develops a vested interest in the company as it was then, is now and ever shall be, a fondness which can prove fatal if events (as they must one day) overtake the formula: but on the other hand the family manager – being proprietor, shareholder and executive rolled into one – finds it easier to take the long view, while continuing to watch the short-term pennies (because they are his own).

Behind every failed family, moreover, there is a failed adviser – or an adviser who wasn't heeded, which amounts to the same thing. Bankers, accountants and other well-paid courtiers were close to the Eskow elbow, as they were to the Lines toy family. The performance of the managing (or non-managing) kin, moreover, was sustained by the professional managers in the banks and institutions with cash belonging to their depositors, most of whom are far from being millionaires.

Between the end of 1960 (their last good year) and late 1971 (their last year, period) the Lines' borrowings from their friendly neighbourhood bankers leapt from £270,000 to £9.5 million. The family went on paying out higher and higher dividends, and pouring more and more borrowed capital into the firm, despite the fact that profits only once, in 1966, crept past the 1960 level. Not content with this exhibition of speeding good money after bad, the City staved off the family's moment of truth for four more years by flogging £4.2 million of securities to an innocent public in mid-1967.

Advisers, financial and otherwise, are indispensable to the owners of silver spoons. But they must be tested anew by each generation for their acumen, their effort, their results, and their toughness, and fired if they fail the test: it costs nothing to get a new lawyer. Social connections (remember Churchill and Sir Ernest Cassel) are neither here nor there. If their advice is imperfect and their opposition either purblind or easily pushed aside, advisers are about as useful as the eminent physicians who, in the early centuries of medicine, resolutely bled their royal patients to death.

When the Lines bankers finally came to their senses, no fewer than six directors, four of them named Lines, lost their managerial heads at one blow. It was far too late in the company's day. According to Peter Drucker, they organize things better in Japan, where the family fortunes are watched over implacably by the elder womenfolk (a much tougher breed than bankers). If any honourable nephew is no good, grandma gives him the chop.

Since this variety of Women's Lib is unlikely to wear well in the West, families have to exercise self-discipline in other ways – although Guinness may have a western variation. For some decades now the magic stout, having brewed incomparable riches for the Guinnesses and transformed them into Earls of Iveagh, Viscounts of Kelvedon, and various other nobilities, has been managed by non-titled non-Guinnesses with such care and attention that in 1972 a French magazine, to Guinness' amusement, elected their company as the most dynamic in Europe. A watchful board festooned with Guinnesses includes a nub of titled ladies, representative of large family holdings, whose appearance at the annual general meeting has been likened to "a forest of cock's feathers and fur".

The rules of family discipline are easy enough to find – they are exactly the same as for firms of the non-family variety. Never appoint incompetents, related or unrelated, to any position of significance. Never allow the board to become overburdened with age, even if it means forcing the dominating father-figure to retire at the same age as the lesser fry. Bring your talent into positions of real power while it is still young: but always ensure that wise, prudent, unambitious and trusted elders watch what the young are getting up to, especially with money. (The Texan oil millionaire Tom Wagoner, chided by a barber for tipping less than his son, pointed out that "my boy's got a rich daddy, but I ain't.") Don't let indifferent performance drift by. The iron law is that stagnation leads to decline. The time to act to avert the former is when the signs of stagnation first appear, before huge deposits of inertia have had time to silt up the entire works.

The crunch comes when stagnation cannot be averted without severe discontinuity, and discontinuity is the process that heirs are worst at achieving. They can be superb at developing a great and soundly-based business along more or less established lines: thus did the Sieffs at Marks & Spencer triumphantly overcome the difficulties, for a bunch of hereditary millionaires with expensive tastes, of serving the desires in food and clothing of their mass market. But never let heirs try to prove that they are better than good old dad, or grandad, by striking out in brave new directions.

That's what Gerry Eskow attempted at Yale Express and, in an even more bizarre episode, Herbert Hoover Jr. at Hoover. This would-be chip off the old block, dissatisfied with the narrowness of the view from North Canton, Ohio, set up an expensive international headquarters in New York, staffed by his own protégés, to revolutionize the company. Sadly, the only obvious focus for young Hoover's energies was the British subsidiary, which Hoover neither wholly owned nor ever controlled to much effect.

The architect of Hoover's British upsurge retired, with an £83,000 pay-off, to make dishwashers and Hoover's US and UK halves stewed together in so complete a mish-mash that the suffering professional managers in North Canton finally mobilized the family and gave Herbert Jr. the old heave-ho. That is the only correct treatment for any descendant who rocks the family's solid silver boat, is rude to its servants or wastes its compounding wherewithal.

There's nothing heinous in the rich heir who shuns the business (like most of the assembled Du Ponts): the only son of Lord Marks prefers painting to stores: the top Rothschild, socially speaking, preferred biology to banking – and ended up in his sixties running the Prime Ministerial think-tank in Downing Street. But drop-outs should be discouraged from over-spending their income or dissipating their capital in support of expensive hobbies – unless, that is, the family luck sticks to their fingers.

One sprig of a British fortune was having a boat built when he heard to his fury that the builder was going bankrupt. He thereupon told his factotum (good factota, stewards or bailiffs are a privilege of the rich) to buy the business. On completion of the deal, the heirs found to their horror that the company also made nasty little wingless aircraft whose propellors were in the wrong place, whirling above the fuselage. They stuck with this unfortunate acquisition until one day a British government decided to merge the aircraft industry, helicopters and all, into fewer companies. In the reshuffle, the family found itself several millions better-to-do: all because originally one prince of the blood wanted his boat finished. There is justice in the world. But it tends to favour the rich.

SCENE 2

THE REWARDS OF EXPLORATION

or

Finding's Keeping

In which we discover how the new explorer after mineral
wealth both has his cake and eats it by exploiting the
fabulous lodes offered by the stock markets of the world
... a way even wealthier than the disregarding of
received opinions on where rich deposits may be found.

The clearest-cut way to new money is finding it, and always
has been. The forty-niners after gold, the East Texas wild-
catters pursuing oil, the Geiger counter gangs hunting uranium
— all had the same, and the right, idea. Those who lack any
other form of financial ability may still have just enough wit to
find a pot of gold, and just enough strength to pick it up

The shrewdest and strongest of them have founded the
lasting empires. The truly interesting and powerful Hearst was
not William Randolph, the czar of San Simeon, for all his
newspapers and noise, but his father, exploiter of the Comstock Lode, a hard warm man whose interests expanded into
most of the unmined metals and untracked deserts in which his
day abounded. Hearst Sr functioned in a more primitive age,
when finding had an annoying drawback: the finder (unless he
sold out smartly) had to wrest his mineral from the good earth;
then he had to exchange the wrested rock for hard cash. He
couldn't find it, sell it, and still keep it — a trick which modern
Hearsts manage with prestidigitatory ease.

The truly modern and imaginative prospector sets forth on
his mission armed with a bundle of share certificates, along
with the more traditional tools. If he strikes it rich, the next
stage is to engender enthusiasm for shares in his company.
Mining shares can soar to more fantastic heights at a faster
speed than any other form of paper wealth as investors all over

the world, although personally unable to distinguish between nickel and molybdenum, or to separate geographically Wagga-Wagga from Addis Ababa, flock for a piece of the finder's action.

Before long the momentum of the share price ceases to bear any relation to the prospective value of the new hoard. The shares themselves, though made of nothing but engraved paper, become the equivalent of the Comstock Lode: buyers desire and devour the stock because they find it so amazingly valuable – and it is valuable solely because buyers desire and devour it so avidly.

While this bubble swells to prodigious size the finder and his friends can take generous reward in cash – and still retain total control of the claim and all that lies therein. Without an ounce of their metal on the market, they are already rich and can only get richer when the wonder company actually comes to have some wonder earnings.

This convenient arrangement makes the methods of earlier prospectors, like Vernon Pick, seem positively self-abnegatory. Pick believed in both the "self-sustenance homestead" and the existence of uranium in the Four Corners area, where four of the States neatly come together. He was proved right, and was amply sustained by the $9.37 million handed over for the property by the Atlas Corporation. A whole army of would-be Picks promptly descended on the US deserts armed with Geiger and scintillation counters. But many years passed before other self-sustainers discovered the still greater surface riches lying around on the stock exchanges of the world.

That discovery wonderfully enlarged the horizons of the finding industry, which previously lived off the no less wonderful profit margin between the cost of discovering, extracting and refining a mineral and passing it on to the customer. In the good old days, before the Arab natives got restless, virtually the entire price of a barrel of oil extracted from the Middle East sand was pure (or, as J. P. Getty would put it, "clear") profit. The ineffable oil fortunes, like Getty's, are mostly private, despite the stock maker's multiplying chains, partly because their owners largely come from a past when a man's well was his castle, and what you had, you held, entirely and in perpetuity.

Getty himself lovingly charts his own progress from the first $12,000 profit on a well in 1915, to the $6,387,946 clear profit on the Nordstrom Lease from 1921–37, with stopovers like the $400,000 plus "excess recovery" on the Athens Lease in 1924.

But what made these excess finds the foundation of an excessive share of the USA's wealth was not simply the initiative, intelligence and industry of its finders: it is fine, old-fashioned freedom from tax. Not a single writer or thinker on taxes or oil has been able to explain precisely, let alone convincingly, why the oilmen of the USA should have received (as they still do) the blessing of an exemption which does for them by law what latter-day mineral explorers must achieve by dint of hard stock market graft.

The sovereign notion is not merely that, before getting round to paying tax, oilmen should be free to deduct the cost of drilling all their wells, wet or dry. A beneficent state, noting that a barrel of oil, once removed from the ground for sale, cannot be replaced, decreed that its owners should be compensated by tax relief for this "depletion of their resources". It is as if a man finds a Ming vase buried in the woods, sells it for $10,000 and is then allowed to knock $2,000 off his tax because he no longer has Ming to market.

Until 1969, the oilmen got $2,750 in every ten grand knocked off their Ming equivalents: and great was the outcry at this reduction of the sacred depletion allowance, as American as apple pie but many times more fattening, from $27\frac{1}{2}$% to 22%. At the former rate, an oilman had trouble getting into a tax-paying position, no matter how hard he tried – and most didn't try too hard. One of the least determined triers must have been Robert O. Anderson, chairman of Atlantic Richfield, which in four years paid no taxes on $465 million of profits – and ended up with the US government owing it money.

What's sauce for the corporation is also ketchup for the individual. If the finder can retain all his income free of tax, reinvest the surplus in still more properties that will yield even greater tax-free earnings, and borrow heavily against the security of the proven oil in his ground – in that happy combination of events, his need to let the public or anybody else into his act is minimal.

This impeccable fiscal logic has enabled the oil barons to form a separate, politically powerful kingdom within the empire of the rich: their realm is as important, relatively speaking, as that of the Dukes of Burgundy in medieval France. Of the thirty-five richest men listed by *Fortune* in 1957, no less than fifteen were either oil-finders or entrepreneurs who had grown rich from the tidbits from the oilmen's table: suppliers of services, bits and pieces, valuable odds and ends. H. L. Hunt, Sid Richardson, the Murchisons, John Mecom (who sold a mere fraction of his properties in the early 1960s for $27 million) – all these ducal figures of the new plutocracy owe their eminence and their fortunes primarily to the oil riches of Texas.

The supply of satrapies from this source, however, may be drying up, which is the result of greed outdoing itself. As the richer fields of the USA were steadily sucked dry, new and lush finds became far harder to hit, and costs of production climbed inexorably closer to world prices: the latter were now determined, not in Texas but by the super-abundant oilfields of the Middle East.

The reaction of the oil moguls, aided and abetted by all the political friends oil money could buy, was to get the oil out while the getting was good – at the highest possible price. Quotas were slapped on by President Eisenhower to minimize imports of cheap foreign crude (selling at prices of, say, $2 compared to $3.75 for the Texas variety). How much money the quota system pumped into the US oil industry's bulging pockets, nobody can ever calculate – one estimate runs between $40,000 million and $70,000 million over a decade. The cold certainty is that it rushed on the day when the USA would run short of energy.

The affluent Americans who found their oil supplies rationed in the winter of 1972, following which crisis the quota system was finally scrapped, were the direct victims of the brilliant deployment by the oil lobby of the millions which their previous lobbying had won. As the shortages of that winter developed into the Arab boycott of the next one, Americans had even more cause to regret their failure to grab all the Middle East oil that they could, when the sheiks were quiescent and the price was four-fifths lower.

If there is any consolation, it lies in the fact that few of the Texas fat-cats, mostly being too old and too rich, had the sense or muscle to follow the oil trade's trend and head East. For those who did – notably Nelson Bunker Hunt, a partner in British Petroleum's great Libyan fields until they were expropriated, and J. P. Getty in the Neutral Zone of Kuwait – the richest rewards of all were still to be made. In his advice to would-be executives Getty stresses the pain of paying $12.5 million for the Kuwait concession, and of investing many times more before a drop of oil came to market. He fails to mention, however, what financial pleasures he received in return for all that pain.

As a rough idea, British Petroleum sold under half – 45% – of its stake in Abu Dhabi, another lately-developed gusher region of the Persian Gulf, to some eager Japanese in 1972. The price tag was $780 million. That kind of money, and the income flow which it represents, gives Getty a return hardly less wonderful than that from Scott Fitzgerald's solid gem of a mountain in *The Diamond as Big as the Ritz*. But Getty was lucky, or wise. He got in early, when a sheik was still a sheik – and not the next victim of a nationalist, ex-military, revolutionary politician.

The Arab rulers, men like the lecherous Ibn Saud or the complaisant Sheik of Kuwait, were notably (although the competition for this title is stiff) the least deserving of all the multi-millionaires. Even though the oil companies kept the rulers on as long a string as possible, the latter inevitably became so loaded with unspendable loot that the simple process of investing their wealth itself generated new fortunes – the $12,000 million that poured into Arab coffers in 1971 was expected to quintuple by 1980, even before, in late 1973, the Arabs craftily quadrupled the price. As the sheiks grew greedier and the Arabian political climate grew hotter, the tax take grew greater – and it has now become genuinely hard work to wrest a decent oil living (decent by oil standards, that is) from the desert.

Dr. Armand Hammer, for example, landed the industry's big fish when he gambled on Libyan crude. But the replacement of a compliant monarch by a cross colonel contributed mightily to the financial embarrassment of Hammer's Occidental Petroleum. Just as Texas has probably run out of future H. L. Hunts, and the West Coast of future Gettys, so the Middle East has probably seen its last big operation.

Big, lucrative plays remain in areas less politically tempestuous than the Middle East – in the North Sea for example, where the British public discovered, to the chagrin of many citizens, that private oil firms, mainly American at that, had

36

been allowed to gobble all the cream, and much of the milk, under tax conditions which the most stupid oil sheik in old-time Araby would have considered generous. North Sea plays, however, require astronomical stakes: thirty-one drilling concessions sold at auction by the British Government cost £37 million, and drilling one well can easily take $600,000. The action has inevitably shifted to the giant corporations: the individual has had to look still further afield – for instance, to the wilds of Australia.

Here, a new generation of prospectors in the 1960s exploited the prime advantage of finding, as opposed to making, wealth, which is that the wealth is created almost from the moment of discovery. If the finder can prove (or get somebody to believe) that he has located a million tons of mineral-bearing Mother Earth, that find or purported find immediately has a value – not the price times the recoverable quantity, unfortunately (even the suckers know it costs money to get the stuff out) – but a very reasonable proportion of what can be a staggering sum. Mining discoveries are thus the perfect material for a speculative share boom, as demonstrated by the movements of two linked stocks, one heavy (Western Mining), one light (Hampton Areas). It was from Hampton that Western Mining acquired fourteen square miles near Kambalda, the seat of a spectacular rise in earnings. In 1966, the year before the deal, Western was earning twice as much as ever before – but that still meant only $692,323 in Australian currency. By 1969 the profits had almost trebled: the next year they were twenty times the 1966 figure: in 1971, at $22.7 million, the multiple was thirty.

In 1967, the shares paid to Hampton for the right to drill its land rose in worth nearly sixfold: at the peak, the stake was worth forty times the low price in the year of the big deal: thus showing how rosily a rise in profits can be magnified at the share price level. In later years, the bloom went off the rose somewhat, with dollar devaluation adding to the problems of nickel over-supply. But by then the harvest for Western Mining's insiders had already long been reaped.

This great Aussie boom had one peculiar economic characteristic. It was founded largely on finds of nickel, a metal which, at the start of the saga, was in short supply. With all those lovely new discoveries being announced, however, you didn't have to be a World Bank economist to forecast that

37

before long – before, indeed, all the new mines could even open – the shortage would turn to glut. In the world of commodities, as many burnt-out speculators ruefully know, a little glut means a large price fall. Yet the shares of any company that had found, might find, or even thought of finding nickel in the outback went on upwards as if the demand and price for nickel had been guaranteed by the US Treasury (a guarantee which in those days, before several dollar devaluations, had some value).

Fortune always favours somebody, including sometimes the brave. Although the gravy was ladled out in the main to local Aussie prospectors, promoters and brokers, two likely English lads, Richard King and Colin Forsyth, got into the act. Their original idea was to launch a unit trust invested wholly in Australian shares, Australia being a country that was largely white, definitely growing and vaguely English-speaking. The launch was neatly timed for an Australian market slump, and the trust languished for an uncomfortable time.

But the duo's ears, close to the Australian ground, picked up the first nickel noises: largely because Forsyth, some time before, picked up something much more valuable, shares in Hampton Gold Mining Areas, which were then so much wallpaper. These purchases alone made Forsyth rich. But the trust, too, suddenly found itself the focus of the world's fastest stock market action and achieved wonders of super-growth: its two founders finally sold out for seven figures, a reward which represented only their indirect gains from the Antipodean avalanche: and even so they missed the best of the tide.

The phenomenal Poseidon, "the share of the century", was a share in which the Pan-Australian partners got interested early on, but after actually going to the Windarra nickel site which explained all the excitement, Forsyth turned cool on the project. Failing to preserve its own cool, the trust's investment meeting nevertheless decided that the shares, then selling at £120, couldn't possibly fall below £80, which was still vastly above the trust's buying price. Had not one broker written that "at any price under £180 they're a snip"? In fact, they crashed to £5: and 19% of the fund was in this one stock.

It requires faith, as well as other people's money, to put trust in geologists' reports couched in meaningless technicalities and emanating from the back of beyond. For every honest prospector, there's always one who isn't above salting the

38

mine. No salter ever swung the trick more daringly than one keen entrepreneur, who got hold of an insignificant little company by various means and persuaded much of the populace, including normally shrewd financiers, that he had found a mine which contained almost every valuable metal known to man (a cautious type, the promoter stopped short of diamonds).

A brilliant scientist had discovered a new secret extraction process which only stopped short of turning dirt into gold. In fact, it would have had to. Visits by curious pressmen to the Eldorado which was valued at numerous millions, discovered a ramshackle lab, but no scientist: and a mine of uncertain title, more or less in the middle of a housing estate, but no gold and no mining. Even then there was a delayed reaction before the promoter decamped with his loot for the sadder and wiser investors to contemplate the wreck of his company.

It pays to be sceptical. The catch, alas, is that it sometimes pays more to have faith. In 1961 an Irish-Canadian prospector named Pat Hughes, then thirty-seven, made a sentimental return to the old country bent on doing it and himself a bit of good by finding some mineral wealth. Now, the Republic of Ireland, as everybody knows, is good for cows, Guinness, Arran sweaters and leprechauns; but the idea of a Klondike in those soft green hills was plainly the wildest Irish-Canadian blarney.

Hughes announced, however, that he had indeed made a find, of lead, zinc, silver and copper to boot, and shares in his company, Northgate, began to move in the accustomed manner. In the bars of Dublin, where many wonders have been seen, the discoveries seemed perfectly acceptable. But elsewhere people were harder to convince that there was anything more valuable than fairies at the bottom of Irish gardens.

Hughes even went to the extraordinary lengths of flying in and entertaining right royally journalists and investment men from all over Europe and the Americas to inspect his new mine. The inexpert looked at Hughes, arm in sling after a recent accident and looking even more like the pirate king than usual, observed a newly mined pile of dirt, noticed a few suspicious silvery twinkles in the heap, and went back to their Old Bushmills whisky as unconvinced as ever. But the silver was of sterling reality: and Hughes went on to discover yet another crock of gold called Silvermines.

Those who invested in these two companies, and Hughes in particular, did better than a lucky draw in the Irish Sweepstakes. By the end of 1970, Northgate was earning $6.3 million a year – and in 1972 Hughes sold just 6% of another find for $5.6 million. Unfortunately, there is no guide, no touchstone, to help the outsider to distinguish between the phoney and, as here, the fruitful claim. You need the same tool as the prospector himself; a sensitive, quivering nose.

Expertise in the geology, characteristics and technology of whatever mineral you are hunting, and in whatever terrain the hunt has reached, is of course useful. As Getty tells it, he and his father spotted one of their most lucrative hauls by noticing a locomotive labouring uphill: this convinced them that they were looking at the top of a dome full of oil. Normally a prospector (provided he can afford the fee) turns to an academically-equipped expert to tell him the good news. But experts have a disconcerting habit of being wrong – and you never know when.

Their failure is understandable. An expert is somebody who has been taught all that is already known about a subject. But he doesn't know what *isn't* known, and he tends to dismiss any information or observation which contradicts his knowledge. The true prospector – indeed, the true business genius of any kind – listens carefully to the expert; but he goes right ahead when instinct tells him that the expert may be wrong.

The great D'Arcy was almost alone in believing that oil could be found under the sands of Arabia: Dr. Armand Hammer made one of his Libyan hits on a concession which Mobil Oil quit after drilling nothing but dry holes: British oil experts turned up their noses at Kuwait, the richest pool of them all. Two of the world's great oil companies, Shell and British Petroleum, are based on England, a country which for decades was devoutly believed to contain no oil or gas whatsoever. All that time the British moguls were sitting in blissful ignorance within seventy miles of some of the world's biggest untapped deposits beneath the North Sea.

True, the drilling and extraction of this bonanza would have presented insurmountable problems to the technology of an earlier age. But a US company even turned up a major field in Yorkshire, of all places. Geologists are not trained to look where they don't expect to find – but that is often where the true finder finds what is truly worth keeping.

40

As time goes by, however, the ignored and overlooked areas and chances must get fewer and farther between, which has the unhappy result that the prospector has to try, try, and try again with a patience that outdoes Robert the Bruce. Robert Anderson is said to have drilled two hundred dry wells before he made his first New Mexico strike. That kind of hitting and missing is a rich man's pastime. Without the possession of a small refinery, financed by a $50,000 loan from a banker father, Anderson could not have afforded the wells (nor, simultaneously, have built up a million acres of landholding, which add up to a useful reserve in his piggy-bank).

Anderson was forty before his crude oil holdings were impressive – and even then a shrewd property-cum-oil deal with some California gas stations was his chief claim to industrial fame. Anderson bought the chain for some $4 million and sold it for $25 million eighteen months later to one of the helpful giants, Gulf Oil, to whom the individual rich should daily sing hosannas. The big play, however, was again in the stock market. Anderson got seven hundred thousand shares in Atlantic Refining for his oil business: the leverage he applied to this holding, by merging Atlantic with Richfield and making the big strike in Alaska, pushed his oil fortune, at its peak, to something like $100 million.

The old days of the lone desert prospector with his pick or Geiger counter, are no likelier to return than those of the fur traders from whom John Jacob Astor made the first of the great American fortunes. The Hochschilds, whose molybdenum mine in California stood in their books at $3,000, netted $15 million more when in 1957 they merged it into the corporate complex of American Metal Climax. Like Bob Anderson, Joseph H. Hirshhorn, the richest of the Geiger men, went corporate, turning over his massive Canadian uranium interests to Rio Tinto Zinc: and like Anderson, too, Hirshhorn was already a long way from the breadline. He is alleged to have read the storm signals in 1929, and to have left the stock market to its slump with $4 million in his kitty.

As a miner and speculator, Hirshhorn was big in uranium by 1950: from this base he made the super-strike of 1952–53. He obeyed the sound principle of listening to a maverick expert, one Franc Joubin, who was almost alone in suspecting that the Algoma Basin of Ontario contained uranium. It cost Hirshhorn $30,000 to prove Joubin right – in return for which proof, transmuted into a mining giant, Hirshhorn was worth over $130 million in 1961. He sold out his stake for Rio Tinto Zinc shares, whereby hangs another story.

In the palmier days for the mining corporation, before the management ran into troubles with environmental pollution at a wildly uncontrolled plant investment in Wales, the shares boomed to give it a value of £640 million in April 1970 on the stock market, which subsequently dwindled to almost half. It must be galling for a gambler to see his winning chips dwindle in as mysterious a manner as they grew. Anderson had just this experience as Atlantic Richfield ran into the massive Alaskan pipeline road-block and the general unhappiness of US oil in its degenerating phase. The owners of Western Mining too, saw their shares plunge. By playing finding's keeping, then, you can have your cake and eat it: the catch is that you can no longer control the size of the cake.

SCENE 3

THE PRIZE OF PRIVACY

or

The Grave's a Very Private Place

Containing the true reason why owners of great private
fortunes allow the public into their coffers, at a pretty
price ... and why even prettier rewards may accrue to
those who keep their economic achievements exclusively
to themselves.

At regular intervals private companies which have deposited
great wealth into the hands of their private owners yield their
virginities and become public. Their proprietors, with many a
sigh and heaving of the breast, sell a modest chunk of their
shares. The suffering is mitigated by the fact that they receive
a goodly volume of cash for their pains.

There is always some plausible explanation of this self-
sacrifice: fear of death duties, difficulty of raising money for
expansion, trouble in attracting or keeping smart enough hired
help. But none of these obstacles is insurmountable: and the
clear proof is that so much of the world's wealth is in wholly or
largely private hands. The public has no more than a look-in, if
that, at the fortunes of Howard Hughes, D. K. Ludwig,
Forrest Mars, or H. L. Hunt in the USA: or of the meat-
packing Vesteys, the mail order and football betting Littlewoods or the shipowning Sir John Ellerman of Britain. The
latter died in 1973 with a £100 million fortune in ships alone –
part of the proceeds of £37 million bequeathed by his father
forty years before.

Few people outside Eire and Palm Beach, Florida, have
heard of Mrs. Ambrose Congreve, for example. More have
heard of Humphreys & Glasgow, a British chemical plant
constructor which was founded by a US immigrant (the
Glasgow of the title) using US know-how. The huge profits

43

made over a long life – father died at ninety-six – were invested with high success in the USA, and the entire fortune was bequeathed to Mrs. Congreve, putting her among the world's richest women. Her husband, Ambrose Congreve, did a sterling job in building up the value of the original business, controlling it from a legendary Irish estate, Mount Congreve. But of the shares in the firm, Mrs. Congreve owned 119,991 and Mr. Congreve just one.

None of the standard excuses for selling shares to the public has any convincing validity: the only point in doing so is to exchange assets for real money at a time when the switch is advantageous. The advantage of publicity is clearest if the private owner has it in mind to take his money and run. But even if the private owner has every intention of staying put, going public has considerable financial benefit: simply because the parts can be made wondrously more than the whole. Nobody ever got richer faster than a former wizard IBM computer salesman named H. Ross Perot. But this wasn't simply because his computer software business grew like the giant mushroom (as it did). The US public fell over itself to buy the tiny amount of shares which Perot generously released – 15% of the total equity. At its palmiest, this was valued at over one hundred times earnings. Nobody in his right mind would have paid that kind of multiple for the whole of Perot's company: if he was exceedingly lucky, it might have fetched a third of the putative but fictitious market valuation.

Giving the public a piece of some desirable action not only multiplies its purported value in a delicious manner – it enables the owner, while grabbing some real money, to retain total control over the cornucopia. The mystery therefore isn't why so many wealthy citizens, on generally spurious grounds, give away part of their privacy: but why so many cling to absolute ownership of empires like the *Reader's Digest* or the Ellerman Line.

The practical advantages are minor compared to the loss of financial flexibility. Even Howard Hughes found the public route indispensable when he wanted several millions, presumably to cover his legal dispute with TWA. In the event, Hughes won his case, and needn't have bothered. But note that the crafty recluse hung on to all of Hughes Tool, except his daddy's former oil-drilling bit business; he got $140 million for that (off the stock market) – although its profits had dribbled down for three years and three once commercially significant patents were shortly expiring.

The Hughes case is self-explanatory: the private person avoids public ownership because of his very lust for privacy. This lust can be obsessional, blotting out common sense as well as financial self-interest. John Moores, the dictatorial boss of a Littlewoods empire that pulls in £300 million a year in retail sales and has an astronomical turnover in football pools, once explained his position, in language worthy of a small shopkeeper: "If we were public," he said, "and I didn't make enough money, they [the shareholders] would be after me."

Useless to tell such a Midas that a holding of well under 50% will yield absolute control: that shareholders don't even speak when they are spoken to: that large public firms have reported indifferent results for a decade without the directors attracting anything more than a unanimous vote of thanks at the annual general meeting (an occasion which vies with a pre-Watergate Nixon press conference in its irrelevance to anything of practical import).

The Midas is motivated by deep, inward fear: anxiety lest his personal control be weakened by dilution. The proprietor has a simple, all or nothing, approach to proprietorship: and this same attitude underlies the privacy of all other enclosed tycoons, even though they range from men who all but keep their money under the bed to international jet-set sophisticates like Aristotle Onassis.

This private passion is no prerogative of the ultra-rich. One of the main causes of bankruptcy is the refusal of the infant entrepreneur to let others into his action at an early stage. The explanation is human enough. The man knows how wonderful his idea is, how irresistible his own managerial force, how dynamic his growth rate (if you start from zero, almost any growth looks marvellous). If he lets somebody else in on his ground floor, no matter what that person provides in capital or knowledge, the interloper is getting in dirt-cheap: cheap, that is, by the standards of the unrealized future super-growth.

This denial leads straight to the dread condition known as over-trading or under-capitalization, in which the sufferer tries to cure his shortage of money by desperate means – like not paying his bills to suppliers, and praying that his customers pay theirs on the nail. If these makeshift means fail (they do, with depressing regularity), the proud and private independent casts around, at last, for outside money. Only it's too late. The time to swallow private pride is when you are not forced to do so; diplomats call it negotiating from strength.

By all odds the craftiest exponent of this art was the wily Armenian, Calouste Gulbenkian. Zen masters are rumoured to teach pupils the essence of swordsmanship by striking at them with sticks when the student isn't watching. The Armenians in much the same way have acquired such dexterity from dodging their persecutors down the ages that only the fool-hardy ever tangle with a businessman whose name ends in "ian" or "yan" — and that prohibition included Anastas Nikoyan, the craftiest trader and most professional survivor thrown up by Soviet Russia.

Gulbenkian's contribution to the world's welfare was to lay his hands on the rich oil concessions in Mesopotamia. His wiliness emerged in his readiness to give up all but 5% of this treasure trove to the mighty oil companies which were anxious to share the gold. That 5% not only gave Gulbenkian his nickname: it generated, painlessly and annually, one of the world's great fortunes, and it demonstrated the truth of an unforgettable maxim — that a little of a lot is better than all of a little.

The small, would-be-big entrepreneur ignores Gulbenkian's gambit to his own detriment. In any event, giving away some equity early on isn't a final, fatal step. If the business flourishes like a green bay tree, the entrepreneur can always buy his partners out. That was the course favoured by Henry Ford I, who began his rise with a motley crew of faithful supporters and devoted much of his time in later years to liquidating their interests.

By and large, despite Henry's appalling mismanagement in the 1930s, the other shareholders were wrong to sell out. Ford shares were worth more than dollar bills. But few people can resist the lure of cash, even in small amounts. The great majority of the oilmen who, at the point of John D. Rocke-feller's economic gun, were forced to sell out either for cash or for Rockefeller shares, took cash: it was a ludicrous error. Keeping a Gulbenkian-sized corner in somebody else's gold-mine is one of the easiest ways to wealth, so long as, like Gulbenkian, you are in a position to safeguard your interests.

The private imperialist values his privacy partly just because there are nobody's interests to safeguard save his own.

This enables him to build the company in his own image and for his own sake. Power, in these circumstances, is plainly more important than its full expression in money terms. Britain boasts one Quaker company which is kept resolutely private by the will of the family – or, to be more precise, the managing members thereof. As usual in these circumstances, a formula exists to put a price on the shares in the event of death or dissolution. It prices the holdings far below even a conservative estimate for the company's stock market value. This under-valuation robs the family of a cool £30 million: the price-tag on allowing the few actively ruling family members to preserve totally untrammelled management control.

Why do the family outsiders suffer such penalties? Aunts may be intimidated by cousin Eric; nephews may fear that, unless they comply dutifully with uncle Al's wishes, he will up stakes in a huff and retire to the nearest tax-free island. Apart from paranoia, they are victims of ignorance. Almost as if they were uninterested in their money (which, in a sense, they are), they are happy to have the anxiety of its care lifted off their shoulders. Tell them that they are being defrauded of the odd million and you turn contentment into a state of acute anxiety. It is kissing cousin to the equally ill-founded apprehensions of private family managers that, without the protection of all-family ownership, their management grip will first be loosened, then contemptuously knocked away.

If their abilities are defective, so much the better for one and all – including themselves as shareholders. But managers of the blood are seldom anxious to recognize their own incompetence, no matter what it costs. The beauty (or horror) of privacy is that mistakes are more easily buried here even than in big public corporations (where funerals can be fully as discreet as Mafia disposals in the East River). Only rarely does a scandal reach such dimensions that the veil is lifted, not merely from the management failure of a family business, but from the very facts of its life.

When Tino de Angelis, the great salad-oil swindler, finally ran out of empty tanks, a company called Bunge discovered to its horror that $15 million of the non-existent oil belonged to it, so to speak. Another $3 million had oozed away in a simple cheque fraud. To mislay $18 million, even to the second greatest swindler of all time, you have to be adequately rich – and Bunge was and is part of what may be the richest private kingdom of them all. At that time its sales were £800 million a year; it held one-fifth of the entire American trade in grain, oilseeds, oils and fats; the whole Bunge y Born earthly paradise, known in its Latin American home as "The Octopus", was in the ownership of two families, the Borns and the Hirsches.

Mario Hirsch was said at the time to know "if a typist blows her nose in Sao Paulo" – despite the fact that he had never visited Brazil. Yet here was a single suborned employee in New York waylaying cheques to the value of $3 million – and nobody noticed.

The family fury, when informed that of four tanks supposed to contain 160 million pounds of salad oil, three contained petrol and the fourth was empty, epitomized the close-fisted, close-controlled approach typical of the private empire.

Bunge y Born was, in fact, having a management overhaul by British consultants at the time, a process which inevitably took it further into the world of public exposure, with all the disadvantages of lost secrecy. As a family member complained, "the bigger you are, the more tax you pay. The smaller you are, the more tax you evade."

The quieter you are, what's more, the better your chance that nobody will notice your size: like Michelin, which in 1968 was still trying to pretend that its turnover, entirely privately owned, came to only £12 million a year; the true figure is now around $1,500 million.

For many years the ace London property developer Harry Hyams concealed a £40 million fortune behind total inaccessibility: by a quirk of fate, his Oldham Estates had a few outside shareholders, which compelled Hyams to hold uncommunicative annual general meetings: at one AGM he turned up wearing a rubber face mask to protect his anonymity. By then it was too late, however. Hyams had blown his own cover by erecting Centre Point, for years the tallest, emptiest and hence most notorious, office building in London's West End – publicly attacked for its emptiness by a Conservative Cabinet Minister, no less. From the publicity angle, Hyams would have done better to stick to bungalows.

Privacy not only protects the tender personality from bruising. It allows the truly gifted proprietor to practise management experiments without let or hindrance. Whether the subtleties of Howard Hughes count in this context is

48

debatable: but, in the age of passion for communicating, for man to man, eyeball to eyeball confrontation, Hughes has proved that a monster conglomerate can be managed via a Mormon bodyguard, telephone kiosks and a tame lawyer or two: practically the only business which Hughes botched up, in fact, was the one to which he was nearest: right on the proverbial spot, in Las Vegas.

Possibly the most successful satisfiers of mass tastes in Britain are the D. C. Thomson family, which, despite making a very public mint from children's comics (*Dandy, Beano*, etc.), Dundee newspapers, women's magazines (*My Weekly, Annabel*, etc.), maintains one of the lowest profiles in world commerce. A spokesman (something of a misnomer in the circumstances) told the *Sunday Times* that "we never give information about anything to anybody" – and he was telling the literal truth.

The law does force the revelation that the Thomson family, whose personal life-styles are no more conspicuous than their publicity, earned £3.2 million after tax in the latest year. That alone adds up to a stake worth at least £40 million, which takes no account of the sums piled up in investment trusts, commercial television, paper and property in the years (many of them all but tax-free) since 1905, when three brothers and three wives initiated the saga. The reigning Thomsons even had to be photographed in the environs of Dundee covertly with long-focus lenses like royalty sunbathing.

Another equally secret tycoon has no head office at all (unless you count a Washington hotel suite), but certainly operates one of the most effective management machines: Forrest Mars of Mars, who has been photographed hardly more often than the Thomsons or Hughes.

Rubbing in the fact that second generation incompetence is a myth, Mars left a successful father behind in the USA and went to Britain to build a confectionery giant so rich that, reversing the usual compliment, Mars finally took over the original parental business back home. He provides his disciples with a management grounding which is direct, steeped in common sense and founded on a simple notion, as expounded by another émigré to Britain, Canada's Roy Thomson, in an immortal phrase, "You make a dollar for me, I'll make a dollar for you." Within that scheme of things, Mars has felt free to experiment with marketing approaches, produc-

49

tion methods, incentive ideas: knowing that, if they worked, he would benefit; if they failed, he would foot the bill.

Innovation in the technical sense seems to spring more readily from private lives: Pilkingtons was still entirely private at the time of the float glass brainwave. The Pilkingtons in 1970 realized over £9 million by selling two and a half tithes of their shares, and thus no longer endure the fate of wholly private emperors, who always lose some money, certainly in cash terms, probably in borrowing power, by retaining their privacy. Only if they deal primarily in solid assets – ships as well as oil in the ground – does the problem become minimal. Any banker will gladly lend on such triple-barrelled security.

The fix may become genuinely painful if, like the Sainsbury family in Britain, which pocketed over £14 million by going public in 1973 (and still had £103 million left in paper), the solid assets in the form of shops are small in relation to the volume of sales which pours through: or if, again like the Sainsburys, there is trouble earning fat enough cash margins to finance further expansion. In contrast, the great shipping fortunes – like those of Onassis, or the shy Daniel K. Ludwig (who runs an empire worth $3,500 million, or more than Howard Hughes' little lot, from locales like the thirty-fourth floor of Burlington House in Manhattan), with their supporting cast of hundreds – have remained almost entirely in private hands. Their owners have no incentive to share their assets, their borrowing power, their tax advantages and their gigantic profits with the suckers.

But what the private business always lacks, unless the family is exceptionally gifted and the racket especially rich, is the ability to generate decades of unlimited growth and diversification. Exxon no longer even bears the Rockefellers' Standard Oil brand, though it still keeps plenty of Rockefellers and allied families in caviare: but its $21,558 million of assets leave even the wildest Texan fortunes in the minor leagues. Like Krupp in German industry, or the Rothschilds in finance, the private business gets inexorably overtaken by the public concern as the years roll by. Big-time corporate managers can create money out of the air by issuing shares. The big-time privateer, like his golden age exemplars, can only create his loot by some form of real economic achievement, and that must be a harder trick.

SCENE 4

THE JOYS OF NEO-NEPOTISM

or

Let Your Nephew Try

How three sons-in-law achieved great deeds with three huge businesses, with some helpful hints on how both sides may successfully exploit the chief advantage of an adopted protégé ... the fact that the employer is not the adoptee's father.

In business, as in genealogy, adoption has much the same effect as birth. The main difference is that sons mostly inherit the trappings of office, and its loot, by divine right. The adopted protégé – usually, but not always, the lucky fellow who married the right daughter – really has to work for his keep. Rich fathers-in-law are generally suspicious of sons-in-law, especially poor ones, until the nuptial acquisition proves himself in battle.

Like Tamino in *The Magic Flute*, the adoptee has to pass through ordeals by fire and water before receiving full initiation. Once accepted, however, the son-in-law has all the advantages of his rich protector, including cash and power, strengthened by his own drive and guaranteed relative youth (girls tend to marry men younger than their fathers). Compared to a natural son, moreover, the daughter's loved one has an irreplaceable asset – the old man isn't his father.

This doesn't remove the possibility, even the inevitability, of conflict between generations: but with luck it subtracts from the brew the ingredients of inferiority complex, dark primal hatreds and contemptuous love. Many a son-in-law has found that Tamino's trials don't cease with initiation. But many a father-in-law has had reason to bless his daughter's natural instincts.

The great Philips electrical business was run successively by two sons-in-law. When the founder of Matsushita, another wondrous electrical enterprise, retired to the position of "rear échelon chairman", he was succeeded by his son-in-law — who adopted Matsushita's name (in much the same way as the Krupp in-laws added that family's patronymic). Three of Britain's greatest post-war successes, too, owe much to the in-law stratagem — and, by strange electrical coincidence, the country's huge power-station to plugs combine, the £1,023 million General Electric Company, is among them.

In British retailing, Simon Marks and Israel Sieff, the second generation which transformed Marks & Spencer, were brothers-in-law: and it was the Sieffs, not the Marks main line, who provided the management succession. The £359 million chain of Tesco supermarkets is another admirable example of the son-in-law variation — in fact, Sir John Cohen, the Tesco founder, had no less than two specimens of the genus on the premises, a doubling-up which provides additional problems of avoiding favouritism, or at least being seen to avoid it.

Nobody knows whether Tesco would have completed its Darwinian evolution from barrows to open-fronted stores to lock-up shops to supermarkets (a ladder from which many others fell) without Hyman Kreitman. This son-in-law, after a visit to the USA, became enthused with the supermarket notion and is credited with imposing orderly business ideas on the "pile 'em high and sell 'em cheap" philosophy which Jack Cohen had trundled along in his original barrow.

Another moot question, however, is whether it's always comfortable for a son-in-law to have his wife's father hanging around the shop when the latter's day is officially done. It takes more than the honorary title of president (in Britain normally the corporate equivalent of the Holy Roman Empire which was neither holy, Roman nor an empire) to keep a self-made family super-boss quiet.

In his pugnacious seventies, Cohen defined his role succinctly: "I'm a nagger. All I do is find fault." Performed tactfully, that's almost as valuable, in business terms, as finding gold. One slip on the wrong side of discretion, however, and the son-in-law can readily be driven to drink or hibernation — after all, the man has been made rich by his father-in-law's shares and his own efforts, and he doesn't actually have to work.

The most prominent son-in-law in British business, Weinstock of GEC, is famous for giving the impression that he hardly works at all. "I've always got time," he has been known to say. No doubt, the pressure was greater in the days when his father-in-law's Sobell radio and TV business was stuttering along, and Weinstock's mind was the most valuable of its intangible assets. Weinstock finally led the firm out of the valley and into the broad uplands, where the old GEC, a company that could ill afford it, paid a price for the Sobell business which gave the family and its friends 15% of the entire, creaking GEC edifice.

Weinstock, as boss of the merged TV and radio side, was supposed to sit amenably on a small committee which, in theory, ran a group that, in reality, was marching inexorably towards £30 million of bank debt and beyond into the great hereafter. When the Sobell son-in-law (backed by his equity) announced that the committee was a waste of time, and that he would attend no more meetings, the thin red line which held GEC's top management together wavered, stretched and finally parted completely. Within a couple of years, Weinstock and his Sobell sidekicks had the profits and the share price zooming upwards.

In 1963–68, the shares advanced ten times: and it followed, with gratifying reciprocity, that the Sobell family share-out rose in step. Each 100% hop in the shares, indeed, must have been worth several millions to the Weinstock entourage, taking Michael Sobell's gains from this phenomenal second-stage blast-off easily past his original fortune.

In truth, entrepreneurs are thrice blessed to have managerial talent visited on them from heaven by matrimony. Their luck lies in the essential difference between the creator and the critic. When Picasso died, the supply of Picassos (genuine ones, that is) ceased for all time: but the supply of critics of Picasso is timeless and inexhaustible. Business breakthroughs, too, are a form of creative art, and therefore often fail to conform to theoretical formulas – which is why so many wildly unorthodox approaches have achieved highly orthodox fortunes.

The critic mentality, and the son-in-law syndrome, come in at the next stage: when the big idea has turned into reality, when the small-holding has become a fertile, king-sized ranch of many acres, or has the chance to spread. At this point the creator finds himself in the additional, and often unwelcome, role of administrator. He needs a supply of managers, the artisans of business, to run his artistic shop. And he needs an analytical, understanding critical intelligence to run the artisans.

These henchmen, of course, are disposable and replaceable: but, then, so is the Picasso himself in his new role of manager-in-chief. Very few masters are detached enough, or sufficiently interested in the wide world outside business, to recognize this reality – unless a son-in-law (real or metaphorical) fits naturally into the slot. The West Coast Croesus, Norton Simon, is a rare example of total abdication – maybe because this one-time scrap-metal merchant had developed rare, expensive and profitable tastes which absorbed more and more of his attention.

Simon progressed from metal to Old Masters on the unlikely back of the tomato, becoming the dominant force in US ketchup with scarcely a false step – except, notably, for an ill-judged venture into non-scrap metal, when he bought a big steel firm. The house that Norton Simon built had in its rooms the usual batch of misfit investments which the Croesus type always collects: all collectors, even of businesses, are magpies.

Simon found the man to tidy up the collection in a hard-jawed former advertising agent, David J. Mahoney. Quickly satisfied by the latter's performance, Simon sold virtually all his stock and quit his own board – leaving little behind but his name. Mahoney minds the store, while the retired Simon devotes himself profitably to paying (and, when he sells off stock, getting) the world's highest prices for paintings.

Few founding fathers have the forbearance or the sense to retire from the scene so completely. But the logic is immutable. If a Weinstock or a Mahoney appears, by matrimony or by management selection, the elderly magician should retire to the wings and leave the sorcerer's apprentice free to multiply the brooms.

This policy has never worked better than for a British miller named J. Arthur Rank, whose flour had already earned him more sterling than he could conveniently spend. An ardent Methodist, Rank wanted to make good, wholesome films to counteract the insidious evil which he saw creeping over the screen. Making films was one thing: getting them shown was another. By putting the two necessities together, Rank ended up owning the largest cinema chain in the country, plus virtually all the local Hollywood (a midget, hand-me-down copy of the real thing).

There's a fascinating contrast between the Jewish immigrants, motivated principally by the money which they made in such preposterous quantities, who built Hollywood, and the reluctant Methodist who dominated British films – possibly the contrast explains why the American films were so much better. Rank found, inevitably, that movies weren't like mills, nor film stars like flour bags. He came to rely on a young professional man named John Davis, to whom fell the investment opportunity of several lifetimes.

As Hollywood's moguls foundered before TV and the death of the star system, the Rank Organization shared their sinking: until a small Rochester, New York, company, desperate to exploit the expensive new invention on which its survival depended, made Davis an offer he could easily have refused. For £600,000, however, David bought half the world rights outside North America in the unwieldy document copier which the boys from Rochester had humbly lugged over to London's Piccadilly Hotel.

In no time at all, from that unlikely start, Rank found itself riding the biggest bonanza which British business has ever seen. Profits from Rank Xerox, less than half a million pounds in 1963 blossomed to £55.5 million in a decade. As Americans seeking a backdoor into Xerox bought the shares heavily, the Rank Organization was worth around £840 million in the stock market early in 1973.

Note, moreover, who has profited most lavishly from the arrangement. Davis is not without honour in his own bank balance: at the same point in time, he had half a million pounds in Rank shares alone, and another £1 million elsewhere in the group. While something more than what the Victorians called a modest competence, it hardly compares with the nest-egg of £400 million odd in the various Rank trusts at the 1973 peak, which Davis did most to create. Any more than Dave Mahoney's holdings in Norton Simon Inc, after four years in which its earnings were boosted by 75%, would have bought him too many Rembrandts. Still, $300,000 a year in salary, $50,000 of bonus, $6 million of largely company-financed preferred stock and a wadge of stock options took Mahoney to a net worth of $14 million, which is enough, even at today's prices, to cover the odd wall.

Protégés who are unrelated are most unlikely to make the Olympian financial grade on which perch many relatives by marriage or birth. Charles Bassine, chairman of Spartans Industries, made the bad boob in 1966 of merging his clothing conglomerate with E. J. Korvette, the fading and under-managed discount store chain pioneered by Eugene Ferkauf. Spartans not only mishandled Korvette — just as badly as its founding fathers had — Bassine also lost business for his own clothes from customers who disliked being undersold by Korvette on the Spartan clothes lines. But son-in-law help was at hand.

The relative in question, Arthur Cohen, had done business with his wife's father and with Ferkauf for many years in the process of building Arlen Realty into America's biggest property chain, with £2,000 million of real estate under its wings. Worth a million in 1955, this boy wonder, who had started with $25,000, rose to $5 million in five further years. Cohen now merged with Spartans-Korvette, freeing its management from paying tax (property depreciation saves Arlen from this horror), getting the benefit of $100 million cash (obtained partly by selling Spartan's money-losing factories); and grabbing management responsibility. Armed in return with a stock exchange quote on the big board in New York, Cohen could then call for a most satisfactory recount of the family stake: it came to 30% of the entire caboodle, which contained a shareholders' equity of $160 million.

This was an achievement almost fit to rank with that of Philip Graham, whose father-in-law, Eugene Meyer, had lost $20 million on the *Washington Post* before his daughter Kay had the sense to marry a man who turned the property into a gold-mine; after her husband's suicide Mrs. Graham turned the paper into a scourge of presidents. Of course, to lose $20 million you have to be reasonably rich to start with.

To him that hath, much shall be given, remains the golden law, even in enlightened nepotism. Where the nepot should look for a surrogate son, if neither genetics nor matrimony have obliged, is a tricky question. Selecting some stalwart who has risen from the ranks seems the safest step. But there are a couple of hurdles (not counting the first of all, which is that the struggle for the crown prince's diadem will waste much energy that is better dedicated to the care of the founder's fortune).

One higher barrier is that the prince will have served so long at his master's feet that he may find it difficult to stand up straight, even if the master does a Simon-like abnegation (which he probably won't). The other main disadvantage is that tycoons are often unwilling to put total, unquestioning trust in a man whom they have ordered about for many years. The logic sounds Irish, but is akin to the inability of fathers to have uncompromising faith in their sons. One such overlord, having finally been persuaded that his newly named, loyal and able president was underpaid, reluctantly told him to put through a salary increase. After deep thought, the man gave himself $25,000 more.

The aggrieved chairman promptly summoned him and demanded an explanation. "You've only been in the job a few weeks," he expostulated, "and you've already cost me $25,000 of profit." If the tycoon looks outside for a protégé, he is less likely to show contempt and is certain not to get his man on the cheap. But unless he stumbles on a Davis or Mahoney by chance (Mahoney was working in a Simon acquisition, Canada Dry, and climbed to the top over the recumbent body of an adversary), the tycoon is apt to be terribly disappointed – and it's usually all his own fault.

He draws up an ideal blueprint, a job specification, for which the combined skills of Napoleon, Henry Ford I and Winston Churchill are required – along with the humility and sweetness of Little Nell – and then is terribly disappointed when his choice turns out to be merely human. One such visionary was always discovering a new wonder-child, who never had time to don the purple before he was being shown to the door marked exit.

Harold Ross, the editor of *The New Yorker*, was a perfect example of this kind of proprietor. He wore out managing editors at a depressingly fast rate in his endless search for perfection (the choice even fell, in one spate of inspired lunacy, on James Thurber).

Consultants or ex-consultants are especially vulnerable to this treatment. They come, armed with a reputation in modern management, into the camp of a general whose own ideas date back to the business Punic Wars. The general's natural attitude is a sceptical "show me": and he often lacks the patience or forbearance to let his adopted nephew do just that.

In one case, the private vehicle of Sir David Brown, which

57

included gears, tractors and Aston Martins, was bouncing off the road at a pace which alarmed even its bankers. (The men who run banks must be admirable companions on a tiger hunt: even the sight of a £20 million overdraft doesn't normally seem to raise their eyebrows – maybe because it isn't their money.) Brown's natural son was apparently not fully equipped by nature to handle the variegated problems bundled together by his sire. A properly selected professional manager, an ex-management consultant, was duly imported. In the typical battle between pro and proprietor, the former gained the support of the anxious banks. They theoretically bounced Sir David out of all executive power and put their trust in the pro: he lasted only a few more months, after which the knight of industry was revealed sitting once again firmly in his saddle.

Brown paid a palpable price, however: three of his businesses, including Aston Martin and the tractor enterprise, were sold to help clear the liquidity mess and the massive mountain of bank debt, over £15 million at the end of 1971. All in all, the affair was a nasty shock, which could have been avoided had the tycoon put his trust earlier in a nephew of non-tycoon propensities.

A contrasting and better example is another private outfit whose owner, anticipating a move to non-commercial pastures, carefully nursed his unofficial nephew through two or three years of sometimes painful preparation. The family future was then, in effect, placed entirely in the nephew's hands. Within a year, he had made his benefactor a paper multi-millionaire.

There is one magnate of notable capacity who, by great good fortune, conceived a natural son possessed of every necessary virtue: a calm, methodical, intelligent manager, with none of his father's passion for the big deal (of the double or single variety). The son quickly and sensibly developed the business, while his father prowled about looking for anyone whom he might devour. Every now and again, seemingly as a tease for the good son, the father would fall for some simulachum of his own young self: a fast-draw gunslinger who had made millions while still (in business terms) in short pants.

The father's favour would be publicly blazoned forth, often by the new nephew; this new love was cemented by details which were once or twice semi-publicly criticized by the good son. The implication was that Big Daddy, disappointed with his son's lack of adventure, might shift some of the inheritance to the dashing shoulders of Little Nephew.

In all the excitement, few people, even the nephews, noted that the terms of their business relationship were, as was his wont, unduly favourable to the old maestro. His favour, suddenly and warmingly given, could be just as abruptly withdrawn: at which point the ex-nephew would find himself clutching the short end of the deal. A sound policy when dealing with wealthy veterans is to assume that the wiliness and power which propelled them to their wealth has in no wise been dissipated by age. Their favour, like that of any absolute monarch, is fickle: the sane courtier protects his front at all times and never turns his back.

That's why the most successful nephews are the heroes of reverse takeovers, those paradoxical corporate devices whereby the sprat swallows the mackerel. The GEC big deal, while a perfect example of the son-in-law gambit, also worked out as a reverse operation: the much smaller Radio and Allied battle cruiser in effect took command of the entire GEC fleet.

In these cases, the nephew, the boss of the smaller concern, is backed up by his shareholdings, by his wealth (he is usually smart enough to extort a heavyweight price from the purchaser, who is by definition dumb enough to pay it) and by his reputation.

More pliable nephews can be found almost anywhere – one mail order king, a relaxed fellow who likes time to count his money, picked on his old commanding officer, hiring him for £950 a year. The ex-colonel built a business worth £36 million just twenty years later. If the paragon can be found among your kin, so much the better: it keeps all, instead of nearly all, the money in the family. But the remoter reaches of nepotism are probably a mistake in businesses which have already adopted all the standard corporate characteristics, including the routine defence mechanisms. The Du Ponts may just have got away with naming Crawford H. Greenewalt, a Du Pont by marriage, as president, although the results, the start of a long Du Pont profit stagnation, don't fully support their case.

Where professional, hired managers will accept a son, especially if they have been schooled to do so, they may jib at seeing nephews, cousins and sons-in-law stepping on to all the top rungs. In family business, it's all or nothing. Nepotists try to get round this by adopting the odd henchman as "almost one of the family": in one case, where blood was not only thicker than water, but strongly Sicilian, the few stolid Wasps who had been admitted to the inner councils were forced to become honorary Italians. One even grew a Godfather moustache.

The acid test is whether there is any chance in this life of a non-family insider being promoted over the head of a family member, as happened after 131 years at the F & M Schaefer brewing giant: a seventy-two-year-old father plucked a management expert-cum-academic from outside to replace himself as chief executive, passing over a forty-two-year-old son. If family boss follows family boss for ever more the non-kin will never be better than faithful family retainers – and some other, brusque solution, à la Schaefer, will have to be found, one day, to the inevitable succession problems.

The childless or effectively childless emperor is luckier than he knows. If he can stumble across the right protégé, the man who can make sense out of success, he can leave a lasting monument and enjoy his own last years. If he can't, or if it falls into the hands of feckless sons, the empire will eventually dissolve.

Men seldom toil to create gold alone: the business itself, their creation and dearest child, is the name of their game. Rather than lose its glory, it's far better to "let your nephew try".

ENTR'ACTE

THE CRISIS OF CONSERVATISM

or

What's Bad Enough for Grandpa

> A miserable fate overtakes the czar of European ship-
> builders, the lords of the Italian appliance industry, a
> British holiday camp king, a Casino at Monte Carlo ...
> as it overtakes all others who slip off the tightrope
> between conservatism and change.

Every business has to tread a frayed tightrope between conservatism and change. If it fails to move with the times, it risks
falling behind, as Krupp did during the forlorn effort to
prolong a nineteenth-century patriarchy into the 1960s. If an
old established company tries too hard to turn new-fangled, as
Hoover did under Herbert W. Hoover Jr., it risks destroying
the very strengths which made it great.

Theoretically, it's a toss-up which course is more dangerous, sticking too long to the old or shifting too zealously to the
new. But more once-great companies have vanished from sight
through being swamped by the tides of history than through
swimming too hard in an effort to keep up with the Marxist
dialectic. That famous news photograph of the aged Sewell
Avery being carried, chair and all, out of the Montgomery
Ward offices to end his resistance to President Truman's price
control symbolizes the fate of all firms and financial heroes
who resist history. They get beaten – Montgomery Ward, once
a name to mention in the same breath as Sears Roebuck,
became but a shadow of that mighty shape.

The issue isn't only that what's good enough for Grandpa
can't be equally good for every succeeding generation. Often
it's the old boy himself who is the purblind villain. All great
entrepreneurs have grave weaknesses, the blindest of spots,
both in their business attitudes and in their treatment of other

61

people. As they grow older and more hallowed and even wealthier, the partial blindness tends to become more severe and to affect the way in which the company does its business.

The natural belief of the rich, shared by the publicists and their public, is that the methods which brought them their yachts, mansions and Monets are not only right, brilliant and socially desirable, but everlasting. The heirs of founding fathers and grandfathers usually share this pious delusion, but worse damage may well be done by the old gentleman himself as he pursues his star to the illogical conclusion.

The post-war history of European business contains some ripe examples. A devastated Continent catching up on US standards of living, with the aid of US finance, offered inordinate opportunities to men of courage, men who often, because of the lost wartime years, came into their glory late in life. They were older in years and in background than the men who ran US business, and the concepts of public ownership or what passes for modern management were as far removed from their minds as Mars is from Earth.

Cornelius Verolme, once the czar of European shipbuilders, only began his career in his later forties. The seventh child of ten in a Calvinist family, whose mother believed in not sparing the whip, Verolme began in a small shipyard near Rotterdam, aged sixteen: he spent most of his working life with a machinery firm, and only broke out after a monumental row. He then conceived the notion that, since 5,700 Allied ships totalling twenty-three million tons had gone down during the war, an insatiable replacement market must exist – which he set out to feed first by reconditioning old marine engines.

Verolme made fast enough profits in four years to buy an old shipyard, demolish it and build a new, modern yard – much to the disgust of established Rotterdam shipbuilders, who blackballed the upstart from membership of the exclusive Rowing and Sailing Club De Maas. Blackballs notwithstanding, Verolme built over a hundred ships in under two decades to a value of more than £230 million. His was the archetypal cry of the victorious grandfather: "Never have any doubts about your own ability. Never ask, can I do it? No, do it!"

The catch was that, like most powerful self-made men, Verolme not only did it, but sought to do it all himself. Virtually all that anybody save Verolme knew about profits was that they were mostly ploughed back. (As for capital and reserves, they were as secret as earnings.) At this point, the twin grandparental diseases of inordinate ambition and over-weening self-confidence over-ran the system. Verolme got caught with an uncompleted monster shipbuilding dock, a difficult merger with a loss-making partner, and a pile of supertanker orders taken at unfunny prices.

The old man, turned seventy, had to be bailed out by the government from a desperately leaky situation – total losses in 1969, the new régime reckoned, came to £14.7 million. An ex-Philips manager, called in to man the pumps, put his finger on the nub of the problem. "I warned him several times that in the end he would not be thanked if he went on running the show himself as long as possible . . . It is nonsense for a man of almost seventy to travel around the world personally to win orders."

But Verolme knew no other way of life: even from his big yacht, he had kept constantly in touch with his office on shore: even with his group virtually bankrupt, he kept on fighting to regain control of the £100 million empire which he had created and all but destroyed. The Greeks would have loved the epic tale of the old king who pulled down his kingdom about his ears by clinging too long to the methods which had originally raised him to the throne.

Similar doomed kings abound in business history. The Italian appliance industry had one of the sharpest rises and falls. After the war, consumer durables in Italy lacked both a market and manufacturers: the future lords of this slice of creation had begun by making iron-age products like wood-burning stoves, the original speciality of the Zanussi family. Another future giant, Ignis, began in 1943, when Guido Borghi, with sons Gaetano, Giovanni, and Guiseppe, started making electric stoves.

As Italian housewives began to clamour for more electric labour-saving, the manufacturers expanded at a furious pace, built the most efficient and productive plants in the world, and barged so heavily into other European markets (they had to, to keep the productive monster satisfied) that they virtually destroyed much of the competition. In the process they so saturated their own market that the Italian boom in refrigerators was over by the mid-1960s; that in washing machines ended by 1967–68. The rest of Europe peaked out only slightly later, and the Italian tycoons were left with a tortuous management problem – and no managers to solve it.

63

Fortuitously, the families were hit by dynastic and business disaster simultaneously. Lino Zanussi, the entrepreneur nearest to managerial stature and builder of the strongest group, died in an air crash with his heir apparent. Only one Borghi survived to take Ignis into the all-enveloping embrace of Philips. The three Zoppas brothers died within twelve months of each other, leaving £50 million-odd of bank debts and a company, taken over *in extremis* by Zanussi, losing about two-thirds of a million each month.

Another Zanussi buy, Triplex, was losing only marginally fewer millions, as the workers, the original beneficiaries of the appliance boom, acting as the final wreckers by staging a spate of strikes, staved off only by ruinous wage increases. Accidents aside, the families paved the way for their own dissolution by continuing to manage businesses of international scale with methods insufficiently remote from the old wood-burning days.

The appearance of simultaneous dynastic disasters emphasizes the chief danger of family enterprise: a bad genealogical run can ruin the act. In Lancashire textiles, where the heredity seems to have been no great shakes, the saying used to be clogs to clogs in four generations. These days it's far harder to return to square one: tycoons may lose their businesses, but seldom all their baksheesh.

There are cases of yacht to dinghy, triplex apartment to farm, Rolls-Royce to Rover or Pontiac in one generation, more often in one lifetime. In the Age of the Common Millionaire, few families are foolish enough to leave all their eggs in one locked-in basket, and few husbands imprudently forget to set up their wives in the manner to which they have both been accustomed. The two devices which have created and perpetuated the Common Millionaire, the partial sale of equity to the doting public and the "provision for the family" in a man's lifetime by the formation of trusts, both also serve to keep the family in bread and butter in the event of failure, by grandpa or his heirs. You wouldn't know, from his style of living, that Bill Zeckendorf's Webb and Knapp property empire had ever gone bankrupt – he even preserved the same once-famous, circular office.

Following the draconian law of business, that incompetence breeds more incompetence, few sights are more awe-inspiring, however, than the completion by heirs of the crumbling begun

64

by the progenitor. Had William Randolph Hearst possessed less megalomania, less talent as a newspaperman and more business acumen, the Hearst empire would today be fit to share the same paragraph as Ford or possibly even Mellon. But Hearst's dictatorial methods and disdain for economics left his two sons a dwindling empire with a managerial heritage which they proceeded to dissipate by squabbling with the managers.

The thirty papers which remained at the old man's death, still a formidable collection, shrank to eight. Unheard-of and relatively diminutive figures like Samuel I. Newhouse overtook the giant with stupefying ease. In one generation, it was almost as if W.R. had never rejected an editorial: after two generations, there was even less evidence that W.R.'s father had ever exploited the Comstock Lode.

The Hearst money was big, the biggest, and it's this size of accumulation which was thought all but impossible to destroy: as Henry Ford I proved by the survival of a colossal family inheritance through a decade of grotesque mismanagement and inept financial provision. But modest money takes a great deal of destruction too: as shown by the fate of one fascinating phenomenon of Britain in the post-war period, the proletarian passion for taking holidays en masse, in holiday camps which recreated something of the atmosphere of the wartime services.

Campers were woken at military hours with screams of "Wakey! Wakey!"; dragooned into enjoying themselves by staff actually called "Redcoats", a name strikingly reminiscent of the "Redcaps" or military police; fed in gigantic refectories with food which the Army Catering Corps wouldn't have (though it should have) been ashamed to own. But the holidays were cheap, matey, fun for the kids – and a Canadian named Billy Butlin (who became Sir William for his pains) made many millions from the game.

Departing for the Bahamas, he handed over to his son at a time when the business clearly needed new ideas even more than new blood. Other fortunes were being created from shipping the same masses by the million to Spain, where the cost was comparable, the sun actually shone, the food was edible, the booze was cheap and the atmosphere was not paramilitary. But Butlins management proved unable to solve the problem, partly because Sir Billy had persisted in believing that the British public still wanted his holiday camps with undimmed passion.

In this situation, the heirs failed to see that, from being a majority taste, camps had become a minority trade – and serving a cheap minority market is a poor financial joke. From profits of £5 million at the peak, the chain sank steadily to £3.4 million at its worst; even the turnover slid slowly downwards. The camps were finally sold to the Rank Organization after Sir Billy had made a last-minute, dramatic reappearance on the scene.

Re-materialization was also managed by W. Maxey Jarman, the prodigious apparel acquirer whose buying had lifted Genesco from $360 million of sales to $1,200 million. Just like Butlin, Jarman handed on the mantle to his son: and this son, too, proved unable to wear his father's shoes. When profits more than halved, and then went on downwards, the terrified directors simply called Maxey back. He took one look at his own purchases and concluded tersely that about a quarter of them were "no good" – no wonder his heir, who then had to wage a bruising war to get his father dematerialized again, hit worse trouble than Sir Billy's.

Billy's own shares went when their going value was £2.2 million; they had been worth over twice as much – and were once worth a good deal less than half the price reached when Rank saved some of the Butlin bacon. In much the same way, a young man named Geoffrey Kaye, on his father's death, mismanaged the Pricerite supermarket chain into a state where its internal accounts could show non-existent profits, but cleared nearly £7 million from the eventual bid: this family's stake had once been worth nearer £13 million, and the incidents demonstrate how, even in an undistinguished, one-product company in a declining shabby market, a family can grow poorer, while still staying rich enough to take care of every need of subsequent generations: provided, that is, that the generations are neither excessively prolific nor over-fond of disputation.

In the 1920s the German family of Stinnes possessed one of Europe's premium fortunes, not of Rothschild rank, but fit to vie with Krupp and the like. In the nineteenth century shipping and coal had founded the fortune; with the third generation, Hugo, known as the King of Assyria for his stern black beard, added steel, oil and paper-making to the mix. Within two years of Hugo's death, the family had to turn to US banks for $25 million.

The family kept half the US company, which now held most of the Stinnes assets, but lost these (as enemy property) in the war. Through all this period, and thereafter, the main problem was the total inability of Hugo's three sons to abide each other. One was bought out: the other two had to be forcibly parted by the widow, who sacked the second son. This Stinnes, Hugo Jr., went off to found his own empire in engineering and plastics. When that came unstuck in 1963, the rest of the family interests, still presided over by the King of Assyria's widow at the age of ninety-three, were also on the rocks.

A not so incidental fact is that the final manager of the widow's truncated empire was Franz von Papen, the last German Chancellor before Adolf Hitler. It's nearly always a fatal sign when proprietors bring in political or similarly distinguished figures to heal family divisions or to mend family fortunes. The latter task is always beyond his powers, ability and experience: as for the rifts within, the poor man must either side with one or the other, or be torn apart.

An equally unpleasant and faster fate overtook the heirs of Sir Frederick Handley-Page, one of the great aviation pioneers, who made a bomb out of wartime and post-war bombers. HP's planes were the spearhead of Britain's erstwhile nuclear strike force. He was an autocrat of striking independence and considerable age, who, alone among the aviation overlords refused to accept the government's forceful wish that the industry should merge into larger units. His reluctance failed to endear the company to those who doled out public contracts, without which a defence company is as well-placed as a footballer with two broken legs.

When the great man died, in 1962, he left this dubious inheritance to three daughters, and too many females, in western society as at present organized, make a distinct drawback. One of the husbands took over; Handley-Page, still wedded to the old man's dreams of independence, started looking desperately for some non- or para-military business. It came up with the Jetstream, an airliner which, had it been able to pack in as many passengers for the price as the specification suggested, would undoubtedly have beaten the world. In fact, it could do neither, and all it beat was the company – plus Bernie Cornfeld's IOS. Three of his sales sidekicks had bought unsaleable Jetstreams at $530,000 a throw, all financed by IOS banks.

Contemplation of such cases reinforces the belief that fathers and grandfathers, however brilliant, should be compelled to retire from executive action at the ripe young age of sixty-five, and should only be succeeded by sons on somebody else's decision — even though this contradicts the fact, equally well established in this account, that many lasting fortunes have been supervised day-to-day to a great age by their progenitors.

The clue lies somewhere along that dangerous tightrope between continuity and change. If the progenitor possesses some instinct, even if only the desire to maximize a profit which keeps him flexible into his dotage, he may do more good than harm. Once he gets glued into his ideas and ways, however, disaster is likely to follow: not least because his successors, lacking his genius, will be as heavily indoctrinated in his rigidity.

It used to be a matter for marvel how superbly the successor generations at Pirelli, Fiat and Olivetti had carried on the founder's good work. Men like Leopoldo Pirelli or Giovanni Agnelli (after the latter gave up playboying for business) had heroic reputations. The consequent temptation has been to blame not the sons but their circumstances for the disasters of the last few years. Nevertheless, in the third management upheaval visited on Olivetti in seven hard years, Roberto was retired to a non-executive position — even though the family had 22.9% of the company.

Managements which suffer such monumental reverses can't have been doing everything right. Fiat was, after all, forced to omit its dividend. The Agnellis, whose tentacles spread into every corner of Italian business life, can manage without the money. But could their main company have done better without the one-man Agnelli pinnacle? If your father and grandfather dominated the show, you are unlikely to settle for less. This is rarely a source of strength — the exceptions prove a different rule.

Four successive Johnsons have headed S. C. Johnson, the private wax and polish royalty of Racine, Wisconsin, with world sales of around half a billion pounds. According to one admiring executive, there's "not a drop-out, not a lemon, among them. Each one has been more aggressive than his father in business terms. They've all had different ideas about what could and should be done, and each seems to have had the very strong feeling that anything the old man could do, he could do a lot better."

The Johnsons, in addition to inculcating business sense into their sons, have indoctrinated their scions in a social ethic of good works. This has given the company a frame of reference more specific than the general Italian paternalism, as practised at Fiat *et al*. But Fiat is still run in an autocratic manner which the old Agnelli, and his strongman successor, Professor Valletta, would have recognized. The reasons are not just Italian (although from mediaeval and Renaissance times dynasties have wielded most of the country's real power). The autocracy also reflects a curious internal logic of car companies the world over.

Historical accident produced car companies which were structured around one man, largely because the successful car empires (a handful of survivors from a legion of competitors) were built around one automotive hit: and a wonder car almost always springs from one man's instinct and inspiration. The Ford company under Henry II, though perforce utterly different in most ways from the creation Henry I left behind, still bows its collective head to the reigning Mr. Ford, who is less a *primus inter pares* than a king among courtiers.

Showing, say, the British company's new models to "Mr. Ford" for prior approval is a futile exercise in the management sense — this one American's opinion on what will sell in Europe is almost certainly not worth having. But the trundling up for pats or kicks makes perfect sense in the atmosphere of a court. And if the dynastic firms lag behind in adapting their management styles to changed days and ways — including the irritating wish of the workers to have some say about their work — the fortunes of the dynasties are sure to suffer: as they have done in Italy. Leopoldo Pirelli, returning to work in 1973 after a car crash which killed his brother, had to face the hard fact that management autocracy coupled with technical failure had laid his company appallingly low.

Another strange case of ossified attitudes overtaken by change afflicted the one-time focus of the crowned wealth of the world, Monte Carlo. Prince Rainier III, though substantially bolstered by the money Princess Grace made from movies and being an Irish-American builder's daughter, can't be indifferent to the fortunes of its casino, in which his State owns a 72% controlling interest — a stake dating back to the creation, in 1966, of enough new shares in the Société des Bains de Mer to deprive Aristotle Onassis of the control he sought.

Once upon a time, the SBM was one of the world's great money-mines. One François Blanc in 1863 paid $366,000 for the Casino concession. He died fourteen years later worth over $14 million. Those were the years when kings and grand dukes rubbed shoulders and chips; that was when the expensive favours of the "Great Horizontals", courtesans like Liane de Pougy, Emilienne d'Alençon and Cléo de Merode could be had for the paying. (They were also known as the "Ladies Who Cushion".) Today amateurs have ousted the professional ladies, and other haunts are attracting the gambling money of a lower class of clientele. But the men who ran the bank at Monte Carlo continued to act as if Edward VII were still arriving for his nightly diversion.

SBM actually started losing money: a state of affairs roughtly akin to Kuwait having a gasoline shortage. The year before they reported their first loss, the old guard resorted to the ancient manoeuvre of cashing in some assets (to wit, blue chip securities) to cover up the falling profits, and raise the dividend. The next year misfortune, as it usually does, followed on deception. Gambling income dropped to less than half the normal take.

Rainier had to instal his cousin, Prince Louis de Polignac, as president and to find, of all things, a Harvard Business School graduate as managing director. Even then, the 1972 net of some 7.5 million francs is a long way short of mountainous standards. What goes up, says the law of nature, must come down. And the history of all monarchies, tiny ones like that of the Grimaldis in Monaco or lay monarchies like that of the Agnellis in Turin, demonstrates the working of that natural law in human institutions.

The wreckage a truly determined family can wreak on grandpa's legacy is demonstrated in reverse by the work done on Waterman by the unlikely Mme Francine Gomez. Waterman once enjoyed all but a tithe of US fountain pen sales: but the US company, battered by ball-points, had been sold in 1958, while the French company, which had the European rights, struggled steadily towards the grave. Mme Gomez, taking control of the inheritance from her mother, had to sack nine out of ten top executives, cut the labour force by 485 persons, reduce the head office to a quarter of its former size, move it, buy back the US company and refurbish everything in sight – thus converting a half a million loss into a $1.5 million profit.

If grandpa and his heirs are to hang on to their hats, that ideal balance has to be struck between conservatism and radicalism. The principles are quite easy. First, no cow can be sacred – anything can be changed, and anybody can be put out to grass, if change or grassing appear necessary. Second, there's an obvious distinction between those traditions which are material to the business and those which are merely nice to have around – like a clump of mistletoe at Christmas. Leave the latter alone, so long as they don't cost much and people like them. As for the former meticulously question every one: and if the answers come out wrong, found a new tradition.

Finally, suppose that the business is running quite beautifully: don't succumb completely to the correct urge to leave well alone. Search for one area of inadequately exploited opportunity: find one function or part of the company which isn't running with the same degree of smooth beauty as the rest. Concentrate on these two fields – good grandpas always do, before their arteries begin to harden.

But that leads to the hardest trick of all: removing or immobilizing the old boy (or boys) before he (they) start costing the rest of the family a deal of money. Short of parricide, which isn't legal, there is no sure method. The older the family incubus gets, the harder it becomes to insult him, to intimate that he is no longer wanted. There is only one gun that his juniors can level at his head – a threat that, if he doesn't go, they will. But heirs are generally too intimidated (and too scared, often with good reason, of their chances of finding acceptable employment elsewhere) to fire that weapon. They prefer, unwittingly but surely, to go down with the captain – and the ship.

ACT II

On the Delights of Deception
or
Honesty is the Worst Policy

SCENE 1

THE FORTUNES IN FRAUD

or

You Can Fool All the People

The principles of Pyramids (and the Apple Miracle, the Pig Pay-Off and the Casino Caper), with a short sketch of the careers of two gentlemen, Glenn Turner and Bernie Cornfeld, who raised the art of parting the public from its money to global dimensions.

You can fool all the people — not all the time, but for enough of it to steal their money. The definitions of theft range from criminal dishonesty to false bills of goods, and the penalties range from mere business failure to moderate prison terms. But the punishment seldom fits the crime — somehow or other, the thief nearly always ends up in possession of enough loot to line a gilded cage for his retirement or future activities, even if he is caught.

Mythologists of crime dream of a Mr. Big, the Mephistophelian brain behind the £2 million Great Train Robbery in Britain, the $2.75 million Brinks caper in the USA, the removal of the Nazi gold reserves at the end of the Second World War, the wave of art robberies that have run curators and collectors ragged all over Europe. But only a pervert would suffer the possible prison penalties, the logistic difficulties, the dangerous and incompetent colleagues and the other risks attendant on robbing even a small bank — when he can start his own bank, and rob the depositors in comfort.

Simple thieving is no longer followed by real bankers, on the whole, because they are too tightly policed and regulated (politicians and cops, after all, need somewhere safe to put their own cash). But it's not only the fuzz that keeps the good banks straight — it's the fact that their money is, relatively speaking, so easy to earn.

75

People deposit their hard-earned dollars, pounds, marks, francs, lire, yens or zloty: the bank pays most of them no interest at all or a stingy pittance (if it's a Swiss bank, it makes the depositor pay for the privilege); yet so profoundly do the rich trust the Swiss that they place other loot in non-interest-bearing accounts: then the same bank lends out that same money at rates of up to 16%. If you are borrowing £1,000 for nothing and lending it for £160 a year, you don't need much else to wax rich: even after paying for the marble halls and marble-headed managers with which banks are traditionally oversupplied.

The principal species of millionaire-making fraud is a variation on the banking theme. The gambit is to persuade people to give their money to you, rather than to the bank, by the childish expedient of offering them a return which is higher than nothing. The recorded annals of deception (probably there were variations in ancient Egypt) include the Apple Miracle, the Pig Pay-Off, the Casino Caper, the Pyramid Ploy and many, many others: as soon as one con is destroyed, another (often the same one) rears its head.

With apples, the idea was that the city-dweller should buy himself a piece of the action in an orchard, because (as everybody knows) one little seed will grow into a big tree, showering apples and wealth on its owners for ever more. Pigs were another form of armchair farming: those noble animals have enormous litters, at great speed, so that possession of just one sow, cared for you by the promoter, would confer the benefits of compound breeding and interest for all eternity.

Casinos were for armchair gamblers. You turned over your money to a wizard who had an infallible system for winning at the tables; he creamed off a commission for his pains, and paid all the rest, at stupendous rates of interest, to his happy backers. One such scheme in 1962 offered the suckers a 360% return in theory: in practice none of the twenty thousand of them got more than a fifth of their money back.

The oldest ploy, possibly older even than apples, is the pyramid, adopted with unstoppable enthusiasm in the early 1970s by US promoters like Glenn Turner of Dare-To-Be-Great, a motivational marvel, and Koscot Interplanetary cosmetics, if you please: or the late, unlamented William Penn Patrick, under whom Turner learnt the trade, and whom the Securities and Exchange Commission accused of taking eighty thousand investors for more than $250 million of Holiday Magic – which sold soap as well as cosmetics. These US wonders were exported gleefully to the British, who have always been suckers for a quick buck.

In its origins the pyramid possessed perfect simplicity – best shown by the chain letter idea. Each participant is supposed to find a fixed number of other kindred spirits, who in turn each find the same number, until by the laws of geometrical progression a sum of money vastly greater than the original small amount comes in turn to each link in the chain. The logical defect is that no money is coming into the scheme from outside. Even if the chain doesn't break, the first come are the first served – but break it must. The mathematical fact is that with each person recruiting four people, it takes only a relatively few stages before the entire population of the United Kingdom, men, women, children and possibly even a few dogs, will be in the pyramid.

Precisely the same objection applied to schemes like Koscot. The gimmick of the Koscot-style pyramid is that its structure is linked to the sale of the wonder-product: cosmetics, or liquid cleaner, or whatever. Each link in the pyramid recruits other links to sell the goodies in a carefully-constructed hierarchy of regional bosses, distributors and salesmen.

The subscription is a purchase of the wonder-stock, offset by bonuses for each new link recruited into the chain. It looks absolutely safe: the money hasn't gone for nothing, but for goods you can see, feel, count – and sell at a satisfyingly high profit margin. The mathematics are magical: according to the SEC, if each Holiday Magic distributor signed up as many others as he was supposed to, 305,175,780 people would be flogging the junk (presumably to each other) within twelve months. The existence of the stuff, however, appears to make the pyramid more plausible: but it actually makes the whole scheme utterly incredible.

The combined profit margins add up to several times the ex-factory cost at the start of the chain – a price which presumably includes a profit. What the pyramided suckers should wonder is why, if the product is truly saleable at such gigantic mark-ups, its proprietor should want to let so many others into so lucrative an act. This is the self-same question that should be, but isn't, asked by those tempted by piggies, apples, casinos and so on: if the profits are truly so great, why does the man need my money?

Even when the promised returns work out at an annual rate of over 300% the victims still wonder not. Their own urge to get rich quick blinds them. Actually, if you could invest £250 at 300%, you would be a millionaire in six years – nice work if you could get it. What is more pathetic, however, is that millions of people down the years have been tempted to part with their cash by quite small rates of interest, or (which comes to the same thing) small savings of money.

Two firms which crashed in Britain, for instance, regularly offered interest on deposits 2% or 3% above the going rate. There was no obvious way in which they could earn enough on the deposits to cover the interest: actually, there was no way. One firm, called Pinnock Finance, was Australian-based and was vaguely supposed to be in sewing machines. After its presiding genius had vanished with the boodle, it appeared that Pinnock had worked the oldest trick in the con game, as faithfully practised by the casino and apple boys.

You pay off the first suckers from the money generously provided by the next set, and so on *ad infinitum*. Just as the pig scheme only contained a third of the happily breeding pigs promised to investors, so much of the Pinnock money went nowhere except into the Pinnock money. The crunch comes when the flow of new money dries up, and the owners of the old money start wanting it back.

This painful conjunction caught a slippery specialist named Dr. Emil Savundra in its icy grip. Savundra's speciality was to offer motorists insurance on their cars at premiums well below the going rate. Note that phrase again: if a rate is going, there's a *prima facie* case that it's the correct rate. Unable to resist the bargain, drivers earnestly loaded their cash into the hands of Savundra's Fire Auto and Marine, where the fat proprietor, with even greater earnestness, off-loaded as much of the proceeds as possible into his own pockets (located mostly in overseas bank accounts). When the inevitable collapse came, as accident claims by motorists exceeded the amount of money left in Savundra's kitty, the cops followed fast – and so did his conviction.

Savundra's fraud thus had a serious defect, shared with the devices of even greater removal experts, Tino de Angelis, the salad-oil magician, and Billy Sol Estes, the silo wizard. All three men made, or conjured up, personal profits running into several millions. Both de Angelis and Sol Estes preyed on the Achilles heel of the modern economy, which is its total dependence on bits of paper. If a man waves a document which says there is grain in a silo, or oil in a storage tank, banks are wont to lend money on that security just as readily as a Savundra customer, having purchased a policy, believed that his car was safely insured.

If bankers checked every individual paper transaction for its underlying reality, the log-jam would reach intolerable proportions by noon on the first day. De Angelis fastened on this fact (just as, in an earlier era, Ivar Kreuger issued $500 millions in fictitious bonds) to the grand total of $120 million. Nobody knows how much of these sums – $167 million zoomed out of the de Angelis company in its last six months of life – was stashed away awaiting his exit from gaol. But there's the catch: the convicted con has to face the inconvenience of a spell behind bars before he can enjoy his proceeds.

De Angelis caught a ten-year sentence, meaning seven years with parole. If the estimates of his take are correct and he hung on to half, that works out at $100 per hour of maximum captivity. In fact, that's not a great rate of return. However you look at it, going to prison is a bad technical lapse, a blotch on the escutcheon of an alleged expert in the business of parting the customers from their money.

It took another American to elevate this craft to the status of a higher art. Bernie Cornfeld, caliph and court jester of Investors Overseas Services. At its peak this mega-mish-mash contained $2,500 million of the suckers' money. How much of it ended in the maw of Bernie and his no less eager cohorts will never be known. But the public flotation of IOS Ltd. alone, the final act in its *Götterdammerung*, made the Cornfeld and Co. stake worth $52 million – and that is competitive even with de Angelis.

Cornfeld's advantage over the piggy man, Savundra and Sol Estes was that, while holding out the self-same bait of riches, he actually offered *less* than the going rate. His idea, a stroke of pure genius, was to sell people dollar bills for $2. Any IOS customer in the US armed forces, where Bernie started business, could have bought mutual funds direct. The disadvantage of these investments, especially those of the so-called "front-end load" genus, is that a major part of the investors' money

79

goes straight to the salesman and the management, not into the investment.

With front-end load, the investor loses half of his initial outlay in this wildly unproductive way. On one calculation, the load and the continuing management charges meant that if an investment doubled in ten years, the investor would have had to wait for six of them to get back on speaking terms with his own money. In Bernie Cornfeld's case the customers paid his Fund of Funds to put their money into the same mutual funds which the overseas Americans whom he first tapped could easily have bought for themselves; the funds also paid Bernie and exacted their own toll, before finally depositing the cash into some kind of investment.

The set-up was so glorious that eventually IOS couldn't stand seeing any of the suckers' money going into somebody else's wallet. So it set up its own internal mutual funds. The customer still paid twice for the same service, but (which was a great improvement) he now paid Bernie twice. What's more, the internal funds were not confined to staid, quoted investments whose market value could be ascertained in a trice by reading the *Wall Street Journal*.

This unconfined joy in turn made it easier to deliver what the customers thought they were buying — which was capital gain on (it was implied, advertised and blazoned forth) a phenomenal scale. With funds as large as those of IOS, however, it was impossible to generate this kind of performance. The sheer weight of so much money was bound to bring down the funds if world stock markets fell, and Cornfeld could not suspend this law of financial gravity. Hence his ventures into dubious areas like the oil land operations of another master in the school of parting people from their money, John M. King.

King's bait was oil for the masses. Working on the mutual fund principle, including that of deducting heavy compensation for his pains, King was supposed to invest the money in oil wells drilled by his own corporation — which provided all other services required, at a price. The beauty of this scheme defied imitation: investors naturally had to accept that some oil wells came up dry. If King failed to deliver the bounty, it was an act of God rather than man, deductible (what was more) as a tax loss.

The King of Denver truly delivered for his friend Bernie Cornfeld. IOS invested in some territory found by King: a sale

80

of a fraction of the tract was arranged at a staggering price which, when applied to all of the IOS holding (actually a bauble of dubious worth), amounted to a $145 million capital gain, prudently whittled down to a mere $91 million.

This was the purest fairy gold. But in practical terms, it hardly matters whether a value is fictitious or real, so long as the fiction is believed. This lovable fact spawned an entire new branch of the money-lifting industry. Devoted students of Cornfeld's success plugged the main weakness in his operation: its ultimate dependence on stock markets, which by their very nature fluctuate. Property, on the other hand, is popularly supposed to go up and up as it goes up. A real estate mutual fund could therefore offer an investment paradise on earth — absolute security with everlasting growth, and good income to boot.

The investors (milked from the front-end as usual) were therefore offered little pieces of large buildings in the lush USA. Gramco, the most successful of these operations, would run the properties (at a substantial fee) and would periodically announce how much they had increased in value. In fact, the real value of this real estate was purely putative: you can sell shares at any time, but off-loading a portfolio of up-valued skyscrapers is no easier than selling your house at your own top price.

In other words, the investors who flocked to Gramco (and to even more obviously fraudulent imitators like Jerome Hoffman of the very unreal Real Estate Fund of America) were unwittingly burying their money in the most illiquid form of investment possible. The whole credibility of the edifice depended on the suckers continuing to believe it. If too many of them simultaneously wanted their money back, even in a completely honest operation, their Comstock Lode would have to sell its fairy gold — and if the fairy gold failed to fetch fairy prices, down would come the entire estate, buildings and all.

To illustrate this truth, say that the suckers have paid $1,000 million for their stake: you decide, after a time, that the buildings are worth $1,500 million, when actually their realizable value is $1,200 million. Any not-such-a-sucker who thereupon takes his money out gets 50% more than he put in: it follows that if half the clients ask for the loot, you must pay out $750 million, leaving only $450 million to satisfy $750 million of claims.

Actually, crisis would be reached well before that point. As soon as schemes of this kind start, for whatever reason, to experience a net outflow of investors' funds, the jig is up, their days are numbered, and the vultures gather.

The Gramco fund, USIF, was eventually stuck with a billion in property, twenty thousand anguished stockholders and 1,700 salesmen running to keep a step ahead of the aforesaid investors. John Thackray reports that the El Salvador representative, on learning of the disaster, checked with an atlas to find the furthest spot on the globe from El Salvador and took a plane there forthwith. Many Gramco and IOS customers were Latin Americans bent on sending untaxed money to safer, less inflationary climes. It served them right. Gramco was caught in the IOS backwash — but it would have fallen, anyway.

But the Cornfeld Gambit and its variations not only proved unprecedentedly efficient at putting greedy hands in investors' pockets: they generated so rich a cash flow that preceding the vultures, other fatter fowls of the air came clustering — the brokers, the fund managers, the bankers, the underwriters: all clamouring for a piece of the action. Drexel Harriman & Ripley in the USA, Hill Samuel in Britain and the French Rothschilds (the English ones asked to be excused) were intimate actors in the final stages of building Bernie's Valhalla: and in the twilight of the gods which ensued, many and white were the respectable hands being washed.

Respectable front, back or side names are no protection for the investor. His true defence is simple refusal to believe that money is subject to miracles. His true weakness is envy. Armchair farming, gambling in plush casinos for high stakes, wheeling and dealing on world stock markets, owning oil wells and skyscrapers — all these are hobbies for those who are already rich. Would-be millionaires fall for their own envy, and the Cornfelds of this world shrewdly exploit that temptation: so shrewdly, in fact, that there is no reason why, given self-restraint, they could not have lasted far longer. So much money was flowing into IOS at its peak that merely lending out the cash before it was invested produced a torrent of wealth, all of which would have belonged to the Cornfeld mob if they had known how to stop it streaming right out again.

But the expenses of running a world-wide door-to-door selling operation are also wondrous: the instincts for mob-psychology of these entrepreneurs arise from their own weakness, which rules out any chance of retrenchment or caution: and, anyway, they are terrified of any fall-off of the money flow.

The writing on the wall for Gramco, in fact, appeared even before Bernie's blackout: the Gramco proprietors Keith Barish and Rafael Navarro, as unlikely a pair of boy wonder financiers as ever flashed across the sky, took over two dozen pages in a news magazine to discuss their financial and philanthropic virtues, in full colour. Those sufficiently unenthralled with these gods among men to seek details of the company's system for paying commission (a highly material subject) were cross-referenced to number eighteen of the unnumbered pages; the eighteenth page contained no reference whatsoever to the commission system. But the customers of such speeches don't really want to know anything, except that they are getting richer. And they do not share the instinctive feeling of the experienced hand that if somebody has to buy two dozen pages of advertising to say how wonderful he is, he can't be.

There was, truth to tell, something terribly, appallingly wrong with all the great con artists of our time: something so abominably amiss that any reasonably shrewd child off the Brooklyn streets (where Bernie Cornfeld grew up) could be expected to spot the defect at once. They are not the obvious philanthropic types, these gentry. They are flashy, showy, greedy, conceited: they give themselves away by hiring expensive political names as window dressing: they act like exactly the kind of used car salesman from whom you shouldn't buy; the type which only has to accomplish one trick to sell the jalopy – which is to sell you themselves. If you can believe them, you can believe anything, including their unbelievable propositions.

The collapse of IOS was perhaps the neatest demonstration of this historical process. As Cornfeld's sun sank painfully slowly in the west, no less weighty a figure than John M. King, the Colorado Bull Elephant, made the early running at rescue. As King's empire in turn melted in the glare of publicity, Robert M. Vesco appeared from nowhere like a Jack-in-the-box. Within a remarkably short time, Vesco had disappeared in his private Boeing 707, into the welcoming arms of President José Figueres of Costa Rica, while the SEC sought, in high dudgeon, to discover the exact whereabouts of $224 million in IOS funds.

"We brought down our families," said Vesco, "enrolled our children in excellent schools, and started our new life in this American Arcadia." There was no Arcadian resting place for either Vesco, caught up in the Watergate disaster and hounded by the authorities, or for Bernie Cornfeld, arrested by the aggrieved Swiss authorities on a visit to his aged mother, and popped into a gaol to ponder for long months over the dwindling of his IOS fortune from $150 million to $5 million.

The Joe McCarthys of the business world live off the Big Lie, off the law that the more outrageous a proposition, the more likely its hearers are to suspend their critical faculties altogether. In this the ungodly are aided and abetted by the virtuous – not merely in the way the latter, too, fall both for the Big Lie and the easy commissions it generates, but because the godly also make such hay out of the savings of the small.

Take the most popular form of investment, the thoroughly respectable industry of life insurance. In Britain the insurers take people's money year after year, with no firm undertaking to pay back more than the face value on expiry: if the investor wants his money back in mid-term, he has to take a large loss: he has no information about what investments, in turn, the company is making on his behalf, or how well they have done: by and large, the results are no better than could have been achieved by investing in a unit trust: and the profits to the company are so large that it can afford to pay very handsome commissions to the agent who merely books the business.

In the USA, by the same happy conjunction of circumstances, the men who sell insurance have profited so mightily that they account for a significant crop in the harvest of post-war millionaires. These are men like the tub-thumping super-salesman W. Clement Stone, practitioner of success through a positive mental attitude, open-handed distributor of largesse to Richard M. Nixon and other positive political thinkers, and author of the ripe remark: "If a family has wealth in the neighbourhood of $400 million, what's a million in gifts?"

At least, you could assume that regular insurance companies were honest – until Stanley Goldblum came along, that is. Ex-butcher Goldblum was the genius behind Equity Funding, the "blue-suede shoes, hipster type of outfit", in the posthumous words of one Wall Street observer, which made the immortal discovery that you don't actually need to sell people insurance policies to achieve $2,000 million a year of sales. Far easier to invent the people – then you can invent the policies, too.

At the first count, Equity had fifty thousand phantom policies, and sold the premiums to other insurance companies (so-called re-insurance) to create $25 million of far from phantom income. Not only were the purchasers fooled: so were the investment experts, which, as a matter of unpalatable fact, is their normal form. Equity's dishonesty was bred from the need to feed a stock price which had soared from $6 to $80 in five years, then had dribbled down to $13 a year later. Yet a group of analysts specializing in this area chose Equity Funding as their pet stock among all the finance and financial services bundles on the market. That was at the beginning of 1972 – about a year before the whistle blew on this people-fooler. The whistle always does blow, in the end: but too late to save the people's pelf.

The mainline insurers can continue to collect their easy pickings. Returns of 4% a year on invested funds (which big insurance companies think decent) are well below recent rates of inflation: but the average investor has never had a respectable home for his money which would both defend its real value and return some income for its use.

When the decent, established, accepted forms of investment offer so poor a deal to investors, it's no surprise that a gigantic latent market exists for those who are less scrupulous, but who offer (or appear to) a better bargain. The fact that the offer is always some modern inverted version of the philosopher's stone, turning gold back to base metal, will never deter the unwary: so around that stone, coming out from under it if necessary, will cluster all those with a highly developed nose for the scent of other people's money.

SCENE 2

THE TREASURE IN STATISTICS

or

Lies, Damned Lies and Figures

In which the penchant of people to believe numbers, and the eagerness of accountants to get paid for their labours, are exploited to multiply non-existent profits by incredible factors to create sensational paper fortunes . . . and inevitable collapses.

The economic world is full of engaging, exploded ideas in which everybody believes: none more engaging or detonated than the notion that only governments can print money. Ever since the invention of the banking system by the Italians, banks have been creating paper gold: and ever since some genius stumbled across the joint stock company, individuals have been free to engage in the same profoundly rewarding activity.

Printing money means producing a piece of your own paper which others will accept in exchange for the pieces of paper put out officially by the government. Just as the government's paper no longer has to be backed by solid gold, the paper spawned in streams by individuals and corporations need have no foundation either. That is why the old, simple tests of millionairedom no longer apply – even though so seasoned and flush a hand as J.P. Getty still believes that a millionaire is someone whose assets are worth $1 million.

That depends on what you mean by worth. It can't mean that the man should be able to produce $1 million of his own cash, since a large proportion of the assets won't be readily negotiable and many of them may be covered by debt. Even if he can write a million-dollar cheque, all that proves is that somebody will honour the paper. Getting the paper honoured is the real necessity: and getting the maximum amount of honour is the real trick. It has nothing to do with the underlying economic assets which the paper-pusher possesses, but everything to do with clever mathematical games.

Another of the obsolete, absurd ideas in which all men believe is that figures mean what they say, which is even less true than the idiotic notion that the camera cannot lie. Since the world of paper money is founded on figures, if you can fiddle around with the numbers, you can also manipulate the money to your great and gratifying advantage. The double billionaire H. L. Hunt once remarked (he could afford to) that "money is nothing. It is just something to make book-keeping more convenient." He had it the wrong way round. It's book-keeping that's nothing — only something to make money more convenient.

For instance, a man purchases twenty garages for $50,000 apiece, a price which represents five years' purchase of pre-tax profits: he has profits of $200,000 a year, and he is presumably worth neither more nor less than the million with which he started. That presumption, however, is demonstrably false. Suppose he takes the company to the stock market as Auto-Electronic Developments: he sells a quarter of the shares for $250,000, and the market thereupon values the firm, modestly enough, at seven times earnings. So his smaller stake is *still* worth a million: and he has $250,000 in cash to be getting on with.

Still not satisfied, however, he borrows $1 million at 10%, buys another twenty exactly similar garages, thus raising earnings by the $100,000 which represents the difference between $200,000 of profits and his interest costs. Beyond doubt, the stock market will be vastly impressed by this powerful growth rate: 50% per annum is the stuff that analysts' dreams are made of. So Auto-Electronic gets revalued to ten times earnings, at which point our hero is worth $2.5 million — representing his $250,000 in cash, plus three-quarters of the pile of Auto-Electronic paper, which is now valued at $3 million.

The uninitiated may marvel how a property with a market value of $2 million can suddenly, with no material change, generate a million of new wealth. Equally, just how has the hero deserved or managed to multiply his original million two-and-a-half times? There is no good answer to these questions, merely an incontestable observation: that on this simple statistical foundation have been erected most new fortunes of our time.

Note that the figures in the fable were all uncooked. But suppose that the garage proprietor's expenses included a major Christmas promotion which cost $50,000 just before the year-end: and suppose that his accountants were persuaded that this bundle should be treated as deferred expenditure. The logic is unassailable, if you're not too keen on assailing: after all, the bulk of the sales will occur in the next financial year, so shouldn't the cost more properly be apportioned to the year in which the sales will fall?

This change will have the not-so-incidental effect of producing $50,000 of extra profits. Instead of the 50% profits jump achieved by the merger, the proprietors can now boast a 75% advance. Even if the stock market sticks to the same price-earnings ratio, of ten times pre-tax earnings, the company will magically become worth $3.5 million: and the delirious owner now weighs in at $2.9 million, stark naked.

The beautiful truth is that, if a company boasts a PE ratio of forty (after tax), each extra dollar in after-tax profits equals $40 in capital value. It follows that any device which maintains or enlarges the PE ratio, or which inflates the earnings per share, is worth more, by virtue of the multiplier effect, than any amount of honest toil. That is why profits are so rarely undercooked. The bias in accountancy is always towards producing the highest figure possible: and the possibility of bias exists first, because accountancy is as imprecise as the music of the spheres and second, because accountants know on which side their bread is buttered. If there are few millionaire accountants, it is partly because they expend so much nervous energy and time in making millionaires of their clients.

The deferring of the garage promotion, for example, is no far-fetched joke. In 1972 a London evening newspaper actually commended a paint company for the *conservative* practice of costing its advertising expenditure in the year when it was incurred. That same year, American oil and gasmen waxed indignant because the SEC turned thumbs down on an accounting method that allowed them to spread the cost of dry wells across several years, instead of taking it in the actual year of the expense: in one of the charming euphemisms which litter accountancy, the smellier, partial method was called "*full*-costing".

88

Equally partial were the habits of Britain's bankrupt Rolls twins (Razor and Royce): one deferred the commissions it paid to door-to-door salesmen of its appliances, the other put off the costs of its massive research and development spending. In every such case, a respectable – nay, an eminent auditor – was prepared to approve the approach: and if by any chance your auditor won't approve, the correct response is obvious, get another one.

Precisely that course was adopted by one US computer leasing outfit, whose profitability hinged on renting out its machines for seventy-eight months. Unfortunately, its customers obliged only to the extent of leases which averaged forty-eight months. If the outfit managed to lease the machines for the missing thirty months or more at roughly the same terms and without much extra marketing cost, all would be well. If it didn't, however, heavy losses would stare it in the face.

When its auditors couldn't be convinced that the re-leasing would duly occur, the company found a more trusting set of accountants. In such circumstances, the offended company usually takes the precaution of asking its prospective auditors their views on any contentious points. Surprisingly often, total harmony results. Maybe that divine music is connected with the fact that auditors' fees provide so much flavoursome food for thought – in 1972 one British company, for instance, shelled out £343,000 to its various accountants.

No wonder that Arthur Andersen, auditors to International Telephone & Telegraph, among other colossi, earns two-thirds of a stupendous income from audits. In the year ended 31 March 1973 its twenty-seven offices around the globe raked in $271.5 million: its 750 partners averaged $74,000 a year – and the twenty top partners, being considerably more equal than the others, collected $215,000 apiece on the way home.

You don't pay that kind of money to get your profits shaved away. ITT is a case in much point. Originally its accountants wanted to include the paper profits made on unrealized capital gains in a newly acquired insurance company's investment portfolio. When this ingenious step was barred, ITT simply sold off enough of the portfolio to equal the unrealized gain, and took that into the profit instead. The object of this strange exercise, which has nothing to do with the trading of either ITT or the insurance managers, is "to maintain the continuous rise in earnings per share".

Now just why would Harold S. Geneen, the millionaire boss of ITT, want to achieve that objective? Is it through a passionate desire for symmetry? Or has it any connection with the fact that Geneen and his managerial cohorts are all, thanks to the wonders of the stock option, heavy holders of ITT stock? Remember that the rise in earnings is purest bunkum. The true, underlying earnings of the arch-conglomerate have not altered in any degree. All that has changed is their presentation – as approved by the distinguished auditors.

As a shrewdity test, ask yourself if, should the value of the insurance portfolio drop, ITT would deduct an equivalent amount from its profits. You can bet *The Godfather*'s profits against the proceeds of a piggy-bank that few boards of directors would do any such thing. By an agreeable irony, ITT's auditors are advocates of a brave new accounting world in which accountants might "discard their exaggerated concern for conservatism and objectivity, which have too often resulted in irrelevant, unfair and imprudent information".

This statement can be tested against the case of Four Seasons Nursing Centers where, by disagreeable irony, Arthur Andersen was again the auditor – and where a couple of its own partners were indicted by the US Government for their part in the affair. In their search for millions, the Four Seasons founders had correctly diagnosed that untold wealth lay in wait on Wall Street if the nursing home idea could be successfully marketed. That in turn meant showing a suitably rich and fast-rising profit record. This was duly produced by devices which, so the accusation ran, included sales of nursing homes which never took place: and, still more imaginative, sales of the dud, money-losing homes to a buyer secretly owned by Four Seasons itself. Since figures, not facts, sway markets, the multiplier took immediate and telling effect. The shares zoomed up from $11 in 1968 to $181, before plunging all the way back to the nothing from whence they came.

This wasn't even an isolated case of its time. National Student Marketing, another busted flush, was an even wilder wow. This operation, headed by a hyper-salesman named Cort Randell, was allegedly founded on marketing techniques developed by young marvels selling to the explosive young growth market on campus. As an alumnus of NSMC, Andrew Tobias has revealed this company too was a free-running machine for generating reported or projected rises in earnings per share.

On 5 November 1969 Randell dangled before the New York Society of Security Analysts a forecast that earnings would all but treble in the 1970 fiscal year, and even broke down the rise into 78% from internal operations, 5% from recent acquisitions, 7% from an extraordinary item, 10% from acquisitions under consideration. According to Tobias, the paper value of Randell's stock jumped $6.5 million on such good news, backed by such precise – and utterly meaningless – figures.

More meaningful information would have included the fact, for example, that in 1968, NSMC reported perhaps $1.4 million of sales which were never actually made, as "unbilled receivables" – in a year when its earnings came to $700,000. Another half-million of expenses was deferred to the next fiscal year (there's that deferral trick again). Exactly the same tricks were worked in 1969, but with an extra twist – for, even after the tricks, NSMC had to count in $3.8 million of earnings from companies actually acquired after the end of its financial year – simply to show any profit at all.

In 1970 the spiralling corporate overhead, the heavy loss-makers, and past accountancy stratagems caught up with NSMC: it had to report a first quarter loss, and the shares promptly and properly collapsed. But in the long dizzy ride up from $6 to a peak of $143, how many nests had been feathered? When a twenty-point rise in the stock is worth over $6.5 million, you have a licence to print money – and too many accountants will happily provide the rubber stamp.

Don't suppose that the reporting of unmade sales or the disposal of money-losers to corporate insiders (both used by NSMC) are rarities. Not only did Four Seasons use the same devices, so did a company selling houses, which counted in its turnover figures (approved by its accountants) letters of intent to purchase homes for which no sites existed. The key to many of these larks is the Material (or Immaterial) Gambit. If the accountants are satisfied that a proposed distortion of the corporate earnings won't affect them as much as 10%, many of the sharp-pencilled US gentry will let it through as not "material".

In the case of the crashed Penn Central, use of the most liberal accounting interpretations (all properly detailed in five pages of footnotes) generated a profit of $0.18 per share, before extraordinary items when — according to analyst S. Scott Nicholls Jr. — the same figures, on conservative principles, added up to $1.18 of loss. Another company, AMK Corp., succeeded in turning a twenty-five cents per share decline in earnings into a forty-nine cent gain by no less than three accounting changes.

Or take General Dynamics, where book-keeping changes produced a credit and a debit, both more or less for the same amounts, which were let through the net. The difference between them was a mere $900,000 — but that immaterial amount equalled 36% of the net income duly reported to the happy shareholders. Then there's Memorex, which on its way to the junkyard of dead growth stocks included in its nine months figures a sale worth $14 million, a fifth of its total revenue, to a wholly controlled leasing subsidiary of its own — which, still worse, had not paid for the goods.

The difference which a piece of fast accounting can make is impressively shown by the case of Dr. Armand Hammer after he bought little Occidental Petroleum in 1957.

Occidental in 1963–72 multiplied its sales eighty-three times, one of the most extraordinary rises even in the oil industry's history. Nevertheless, in 1969, according to the SEC, no less than $14 million of the $49 million profit reported for the first three quarters resulted from unrevealed changes in accounting methods. The same source charged that the same profit-inflating technique was used in Occidental's peak year of 1970.

The reason why so rich a man as Hammer should permit such practice is because Occidental wanted, wittingly or unwittingly, to conceal a negative trend: in 1971, it had to report a $67 million loss; 1972 was no great shakes, either; and Hammer had loaded $900 million of long-term debt on Occidental's back.

The beauty of the doing-it-with-figures approach is that it has infinite variations and can be repeated *ad infinitum* — not to say *ad nauseam*. The garage proprietor who miraculously turned $1 million into $2.5 million can carry on buying businesses on the same mathematical basis: each new business acquired, moreover, stands to offer new chances for re-arranging its figures in a more profitable light. And if he gets tired of borrowing money to finance acquisitions, the figure-man can always use his licensed paper money.

One conglomerator, Meshuham Riklis of Rapid American, while on his way to accumulating a rapid fortune large enough to spend on constructivist art and other worthy diversions, observed that "by the time the debentures (Russian rubles) or warrants (Castro pesos) become due, the company you acquire can generate more cash than they are worth". Even without Soviet and Cuban capers, the game looks even more painless than debt. You can actually exchange pieces of paper printed by your own sweet self for the real-life assets of other companies, even for real cash. One paper-counter valued at forty times earnings can buy two lumps of equal-sized earnings in two companies selling on a PE of twenty. The lure of these Riklis mathematics is so seductive that many a bright young thing has been led to his own destruction on the rocks of hard arithmetic.

Assume that you really do have a great $1 million business, growing at 50% per annum and commanding a PE of forty. You have a million shares in issue, so the firm is worth $40 million, of which you own half. You buy a few siblings for half-a-million shares, which produce profits, at a twenty times PE, of another $1 million. This raises your earnings per share to $1.33, boosting the capitalization to $80 million, of which you now own a third – or nearly $27 million.

So far, so marvellous. The next year, however, your original activity produces its 50%, but your acquisitions stay put. The earnings per share rise again to $1,66, and the capitalization rises by another $20 million. A third of that, however, goes to the new shareholders whom you unhesitatingly bought in: and the lost $7 million or so is really a delayed cost of the original purchase.

The situation can get even worse. A progression from $1 to $1.33 to $1.66 looks like a showdown, and that high PE may wobble. So the temptation is to make another set of acquisitions, and buy another $1 million of earnings for half-a-million shares. But that isn't enough – earnings per share will only rise to $1.75. Try $2 million for a million instead – now you're really cooking with gas. That's $1.80 a share, representing another increase of a third in earnings, and pushing the capitalization to $180 million.

Your stake has now, after much huffing and puffing, risen from $20 million to $36 million – but so has that of the new shareholders, who brought in only $1 million of profits. And what will you do for an encore? Another 50% rise in the original business is now utterly swamped. Even an acquisition programme twice as large — $4 million of earnings for two million shares — won't do. You either have to engage in super-colossal buying, or somehow get your $33\frac{1}{3}$% growth rate from the existing businesses.

That is precisely why figure specialists (of whom the conglomerators are the prize breed) are led into ludicrous over-stretching (like James P. Ling's purchase of Jones & Laughlin) or into imaginative accountancy (like NSMC), or both. The mathematical game all too easily turns into an arithmetical treadmill, moving far too fast for the players to stay on.

The beneficent rain of long multiplication, of course, falls on the just and the unjust alike. *Time* magazine in early 1973 printed a roll-call of families who had struck it rich by the easy expedient of watching their shares rise. There was, for instance, David Packard who left President Nixon's defence department neatly in time to take his shares out of their temporary resting place, dust them off, and count the loot. It came to $260 million or $77 million for every year in which Packard didn't work at his Hewlett-Packard company, founded in a garage just before the Second World War. During Packard's Pentagon service the shares sat peacefully in a trust. It is another perfect example of the total untruth of the widely believed maxim that you can't have your cake and eat it. Packard's partner, in fact, ate even more confectionery: his stock rose by $271 million — more than ample reward, even for a 61% profit rise.

That multiplier, alas, has a nasty knack of working in reverse. If the PE is forty, if the profits are $10 million, and if you own half the shares, each $1 million of extra profit is worth $2 million in your safe deposit box. Suppose, however, that the profits fall by £1 million in one dull year; and that a disillusioned stock market consequently pushes down the PE to twenty. That one slight slip will cost your kitty no less than $110 million.

Now, being able to lose a fortune of that size may be gratifying in its way — H. Ross Perot, king of the computer gee-whiz experts, lost almost half-a-billion on paper in a single day as his 85% of Electronic Data Services zoomed down from its high; but that is not how most millionaires like to be titillated. Indeed, the awful prospect of that slide is what keeps the millionaires and their ever-loving accountants on the hunt, not for bigger and better profits, but for something which looks just as good and even works as well, if only for a time: bigger and better figures.

SCENE 3

THE MIRAGE OF TURNAROUNDS

or

It Can't Get Any Worse

Why rotten companies have made have-nots into haves
more often and with greater speed than good companies
... with some unkind reflections on the true achievement
of Harold S. Geneen in equating mediocre performance
at ITT with magnificent reputation and marvellous
reward.

The good reward can come more easily from a bad situation
than a good. Thus quick and risk-free fortunes have been made
by managers seduced to move into deadbeat and dying
companies. They have cleaned up doubly, both for themselves
and for the moribund corporation. Their rewards are out of
decent proportion to their turnaround contribution — because
it isn't easy to heave a corpse out of the industrial graveyard.

Still, the can't-get-any-worse artist has a saving grace or
two. Bad needn't become best to produce the financial transformation he seeks. A mere improvement from murderous to
moderate suffices; provided that the manager is prepared to
use every trick in the trade of adjusting earnings per share
sharply upwards. If investors believe that a corporation is
headed for the slaughter-house, they will shed the shares like
so much moult. The price will slump deeply below the physical
value of the assets. (The one certainty of a deadbeat situation
is that, in effect, dollar bills will be on sale cheap.)

More: since the company hasn't actually collapsed in a
smelly heap of bad debts, the odds are that it won't. When the
Chrysler Corporation was turned round from its mid-1950s
slump, its market share was shot to ribbons, its earnings were
barely visible, its debts were monstrous — but the company
was still sufficiently intact for George M. Love (custodian of

the Hanna heirlooms) and his protégé, Lynn A. Townsend, to mount a swift and enriching rescue operation.

The possibilities for swiftness are another virtue in the situation. Since the company is down on the floor, it's probable that the management which dumped it there lacked even the normal self-preserving executive attributes. Sweeping away the expensive cobwebs, a simple task for an educated manager, must produce an immediate and lush financial saving.

To give some idea of the potential in a really large turnover, the Philips electrical giant, under financial duress, managed to cut its inventories from 36% of 1970 sales to 27% of 1971. If a relatively efficient firm can squeeze out that much juice, imagine the joy which can flow from a rotten apple. And again, any juice will be compounded by the mathematics of the fact that a stock set for a turnaround operation will be in the stock exchange discard.

Assume that the company used to earn $2 million a year, and earnings have collapsed to $200,000, breathing hard. The market may value the entire misfired shooting match at $2 million. In comes Sir Galahad with his team of trusty knights, throws out the old-line management and buries the skeletons in their cupboards in the first year's accounts.

That year a thumping loss results. But the shares, buoyed up by Galahad's reputation and his press interviews, advance 50% to a $3 million capitalization. Galahad & Co don't mind this at all – they have stock options at the old price, a quotation which they now proceed to leave far behind in their gleaming wakes. They push profits up to $1 million: only half the company's old earning power, true, but think of the steep rate and angle of climb. If the knight errants merely return to $2 million, the next year round the course, that will mean doubled profits. No bright squirrel of an investment analyst can resist a proposition of this kind: so the shares go to twenty times the million dollar earnings, or $20 million, a tenfold rise; the knights cash in their options: and, if they are lucky and keep their noses sharp and their lances clean, there are years of pickings to come.

In Britain a whole squadron of raiders came galloping down on the deadbeat hulks of the country's industrial history in the 1960s, led by a master of business backgammon, Jim Slater. Slater moved into a metal window firm called Crittall-Hope (the hyphen was a euphemism for a merger which had never been consummated), sold off surplus and money-losing assets and was left with £5 million of "liberated" cash, plus a business making half its old turnover. But in the process, Slater's personal vehicle, Slater Walker, had shot up from a fringe operator to a big-time conglomerate. In the Crittall-Hope year of 1968, the shares soared by 329%.

Most Slater starlets failed to match these sudden millions (Slater's empire rode on to more mergers and a peak market capitalization of £120 million). The imitators still did well enough to line their fur coats for life. In their hands the game, basically the old conglomerate play, acquired a subtle difference, a new complexity. For the conglomerates ruined a perfectly viable system for the creation of paper fortunes (readily convertible into more solid assets) by misunderstanding the nature of their own rackets.

The essence of conglomeration was, and is, the exchange of paper for earnings: by this unprepossessing trick were the conglomerate millionaires created. But the front behind which they executed this stratagem was a beauteous but totally illusory vision of a new management world, brave and unprecedented, in which finely-honed minds using razor-edged techniques would manage diverse businesses in a manner leaving far behind the contemptible efforts of the older, switched-off generations.

The snag behind this noble façade was that the conglomerators, who (like all con men) believed their own publicity, in reality had to manage convoluted, complex, ill-assorted bundles of companies: at which they had no greater success than any previous generation of managers out of their depths.

The British mutants, however, produced a gentle twist. The conglomerator would only manage the assets to the point where, like the bear cub of mythology, they had been licked into shape. The cubs would then be sold off, preferably for cash, while the conglomerate, its coffers replenished, padded off in search of new prey. Where the simple, straight turn-around artists concentrated on one desperate situation at a time, the Slater mutants could handle two, three, four: each time milking or stripping the surplus assets, revamping the businesses, selling them off, then repeating the cycle in other musty, dusty corners of commercial Britain.

But the lifespan of the conglomerating wholesale salvationist was brief. Most one-off turnaround specialists in individual companies sooner or later run into the same road-block that stopped the previous management in its faltering tracks: the wholesaler simply runs out of road. This happened in spectacular fashion to an Old Etonian practitioner, John Bentley, whose Barclay Securities issued over seventeen million pieces of paper as it rounded-up terrible, run-down companies in toys, media advertising, pharmaceuticals, even films. Over its four years of life Barclay's earnings per share rocketed ahead as the awful companies were made tolerable: and the shares followed suit, shooting up by 852% before the dreadful truth dawned: which is that the higher the shares rise, the less chance the take-your-money-and-run technique has of making a real profit.

Suppose you have a £1 million company with £1 million of assets which issues £1 million of shares for another million. Suppose that it then performs the standard revamp, cuts the unprofitable products, ceases to serve the unprofitable outlets, flogs off the surplus offices, and gets profits back to a respectable height. At that point, a buyer appears ready to pay £6 million in cash for the revamped wonder. (If a buyer is not in evidence when wanted – a handy device is to have a captive customer, a good and true friend, or another company which you control yourself, to take the bargain off your hands.) On the face of it, your firm has a very nice £5 million profit: but that sum depends entirely on what has happened to your shares in the interim.

If they have multiplied tenfold, the effective price paid for the assets now being sold for £6 million is £10 million. Paradoxically the worse the shares have performed, the better the deal. This basic, uncomfortable formula explains a great deal of what happened, not only to Barclay Securities which (in a bad case of biter bitten got gobbled up by another financial conglomerate), but to the multi-market, share-sprouting companies as a whole. Their share prices ran far ahead of the real value of their wheels and deals. The proprietors could, of course, say the mathematics be damned: if you can cash in on a tenfold share boom, who cares about fundamental realities? The promotors, however, were the chief cashers-in: Bentley pocketed the best part of £2 million from the last round-up. The whole game otherwise added up to another method of shifting wealth from the many weak to the few strong.

The prime example of the combined turnaround and conglomerate technique is the great and mighty International Telephone and Telegraph, the pride and the passion of the archetypal mid-century millionaire manager, Harold S. Geneen.

When Geneen came to ITT, it was big, but its bigness was in dreary areas, such as communications utilities, with some illumination from brighter but neglected operations, such as manufacturing telecommunications gear in a booming western Europe. The simple knowledge that Geneen, a man of miraculous reputation, was on the move from Raytheon, forced down the price of the latter's stock and boosted that of ITT by several millions – and Geneen, with a single-minded devotion of awesome dimensions, proceeded to prove the stock market right.

In a decade the sales multiplied 6.7 times, the profits ten times, the assets 6.3 times. Quarter after quarter the wreck that Geneen inherited waxed richer and richer, and Geneen waxed with it, in wealth and reputation. The waxing was accomplished primarily through a corporate acquisition programme remarkable for its catholic, open-minded nature. If it moved, ITT seemed to buy it: the collection eventually included old ITT items like Standard Telephones and Cables, new buys like Avis car-hire, a hotel in Hammamet, Gwaltney Smithfield hams – and still the shopping went on. In 1970 alone ITT added $1,500 million in assets and the next year put on a billion more in weight, as Geneen used what he himself modestly called ITT's "unusual abilities to follow a policy of diversified risks in selected fields of above-average opportunity".

All modesty aside, ITT is the world's all-time champion of the turnaround carried to its logical extreme. 1972 sales were $8,500 million. The original ITT, when Geneen moved in, couldn't have got very much worse without disappearing. The new ITT, so popular belief had it, couldn't get any better: it was the ultimate in modern management, as Geneen himself said. In terms of wealth creation, ITT's progress was broad and strong indeed: at the end of 1972 the former deadbeat was capitalized at a wondrous £5,759 million. Probably any ITT fan told that earnings per share in the 1961–71 decade had grown only by 7.84% annually would have refused to believe so blatant an untruth: but that was the fact. What's more, 197 of the biggest American corporations listed by *Fortune* outgrew ITT in that decade (ITT looked better over the 1962–72 period, but only because earnings fell under Geneen between 1961 and 1962). What's still more, the ITT record resulted in part from some elegant cookery of the books. In 1971 the gain in earnings was a worthy 10%, from $3.14 to $3.45 – save for the little matter of losing the Chilean business after a peculiarly inept attempt to overthrow the host government. Adding in (or taking out) this "extraordinary item" reduced the figure to $2.85, a 9.2% decline. But the essence of making a bad situation good is that the impression created matters more than the reality: and the impression arises from assiduous public relations and assiduous accountancy. The latter art form is easier to exploit when a company is changing its shape and size almost weekly by merger, spreading itself from micro-waves to insurance in the process. In fact, without the 1970 insurance acquisition, ITT's income in the next year (even without knocking Chile off the score) would have been down in 1969 – despite a sales increase of $1,562 million in the intervening period.

But in 1971, for all that fine timing, not only was ITT's growth record modest, so was its return on invested capital (194 large companies did better), and so was its industrial performance. In industrial and consumer products (3.8%), ITT earned hugely less on sales than 3M (11.5%). In food processing and services ITT could only contrive an abysmal 1.9%.

The conglomerate's best performance, to nobody's surprise, was in the business in which it started and which it knew best: 4.5% on telecommunications equipment, or slightly better than a rival like Western Electric. Nobody can take away from Geneen his amazing feat in turning a beat-up old telecoms company into the eighth largest company in the USA. But equally astonishing to the inexpert in mass psychology, is the easy acceptance by the outside world that creative accountancy allied to rapid acquisition equals magnificent performance.

As a textbook exercise in turnarounds, the ITT drama will never be matched, for the political and public mood has turned against this style of conglomeration. But there are plenty of hulks drifting in the rougher seas of commerce waiting for a boarding party that, by substituting strong management for weak, can achieve the kind of first take-off results that sent

101

ITT on its way: in 1961–67 earnings per share doubled, long before the big take-overs. As to personal fortunes, in 1971 and 1972 alone Geneen collected options worth over $3 million.

Every situation, no matter how evil-smelling the egg, contains within it the possibility of a nice, fresh profit. One US operator, Harry Weinberg, once even made $100 million out of the most certain financial death-traps in the big cities: bus lines. In his own accurate words, every urban bus company Weinberg bought was "a cow with no milk in". But people still had to get to work: cities were still prepared to subsidize and otherwise assist any big-hearted citizen who would help his fellow-citizens on their way: and Weinberg's squeezed-out cattle yielded a surprising flood of cream. As long as the market demand is there, there is some device, some new approach, some scheme of rationalization that will convert the demand into tax-free or tax-paid dollars.

The Dictaphone Company, at the time of E. Lawrence Tabat's takeover, was running steadily downhill. It lost money in both 1970 and 1971; it suffered from a sick product line and from the best efforts of the most formidable competitor in US marketing, IBM. In the first nine months of the next year, Tabat got operating income up 24% on a 6% sales rise, not by black magic, but by certain simple changes. He sold off money-losing office furniture companies and brought in a new Dictaphone product named the Thought Tank, engaged in aggressive advertising that committed the *lèse-majesté* of being rude to IBM; and shoved the share price up 50% in two months.

The moves were no less obvious than those which John Bentley, in the hey-day of the hot stocks, supervised at the Chad Valley toy company – where, out of 650 lines, a fifth provided 80% of the profits, and 250 lines could be erased almost overnight without doing anything but good. But another operation greatly enhanced the prizes from the Chad-style gambit: the wonderful, the unique, the now-you-see-it, now-you-don't Shell Game – a shell in this instance being a company so burned out that it has almost nothing left, except the crucial asset, its stock exchange quotation.

The British colonial past has left a particularly interesting set of relics, with names like Galaha Ceylon Tea Estates or Parit-Bruas (Malay) Rubber Co, whose shares sell at infinitesimal prices, when they sell at all. As of 20 March 1973 the last deal in Parit-Bruas had been reported on 31 March 1970, three years before, at the princely price of about one penny. The shell gamester buys control of such an outfit and, when he has a suitable stake, allows the word to leak to others — at the same time revealing that high-earning interests are about to be injected into the empty shell.

If a company is capitalized at £25,000, with hardly any earnings, the injection of £50,000 of net income must enhance the shares by moon-man leaps and bounds, even if the profits are valued conservatively in the market. In fact, a well-manipulated market will value the shares on the basis of their inexhaustible capacity for early spectacular growth.

The two outstanding performers in Britain in the 1970s, Jim Slater's Slater Walker and Ralli International, run by Slater protégé Malcolm Horsman, began life respectively as H. Lotery and Oriental Carpet Manufacturers: of the gains in their share prices over the 1962–72 decade (a respective 2,691% for Ralli and 2,986% for Slater), the bulk of the rise was recorded largely in this early miraculous transformation.

In 1968 the oriental carpet-baggers employed £2.5 million of capital: from 1969 to 1970 the shares multiplied sixteen times as the capital soared to £33.4 million. The little H. Lotery employed a mere half-million of capital in 1962. Between 1967 and 1968, as the action really got under way, the share price multiplied over tenfold as the assets jetted upwards from £4.7 million to £94.3 million. For Slater and his erstwhile lieutenant, both of whom shared fully in this sudden effulgence, capitalism must have seemed a lovesome thing.

For humbler or less expansive toilers in this particular vineyard, the great danger is that the recovery, the upward thrust, will run out of acceleration, and even decelerate sharply: in the same dizzy style, and with the same desolating effect, as the share plunge in fallen conglomerates like Litton and Gulf & Western. Getting back up from poor to moderate is only the first stage of the battle: the distance from moderate to excellent is far longer, and getting there can be as arduous as the journey to the moon. Often the astronaut would be best advised to turn for home before the distance catches up on him.

The calamities of Chrysler are a cautionary tale: pulled up by the Love-Townsend team to $303 million of net income, then slumping back to an $8 million loss and a near-desperate credit crisis. Stock options, cashed-in options, bonus schemes and the like look painfully sick in such circumstances – unless, like Townsend, you have the ultimate turnaround gambit up your Ivy League sleeve.

From 1968 onwards Townsend and his president, John J. Riccardo, received not one cent of bonus. But in 1972 the famine ended. A payout of $413,660 to the chairman and $351,400 to his number two raised their total takes to a new company record of $638,600 and $551,400 respectively. The strangest fact about these peak pay-slips was that Chrysler's 1972 earnings, while sharply up on 1971, actually fell short by some $93 million from the 1968 record. Instead of pushing up the earnings, the directors had simply pushed down the profit level on which the bonus payments were calculated.

The Townsend-Riccardo Gambit only rubs in the point: that in this line of work, it's not how successfully you turn round that counts, it's how efficiently you exploit the angle of turn.

SCENE 4

THE MIRACLE OF MERGERS

or

One's Company, Two's a Fortune

Containing the explanation of why mergers, acquisitions,
amalgamations and unions, which are generally disastrous for fat companies, make rich men richer still . . .
and not only because fat companies pay such men fat
fortunes to acquire their businesses.

The one unassailable truth to emerge from an age in which
every ambitious or half-ambitious corporation sought to improve its affairs by merger is that merging does not improve
corporate affairs. When two Goliaths join in unholy wedlock,
the general result is to produce simply a fatter target at which
the Davids of business can aim their hard, round stones. When
the fat company buys a small outfit, the chances are that the
profitability of the buy, and still more the contentment of its
people, will be squashed by the fat man's heavy tread.

No matter how the effects are measured – return on capital,
growth in earnings per share, movement in the beloved share
price, share of new markets – the merging firms seldom outdo
the corporate spinsters and bachelors, and often get undone
themselves.

The unhappy record isn't just the result of an incurable
corporate tendency to overpay for company purchases (a habit
encouraged by the fact that real money is seldom used –
though full many a millionaire has capitalized on this generous
penchant. Selling out to a fat purchaser, the accepted, easy
alternative to selling out to the public, produces generally less
lavish results, but has the advantage that the proprietor can
grab his money, and all in the form of cash or negotiable
securities.

If he tries to offload an inflated majority holding in his own demesne on the market, its paper value can suddenly crumple in the chill wind of reality. On the other hand, if Corn Products or Unilever can be persuaded to buy, the shares which they issue (assuming that the happy victim's persuasion hasn't extended to exacting cash) are a mere drop in the Pacific Ocean of the total equity. When Unilever in 1973 decided to buy a few British garages, for example, it offered £3.9 million, or twenty-eight times the earnings: the kind of bonanza that even Santa Claus seldom brings – yet it was still only a fraction of 1% of the Anglo-Dutch giant's capitalization.

Those quintessential imperialists, the Americans and the English, gladdened hearts all over Europe as, inspired by the European Economic Community and its glorious promise, they paraded the pavements of the Continent with their hearts and cheque-books open. On the whole, the wanderers did better in France, where generations of tax-evading capitalists had lived out of the cash box and kept down the apparent value of their family nest-eggs, than in Italy, where generations of equally avid tax-evaders had perfected the art of presenting different sets of books which meant all things to all men: no profits to the taxman, huge earnings to prospective purchasers, with the truth (shown only to themselves) somewhere in between.

In one case the buyer of an Italian business was horrified to get a tax demand for more than the company's entire income. This innocent American had submitted an honest tax return, and the inspector had simply assumed that, like all returns submitted by the previous owner, it had grossly understated the true profits. Never deal with an Italian is fairly sound advice to the merging novice. By the same token, always deal with an Anglo-Saxon is the best of counsel to an Italian, many of whom need no second bidding.

By all odds the most vivid proof, even if unintentionally, was provided by Leopoldo Pirelli, the lithe, good-looking scion of the second richest Italian family of industrial aristocrats. The exact nature of the Pirelli riches is hard to establish, since there is a typically Italian convolution of companies: the original Societa Pirelli & Co, founded in 1872 by an inventive genius who simultaneously grasped the potential of rubber and cables, holds stakes in two other companies, one Italian, one Swiss (Switzerland is a favourite resort of well-sprung Italians, who are in the habit of crossing the border with well-filled

106

suitcases of currency whenever the local economic climate gets too hot.)

The Swiss company owns part of the Italian, the two share ownership of the Pirelli interests outside Italy – and there are some other modest investments to be taken into account, like the second largest holding in Fiat. This was the financial hornets' nest into which some brave Britons poked.

The Pirelli interests got half of the Dunlop empire, and *vice versa*: there proved, however, to be more *vice* than *versa*. The Italian business proceeded to lose £18.6 million in the first year of the union and still more in the second, as a wave of labour unrest, managerial arthritis and technical failure devastated Pirelli's profits. Dunlop's eager Britons were forced to write off their entire £41.5 million investment in Italian bad eggs. The Italian basket, however, still contained half of Dunlop – and those eggs, on a fairly conservative assessment, were worth £300 million of solid gold, or £150 million to the Pirelli side. By any standards, it was a remarkable exchange.

The rich individual runs the same financial and managerial risks, whether he is diversifying into some beckoning field of which he is wholly ignorant or merely eliminating some supine or rampant competitor. But the risks are offset by one sovereign fact: unlike the corporation, which is theoretically bent on accumulating higher earnings, the millionaire is predominantly interested in a higher pile of assets – which, apart from other blessings, if they carry no earnings (visible ones, that is), carry no tax either.

The relevant figure is that 30% of £100 million of corporate assets is worth more than 50% of £50 million – to be precise, £5 million more – and still gives control of the caboodle. It therefore pays the accumulator to surrender part of his ownership for fresh piles of assets: so long as the surrenders are always smaller than the piles.

Maxwell Joseph, who rose in the property world via the promising routes of estate agency and marriage to a property tycoon's daughter, probably accomplished more by basic surrender than by any of his astute advances. As recently as 1963 Joseph's hotel interests, consisting largely of undersized properties around Mayfair, weighed in at a measly £9.8 million of capital employed. Seven years later, after buying up hotels, dairies, dance-halls and a sizeable brewery, all in exchange for a plethora of loan stocks, shares and other pieces of paper, Grand

Metropolitan Hotels, the Joseph vehicle, was worth twenty-two times that amount. After adding an even vaster brewery, Watney Mann, Joseph's personal share stake, only 18% of the equity, was worth £19 million – that is, before the stock, bowed down by the sheer weight of the mergers, took a dive.

But the cumulative effect is unlikely to be so overwhelming if the accumulator insists on keeping total control or something like it. Friedrich Flick suffered from no such quirk: this genius, who bridged the Nazi and Adenauer eras, had been deprived of his fortune by the Allies after the war, and so was not in a mood to surrender control of his rebuilt empire in the peace.

The rebuilding itself was a miracle within the wonder of German resurgence. At his death in 1972 at the age of 89, Flick possessed $1,700 million worth of sales in steel, chemicals, paper and odds and ends (including the Leopard tank): and that bundle, which earned $9 million in profit in 1972, excluded the ripest of all – a 40% holding in Daimler-Benz, with sales of $3,700 million. Small wonder that the old autocrat's death sparked off a bitter family squabble.

No one could argue that the Flick family plot was tended with any evident management skill: 0.4% on sales (even allowing for the reluctance of German firms, especially family ones, to show more profits than they need) is not the standard preached by the Harvard Business School. But that is the profound advantage of the personal proprietor in the merger sport: so long as he covers his costs, in borrowings or any other out-of-pocket expenses, possession is nine-tenths of the game.

It's the professional manager, or the proprietor with outside shareholders on his back, who must go for growth at all costs – including the costs of painful mergers.

This necessity in turn means that the professional corporate merger must be made to work. Either the deal has to be pitched on such glorious financial terms that, come wind, come rain, the earnings come out ahead: or the managers must manage their heads off to achieve the hoped-for synergy. It often degenerates into a desperate race between the corporate earnings and the conversion date of the convertible stocks issued to finance the big deal. From the start to the finishing line, however, the corporate jockeys can never do one thing: sit back and relax. But then most of them don't want to.

Acquisitions are a challenge to the professional manager's

innate sense of order and neatness, his desire to subject the entire corporation to the same systems and discipline. Dorothy Parker had a poem for it: "They hail you as their morning star, They love you just the way you are. Then when they've got you safe and sound, They try to change you all around."

One British entrepreneur has never forgotten his shock when the full weight of ITT's planning descended on his innocent head. For his proportionately tiny morsel of the corporate feast, some three hundred man-days of planning were demanded. (As it happens, the effort turned up a potential seven-figure loss in one product, which was duly corrected: this discovery converted the Briton to planning, but later, in a very similar business, he found that three man-days did the planning trick: and the paperwork was the equivalent of *Jonathan Livingston Seagull*, rather than ITT's *War and Peace.*)

Many accumulative individual millionaires are just as incapable psychologically of leaving well alone. But, unlike the managers, the rich have the option. If they pile on $10 million of assets earning a beggarly million, it's a matter of some indifference — within reason — whether the earnings rise or fall (and a millionaire's reason seldom extends to actual losses). The tycoon, if he wants, can afford to treat his interests, purchased or not, as they really are — a portfolio of investments, no different from a hand dealt in the stock market — except that the holder can call all the plays.

He can put up with large minority holdings which would greatly vex any conventionally managed or mismanaged company: like the Flick 40% of Daimler-Benz. He can run every single company in a different manner, or have it run by somebody else — which is the essence of the rich man's approach. It's uneconomical for somebody whose time equals a fortune to fiddle when perfectly competent hands can be hired to conduct every orchestra in the collection. Far better to sit, like Howard Hughes, in lofty isolation, surrounded by silent Mormons, communicating with your managers either not at all or by telephone, while they make millions on your behalf.

The Cowdray family, by some repute the richest in Britain, provides a textbook example of a seemingly haphazard collection of interests: their full complexity was revealed only by the decision to go public. At the start of their consolidation, the Cowdrays owned two public newspaper companies, one of which held the controlling interest in the other; a private newspaper company with no connection with the other two, a book publisher, the obligatory oil and gas, a merchant bank, Lazards, Château Latour, with its fine clarets, a sizeable share of the potteries around Stoke-on-Trent, including Crown Derby, engineering firms – and so on. Not one of these appeared to be managed by any system common to the rest of the family holdings.

Not that the Cowdray group was ill-managed. Profits, at £4.2 million in the year before the Cowdray jewels went public at a total price of £100 million, rose to £10.5 million four years later. The point is rather that management to the Cowdrays and their able administrators bore no relation to the homogenizing, staff-breeding, interference-prone systems of the pros. That fact alone removes a great dose of malaise from mergers, on two conditions: that the merger millionaire must always be prepared to replace a bailiff who mismanages his acres of the estate: and that he be equally ready to sell.

The men who hold the sovereign advantage of personal wealth hate to sell, as a rule. They are acquisitive, and the act of acquisition, like libido in the highly sexed, lasts a lifetime. But, just as they are free to let a valuable investment accumulate more wealth in its own weird way, so are they at liberty to sell without exposing themselves to critics as incompetents, either for buying the thing in the first place or for selling it. In big corporations, disinvestment is usually the pleasurable job left to the next incumbent: pleasurable, because the very deed proves him deft and his predecessor dull.

But even the most dextrous accumulator buys the occasional lemon, if only because what makes excellent sense for a free-lance financier may fit uneasily into a corporate blanc-mange mould: and most great free-lance fortunes all become corporate one day. Norton Simon, in the process of extending his tomato-based empire, picked up not only extra tidbits in food, but also printing operations, trade books, magazines and Talent Associates, the film and TV company: all of which his managerial successor refused to have in the shop.

Individual tycoons do not have the professional manager's love for tidiness. The lucrative lessons of tycoon mergers should not be lost on the professionals (although they usually are). Never buy dear. Manage what you do buy according to its internal logic, not yours. Don't try to manage the new crown jewel at all if some other custodian is already, by your standards, running it successfully. If the selling occasion arises — an offer you can't refuse in good financial conscience, a misfit, a need for resources elsewhere, plain and unadulterated boredom — sell without compunction.

The most unlikely of the conglomerates proved to be the biggest real winner partly because it followed the habits of its rich founder. No sane corporate planner would put his name to a scheme for combining sick textile companies with upholstery cushioning, radar antennae and electronics, all as the base for an "acquisition of the month plan" designed to add forty companies in eight years. This incongruous outfit predictably ended up in a confusion of money-spinners ranging from chain saws to upper-class stationery, from watch straps to power lawn-mowers.

Yet from 1958 to 1973, sales piled up from £244 million to $1,858 million: and when Litton was showing a grisly loss and ITT a feeble gain of 1.58%, this company, Textron, was still boasting a ten year total return to investors of an annual 9.84%. The founder, Royal Little, "didn't see how the textile business" (in which he had started in 1928) "could ever be good again in my lifetime". He did, however, see acutely how the intelligent use of tax losses for an acquisition programme could create the good capitalist life all over again: provided he stuck to good capitalist rules.

His moral principles included keeping the head office down to a small number of bodies in an unglamorous locale in Providence, Rhode Island: Providence is a long way from rivalling Wilmington, Delaware, in sophistication, let alone Park Avenue, New York. That, by no means incidentally, is another asset of the rich empire-builder. His personal and corporate overhead are one and the same thing. While Howard Hughes must pay a pretty dollar in private air transport and the hire of whole hotel floors, his costs don't begin to cover those of a truly ambitious multi-national corporation. To get some idea, one scion of a dollar imperialist, Edgar Kaiser, had $14 million of his money saved in a year by the head office economies implemented by a newcomer at Kaiser Aluminium: which gives an inkling of the appalling burden that bigger companies still must carry on their backs.

Then, Royal Little would never buy for Textron on less than a seven-year payback of its money, and would throw out with

111

unsentimental despatch any acquisition that sooner or later failed to come up to the corporate snuff. This set of policies by no means implies disinterest in the subsidiaries, their well-being and their wherewithal. What gives the individual investor and his imitators such abnormal financial potency is the combination of passionate interest in the balance sheet and the bottom line (which is where the earnings are kept) with lack of passionate involvement in the mechanics of each individual enterprise. The large, managed company cannot in the nature of bureaucratic life sustain this potent combination for as long as the individual. So the corpocrats make rich men richer by paying over-rich sums for the latter's assets: and then proceed to make their corporations poorer by managing these expensive acquisitions into the ground.

On the Multiplication of Millions
or
Many a Muckle Makes
More Muckles

THE PILE-UP OF PROPERTY

or

The Upside-Down Pyramid

How the pyramid, disgraced in the aftermath of the Great Crash, has been resurrected in modern times to make the whole of a millionaire's holding worth more than its parts ... with some hints on avoiding the perils of top-heaviness.

The pyramid, the most elegant of geometrical shapes, has twice in history been associated with great wealth. In ancient Egypt the Pharaohs made the elementary error of burying their treasure, the equivalent of Rockefeller or Rothschild-sized fortunes of today, in these imposing structures. There it lay waiting for the next generation of tomb-robbers to pocket the proceeds: as neat a demonstration of the passage of wealth from weak hands to strong as history can offer.

Pyramids did not reappear until the halcyon days of free and untrammelled capitalism, in the hell-for-leather run-up to the great slump. But in this reincarnation the pyramids were made not of stone but of paper, and their construction served the opposite purpose – the transfer of money was still from the weak to the strong, but this time the weak were many and the strong were few. No device conceived in the great boom and destroyed in the slump provided a more geometric multiplier of money.

If a roaring promoter had a business in the twenties which the stock market, roaring away, valued at $100 million, that sum rapidly ceased to seem adequate in the light of the still more rapturous paper values being created on all sides. But what if a second company were created whose principal asset was a major holding in the first? Bonanza number one was still worth $100 million: bonanza number two could rapidly be run up to the same comforting figure. A third company wow could then be formed whose prime holding was a major share in bonanza number two. If that, in turn, could be rushed up to $100 million, the entire paper fortune had been trebled without any commensurate improvement in the underlying assets.

The practitioners of the 1920s carried the device of the holding company to undreamed-of extremes: in his supreme deployment of the pyramid art-form, Samuel Insull constructed an edifice in which, on one estimate, one dollar invested in a company called Middle West Utilities controlled $1,750 held by the public in the operating companies which actually produced the nation's electricity, or at least 12% of it.

But pyramids, for all their seeming solidity, have a basic weakness. If one lower layer starts to crumble, all those above must fall in on top. Insull's frantic efforts to protect part of his unimaginably complex pyramid from the imagined depredations of a rival financier deposited a $20 million profit in the latter's lap and eventually, after a terrible collapse in his shares, deposited Insull in court, accused of using shareholders' funds for his own pyramidic ends. (Despite having fled before the law to Greece, the old boy, pleading an "honest" accounting error of $10 million, got off scot-free.)

The wily outwitter of Insull was none other than Cyrus S. Eaton, whom a later generation knew only as the capitalist friend of Krushchev, the founder of the east-west Pugwash conferences on nuclear science, and the author, among other tomes, of a work entitled *Is the Globe Big Enough for Capitalism and Communism?* Eaton used his investment bank, Otis and Company of Cleveland, and his holding company with skill and daring – muscling in on Insull and on the territory of mightier forces still, the Mellons and the House of Morgan.

Eaton later memorialized his own exploits under the simple description of "Organizer, Republic Steel Corporation and United Light and Power Company". His was an extraordinary survival into the Age of the Common Millionaire of a man who wrestled with the giants of the silver age on their own terms and with their own philosophy. As somebody remarked when Eaton was building up his huge holdings in Insull stocks, "Eaton wasn't really interested in running things. All he wanted was the money." For Insull, it was the other way round, even when in fifty days of the fatal summer of 1929 his securities were appreciating at $7,000 a minute, day in, day out – which must be some kind of record. He fell two years later for a very simple reason, as his market operator explained: "You can't go on buying your own stocks forever. Sooner or later you run out of money."

Insull's monument was only the most conspicuous of the structures erected by the latter-day Pharaohs. As for others, John Kenneth Galbraith has described the furious progress of outfits like the American Founders Group. It started in 1922 with two investment trusts, which shared a capital of $500 between them. By 1927 the two companies had become three, which between them had sold $70–$80 million of securities to the thirsty public of the day. In 1928 and 1929 the sale of stock, in a group swollen to thirteen companies, reached epidemic proportions: its total resources had enlarged gigantically to a clear billion. A third of that, however, was accounted for by shares in the American Founders Group itself.

The terrible result when the steps of the pyramid crumbled away and the laws of geometric progression worked in reverse, are demonstrated by the performance of Goldman Sachs. This began its rake's career by organizing the Goldman Sachs Trading Company as the base of its pyramid. The public was let in on this ground floor at $104 a throw. After the débâcle, in 1932, the ground floor entrants were deep in the basement: their shares were worth less than $2.

Small wonder that Insull or Goldman Sachs pyramids have not been allowed to reappear. But the holding company is, as we have seen, alive, kicking and capable of generating profit at a most becoming rate. Indeed, holding companies are still the prime medium for organizing corporations. Every big company has a pyramidic legal structure: the critical difference being that, with insignificant exceptions, the apex of the pyramid holds 100% of each layer, a percentage which serves as an effective enough cement.

Every now and again, however, something suspiciously like the old-style pyramid rears its head. The Welsh financier Sir Julian Hodge achieved his first leaps and bounds up the financial ladder with a company called Anglo-Auto Finance, which handled instalment purchases of cars. He then formed another company, Gwent & West of England, which owned a hefty stake in the finance firm. When Hodge moved on to stage

117

three, launching a third firm, Hodge Group, which boasted ownership of a large chunk in Gwent & West, hailstones of criticism showered down.

The critics were disturbed, not only by the structure, but by Hodge's enthusiasm for bringing small Welsh shareholders in on his act. People's capitalism is a wonderful thing, no doubt. But it's a noticeable and regrettable fact that down the ages schemes, honest and less so, for bringing the benefits of capitalism to the masses have tended to leave the latter poorer and their would-be benefactors considerably richer. (The less money the masses have, for some strange psychological reason, the more tempted they are by low-priced shares: companies have been floated off, at huge profits to the floaters, as shilling stocks in London or penny stocks in Wall Street, that would have mouldered into dust at a heavier price.)

True, Hodge let right be done in the end: when the empire began to come apart, he called in expert help to dismantle the pyramid and repair the cracks in its constituent bricks. But anybody who had invested in Hodge at the time of its launch, when (much to its creator's wrath) one financial journalist called it Britain's "most overvalued share", had a desperately bumpy ride. From a peak of 60.8d in 1963 they ended up in 1969 at one shilling, about as low as a stock can get without vanishing altogether. But verily Sir Julian had his reward for seeing the light. His holdings, both personal and through what the legal jargon describes as "the ultimate holding company", were worth a far from cool £13.5 million after five years, and the Hodges had their last round-up when a fat bank bought them out for many millions in 1974.

Lurking behind most holding companies is a private company or trust in which the personal holdings are located. This is a handy device, used by many millionaires to provide more strings for their bows and to erect a decent distance between their dividend income and the taxman.

Some of these devices, like those run by the Rockefeller brothers for their own good and the benefit of mankind, have achieved fame in their own right, although not necessarily profits. The International Basic Economy Corporation, for instance, was founded back in 1947 by Nelson Rockefeller and threw itself into worthy activities like food distribution, housing, marketing and manufacture in various deserving geographical spots, all in an attempt to stimulate the local economies. But in 1971, when Rodman C. (Nelson's boy) took over the helm, IBEC had succeeded in making only $796,000 nine months' profit on sales of $213.1 million − which practically classified it as an outright charity.

The description would scarcely apply to the empire put together by Frank Lloyd, the past master at separating artists from their paintings and, in exchange for the same, million-aires and museums from their cash. The difference in cost between the two processes has given Lloyd enough millions (reputedly twenty-five, calculated in dollars) to buy a French holiday home from uranium king Joseph Hirshhorn and to finance a convoluted legal and fiscal structure. At its head is the Lloyd family trust, based in Liechtenstein: that useful principality is also conveniently the home of the master company, Marlborough AG, and of two associated firms, Art Finance and Kunst und Finance (which means Art Finance in German).

Art Finance owns the two New York galleries, while the master company owns directly the four businesses in Zurich and London, not to mention the four partnerships in Rome, Toronto, Montreal and Tokyo. According to his partner in the latter business, quoted in *Time* magazine, "Lloyd-san almost seems to understand Zen". Be that as it may, Lloyd shows to a fine degree the natural understanding of the process of finan-cial self-preservation − which, in a sense, is why the Pharaohs built their pyramids too.

But no family pyramid entombs more wealth than Chris-tiana Securities, 75% owned by the Du Ponts who have deposited therein the lion's share (29%) of their interest in the family gunpowder store. Paradoxically, as the clan's numbers have increased, so the usefulness of the structure has declined. The Du Ponts have been anxious to exchange Christiana for straight holdings in the family store, but have run into legal obstacles. Their motive is to make it easier to sell the shares: the usual reason for family pyramids, however, is to hang on to the contents. These family holding companies consequently rarely live and breathe: they are receptacles, legal con-veniences, paper pigeon-holes.

Nobody could say that of James P. Ling's Ling-Temco-Vought, which re-invented the pyramid in a most ingenious way and became the ultimate in holding companies.

119

All conglomerates, partly because of their bad habit of buying companies too expensively, suffered through most of their lives from relatively low price-earnings ratios. This irritates their masters beyond reason: anybody who wanted to excite a flow of logical passion from Harold Geneen of ITT in 1972 merely had to ask his opinion of the company's PE.

Anthony Sampson found the perfect description for both ITT and this type of construction. "The whole massive conglomerate, from Tokyo to Chile, from smoked hams to telephones, rested like a vast upside-down pyramid on a pinpoint – the share price on the New York Stock Exchange." If the price on the NYSE rocked, or rocks, the pyramid sways in time: and if the bough breaks, the cradle may fall. . . .

Ling was virtually alone among conglomerators in deciding to take this cradle by the rockers. If the NYSE price stuck at a point where the parts were worth more than the whole, he reasoned, float off part of the parts and you would, by establishing a stock market value, simultaneously despatch some needed public cash to the L-T-V coffers and enhance the balance sheet.

One of the news magazines published an endearing map, rather like a game of snakes and ladders, which showed how Ling, through an intricate series of deals ending with the flotation of the Wilson companies (nicknamed on Wall Street "meat ball, golf ball and goof ball"), paid for the original acquisition and was still left holding control of Wilson's meat-packing, sports and chemical businesses – all for free.

But Ling's empire always sounded too good to be true – and indeed it was. The poor boy from Oklahoma had built up the fourteenth-largest company in the USA by initially developing an electronics and aerospace business: he shot himself down with a sequence of careless and costly purchases.

The sad truth which pyramid-builders overlook is that the underlying value of the business, which resides in its operating and earning assets, is not changed one iota by all their financial architecture. The separate market quotations for meat ball, golf ball and goof ball couldn't increase either their intrinsic value (whatever that was) or L-T-V's: and on the latter score, the market was perfectly right – the sprawling bloated body of L-T-V was worth less than its parts.

That was simply because the parts cost too much money, even if the money was funny, and because Ling could only keep the balls rolling (meat, golf, goof and the rest) by smothering the consequences of each deal in the next. Hence the catastrophe of bidding for the Jones & Laughlin steel giant, hard on the heel of the purchase of Greatamerica Corp from another loaded Dallas conglomerator. The sole point of offering $85 a share for J & L stock which was on the market at $50, was to make certain of the buy. Even if the government trust-busters had not stomped all over the deal, Ling was venturing into an industry where, given its low profits and low-browed management, the bravest and brightest would have feared to tread.

The holding company, with its heavy mass of subsidiary interests balanced on top, becomes like a pyramid inverted and balanced on its tip. The structure is inherently unstable, which is why its builders, like Ling, and like Insull before him, have to rush from side to side in the desperate effort to keep balance and control. As they rush, so the structure gets more complicated, and it becomes harder, even for them, to keep track of the hectic paths they trace from brick to brick.

Far better is the simpler, static life of a little British outfit called A. Kershaw & Sons. Back in 1948 this company sold all its assets, except for under £50,000 in cash, to what is now Rank Precision Industries. At the end of 1972 Kershaw held not quite 40% of the latter company's ordinary shares, and rather more of the preference. A pretty unexciting investment you might think – until you enquired what Rank Precision Industries owned in turn. Among other less substantial goodies, that second holding company owned 5.6 million assorted shares in Rank Xerox, a goldmine undreamed of in 1948, or 1958 for that matter. Even in 1968 the dividends filtering through to Kershaw only came to £387,822. In the 1970s they were running at over a million annually.

The bulk of Kershaw's shares, in turn, are held by the Rank Organization, which owns Rank Precision Industries. What point there is in this perfect circle is none too clear: although there is a clear benefit to the Rank directors who hold a few Kershaw shares, highly desirable pieces of paper which have dutifully soared along with Xerox profits. Thus the chairman of Rank, Rank Precision Industries and Kershaw is the same man, Sir John Davis, who holds only 58,722 Kershaw shares. But since these weighed in at a peak of £16.75 in 1973, that small holding was worth not quite a million pounds. Such are

121

the blessings of leverage — provided always that the underlying securities and profits are truly secure.

The guiding principle for the construction of a pyramid is not necessarily simplicity, but sense. If the pyramid is taken to pieces, as with Hodge or Insull after the crash, what's left must be sufficiently viable to make the innocent wonder why the pyramid was ever constructed in the first place.

The guileless should ponder the case of Jimmy Goldsmith, possibly the most flamboyantly effective financier of the New Europe. When Goldsmith first entered the headlines, as the stripling who eloped with a Patino tin heiress against the furious will of a richly provided Latin American dynasty, the obvious assumption was that the eloper was a no-account playboy. In his own startling right, however, Goldsmith has put together, from a base in the free and easy financial atmosphere of Paris, one of the great New European fortunes. At a modest computation, Goldsmith was worth £40 million on the completion of his super-deal, the acquisition of a faded group of grocery shops which, with the open-eyed but still amazing aid of a fat company, Unilever, cost him nothing at all.

Goldsmith first surfaced in France (his mother is French, but his education was Etonian) with a business called Laboratoires Cassenne, which allowed sales to bound ahead so wonderfully that it ran out of the money needed to finance that bounding level of activity. This condition, over-trading, leads to bankruptcy just as surely as if turnover had been heading for the cellar. Moving on to a chemist chain, Goldsmith made two mistakes: he bought the lemon from an established multi-millionaire (Sir Charles Clore), and in partnership with another young man of wealth, Selim Zilkha, whose subsequent and brilliant career in shops for expectant or recent mothers is a text-book lesson in how the rich can get much richer the hard way.

As Goldsmith later admitted, "I nearly lost my shirt" in the over-priced and under-managed shops. But he bought out Zilkha's interest in some slimming biscuits — and, several brisk deals later, seemed to have the nucleus of a speciality food firm, busy making profits from products ranging from chocolate buscuits to snuff. Snuff, however, is what Goldsmith's Cavenham Foods was not up to. In its second year, the loss was almost £1 million. Only some fast and fancy footwork saved Cavenham from extinction.

In the process, Goldsmith not only turned to the west for rescue from the USA, linking up with a company he found in Memphis, but also committed a serious breach of the millionaire club rules: he sent more of his own money, half a million, after bad, to plug the hole in the boat. But there was method in Goldsmith's bad financial manners. Behind Cavenham, if it could be kept afloat, was the even more compelling *raison d'être* of General Occidental, GO for short, and a go-go holding company if ever there was one.

Goldsmith was not alone in doing the holding – a French cousin, Baron Alexis de Gunzberg, is a partner in interlocking entreprises of formidable complexity. For instance, in March 1968 the pair took control of a former Algerian tramway company, and pumped various interests, ranging from a chunk of Cavenham to banking, into the shell. They also bought, quite separately, another bank, which controlled another group of firms under the abbreviated name of FIPP. By the time FIPP had taken over slimming foods from UTP, and had then been merged with Cavenham, and had agreed to merge with a French food group, GASA, and UTF had been merged with SGF to form GO, almost nobody could keep pace with the initials, let alone the interlocking and unlocking – except presumably Goldsmith and Gunzberg.

At the end of the day the formula FIPP + UTP + GASA + SGF added up to around two thirds of GO, half in Goldsmith hands: its one-third of Cavenham alone was worth £60 million at the 1972 peak, the share price having soared eightfold in a year, partly through the beauteous benefits of two acquisitions, the dyed-in-the-beef food business of Bovril and the Allied Suppliers food chain. The latter cost Goldsmith £86.3 million of Cavenham's money. But Unilever, a big Allied shareholder, obligingly bought the Lipton tea business back for £18.5 million, which reduced the net cost to £67.8 million, most of it covered by surplus and saleable property: within a few months Goldsmith had got rid of two City office blocks for £11 million.

All this gorgeousness had to compensate for Goldsmith's woes elsewhere. While Cavenham was booming, the French interests were dropping a packet on bras and lingerie. Goldsmith's attempt to build up a financial pyramid à la Cavenham, with an obscure outfit called Anglo-Continental fell foul of a mistake made earlier in his career – buying from a fellow

123

millionaire. In this case, Jim Slater, the arch-accumulator of holdings and cross-holdings, off-loaded a mixed assortment on Goldsmith, whose share price promptly suffered a fearful fit of the vapours.

Dealing inevitably complicates the dangers of the holding game, since the impact of a bad deal must be magnified in exactly the same way as that of a poor set of earnings – and the really appalling buy can catch the holder both ways by throwing in some wretched earnings at the same time. The Goldsmith career demonstrates the basic principles both positively and negatively.

Negatively, never buy from strong hands: positively, always buy from the weak, which means, generally speaking, large corporations. Positively, coalesce diverse interests to extract their maximum value: negatively, don't diffuse your activities over unrelated fields. Negatively, avoid backing the wrong business horse: positively, capitalize on your mistakes by learning from them. Positively, remember that the ultimate gain from the ultimate holding company resides in keeping its control in your hands: negatively, don't allow your operating base to become so weak that it won't support the holding structure above.

The essence of the modern pyramid can be seen, as through an X-ray, by examining its opposite – the public company in which the ultimate holder personally owns most of the shares. He is limited to the latter and to their possibilities. The law doesn't allow him to build vertically much beyond one layer. So he turns to horizontalism. The holding company owns the master stakes in all the subsidiary or associated companies, but the latter can own useful holdings in each other and can deal and wheel incestuously as much as the master likes. This is not only a convenient way of realizing investment profits, but of burying mistakes or the so-so performers with which all holding operators are afflicted.

No greater practitioner of this quite legitimate art has ever breathed than Jim Slater, friend and friendly helper of Goldsmith and many other tycoons. The investments held by his master company, Slater Walker Securities, varied so greatly in percentage of the equity and nature that keeping track of them was a task beyond even fast financial minds. The spoor became clear, however, when Slater launched an investment trust whose contents, as City cynics were quick to spot, consisted largely of Slater-held shares which had been making something less than the running in the stock market and the cynicism became so overwhelming that eventually Slater had to buy the whole bundle back.

The cynics were possibly too rude – it's an old trick to hide less splendid assets in some more convenient disguise, as demonstrated by George Weston Holdings, the master company of Garfield Weston's empire. For a group so little known, Weston's pyramid is of stupefying spread, with powerful companies in Britain, Canada (Weston's home country), South Africa (a regime to which Weston is partial) and the USA. In the USA, when National Tea lost money and omitted a dividend, the first such omission by a Weston company for half-a-century, the seventy-five-year-old patriarch whipped in one of his sons to repair the damage.

But terrible troubles in finding a solution to a self-created British problem were less easily dealt with: he had attempted to build the mammoth Fine Fare supermarket chain without adequate management. First he imported a flock of Canadian managers who flopped; then he put the whole collection in the care of an ace Canadian whose supervision was decidely hampered by his refusal to cross the Atlantic in aeroplanes. So Weston neatly transferred ownership of the Fine Fare supermarkets (and their losses) to the Canadian wing of George Weston Holdings until such time as the losses had turned to sufficiently respectable profits.

That day duly arrived, thanks to the discovery of James Gulliver, a consultant who had unearthed and cleaned up a mess in a small part of the Fine Fare stables. At which point Weston had a business well on its way to a worth of something like £120 million, a wonderful profit on his original investment. Fine Fare's ownership was then repatriated across the Atlantic, where it became once again an ornament of Weston's British empire. What an astute millionaire holds, he has.

THE DIVERSITY OF RICHES

or

Too Many Broths Don't Spoil the Cook

The principles of diversification for an intelligent tycoon, one of whom turned a £39,000 family stake into £28 million by following the sideline rules ... which include, above all, that of never committing more than side-stakes.

The fortunate few who climb step by ambitious step to the summit of large corporations are subject to the understandable vice of behaving like grand tycoons when they are nothing of the sort. Lack of tycoonery, with all its aggression, egotism and passion for chopping pieces out of corners, is almost an essential qualification for the long haul up to the top. Once installed on the peak of their local Popocatepetl, however, the corpocrats begin behaving in what they foolishly imagine to be tycoon style.

In particular, they become magnetically attracted to the sight of other baskets into which they can deposit their (or rather, the shareholders') eggs. Although the results usually range from ghastly to middling, the observation on which the mistaken policy is based is substantially correct. A high proportion of the world's rich have variegated interests here there and everywhere – and go on accumulating more like so many thieving magpies.

Their observation, however, isn't matched by sufficiently careful analysis. As we have seen, corporations are best advised to keep as many eggs as possible in one basket: otherwise the outfit itself becomes too diffuse and its senior men – the very same survivors of the long race up the bureaucratic ladder — are forced to dissipate their talents and experience over fields where neither apply.

The rich entrepreneur usually has his base-load, just like the big company. But his accretions are less in the nature of a corporate policy than of a once-yearly bet on the Grand National: and, unlike the corpocrat, the entrepreneur has both flair and personal resources. Consequently, he is betting on himself: and, if the horse limps in the day after the race, he bears any loss or (more accurately) offsets it against his taxes. The corpocrat is betting on other people, the underlings who formed or will execute the plan; the loss, in the event of failure, will hurt his profits, balance sheet or both, but the gain of a million in a $300 million company won't even be noticed.

That same capital profit, however, will look clean and sweet to any individual: and the rich, after all, have to do something more constructive with their money than burying it in the ground. That, however, is precisely what one multi-millionaire did, and to his eternal profit — Kemmons Wilson, who made most of his money by housing the quick at Holiday Inns, but turned a considerable number of extra bucks out of the dead.

Wilson bought into the cemetery plot business, but was put off by the low density of corpses. He bent to the question the same ingenuity which evolved his franchise system for motel multiplication. Stiffs occupied so much ground, he observed, because they were stored horizontally: insert them vertically, and the entire dimensions of the problem would be changed. Wilson then adapted an oilfield machine to bore the vertical holes, and made a special cylindrical coffin designed to fit the slots. His new basket was then ready to receive its golden, if macabre, eggs.

That combination of opportunism and technical innovation is not easily reproduced. But expert entrepreneurs down the ages never seem to have hesitated before a new possibility: they needed only to see that if the barriers between hope and realization could be removed, a rich margin would result. The rewards don't even have to be realized fast: again, the individual investor, as opposed to the corporate one, has the inside track.

Since income is a potential embarrassment to the individual, he can be wholeheartedly content with an unrealized gain, so long as it is sufficiently gainful. Virtually all grades of the well-to-do have these sidelines, extra-mural activities which are bred by the very existence of their wealth. It acts as both magnet and propulsion unit. Propositions are irresistibly attracted to the point of the compass where possible finance sits: and the financing possibilities irresistibly urge their possessor to diversify — often in nutritious fields unrelated to the sources of their bread-and-butter.

Kemmons Wilson's corpses are no further apart from his Holiday Inns than Norton Simon's art collecting is from his tomato ketchup. In that case the sideline has become the mainline activity, and a rich dish on its own. An inescapable truth is that, for those who could afford them, Old Masters of the Simon quality or Impressionists of the foremost rank, have been among the most purse-warming, as well as culturally rewarding, investments of the post-war period. Take the £798,000 price Simon paid for Rembrandt's *Titus* (after the auctioneer got tangled up in Simon's tortuous instructions to the effect that when he was standing he wasn't bidding: when he was sitting, he was, and so forth): it has already begun to look like a bargain.

In a sense Simon, like Duveen in the age of the supreme dealer, made his own market: his prices have been a major force propelling his own art values upwards. This, again, is a privilege of the wealthy diversifier. He can move sufficient resources to the chosen area to force his dreams to come true. (There are, alas, exceptions: times when a market is too big even for Croesus to corner — although that may not stop him from trying. Two offspring of H. L. Hunt, super-rich both from Dad's oil and their own earnest endeavours, in 1973's silver rush cornered over 6% of the world's total stocks, worth in early 1974 a quarter of a billion dollars — close to half of which was the paper profit of Nelson Bunker and Herbert Hunt, enough to make even the biggest Daddy proud.)

The nature and range of a man's understanding determine how far he can diversify, and in what ways. Many men of surpassing wealth feel uncomfortable more than a stone's throw away from their business hearths and think little of happier, luckier spirits who fool around with coffins and casinos. There's a line in a Frank Sinatra film, uttered by Keenan Wynn as a rich promoter offered a Sinatra proposition for a Florida Disneyland, which sums up the attitude. "Disneylands," said the Wynn character brutally, "are for

Disney." (Whose company proceeded some years later to build one, to its great profit, in Florida.)

The choice is truly a matter of temperament as much as ability. The diversifier has to regard himself as an investor, which is an utterly different role from that of the entrepreneur. Those who are content to sit back in their leather-padded swivel chairs and collect the money, however, have made some extraordinary extra piles. The oil-rich Texan Amon G. Carter, for instance, bankrolled American Airlines; the Murchison boys, also from Texas, engaged in some spirited forays into New York finance, notably a battle for control of the giant Investors Diversified Services mutual fund complex.

But oil fortunes, in general, have had less impact outside Texas than might be expected. Part of the reason is that oilmen habitually put their profits right back into oil, which is increasingly capital-hungry these days. Another is that Texas is a large state with enormous tracts of land: those oilmen who have invested in land have done nearly as nicely as those Texan land barons who went into oil.

There's a rueful story about Albert D. Lasker, the Lord and Thomas advertising genius, whose $115 million packet is alleged to be the greatest fortune anybody ever has taken out of advertising. Lasker off-loaded the Texas land bequeathed by his father. Had he kept that rich soil, Lasker would have died $500 million better off.

Even a foot-loose millionaire must live somewhere: and while buying two or three houses, he might as well have a small patch of land to call his own in their vicinity. If that patch contains a farm, or trees, or various other conveniences, moreover, its acquisition will reduce his estate duties, his taxation or both: and while performing its good deed of reduction, it will appreciate mightily. In 1961 Sir Charles Clore, seeking a suitable home for a couple of million pounds, bought sixteen thousand acres near Hereford from a London hospital. A dozen years later Clore's country *pied-à-terre* was worth, on a conservative estimate, £14 million.

In fact, this profit, gathered from imitating the lilies of the field and neither toiling nor spinning, outdid some of Clore's more spectacular achievements founded on real entrepreneurial effort. When he paid £550,000 for the site of the London Hilton, the first building to upstage Buckingham Palace, he was widely thought to be pulling off a masterly coup. But the site vendor invested Clore's thousands in land about as far from the metropolis as Britain can provide, up in Scotland, where his capital multiplied five and a half times in a decade – handsomely beating the profit on the Hilton for much less trouble.

That kind of appreciation has been recorded by almost every member of the well-endowed classes who put money into real estate – and in the USA, where the investor can charge depreciation on the purchase price even of old buildings, this type of diversification is practically obligatory. There is no doubt some screwy logic in allowing a millionaire to deduct from his taxes the notional annual fall in the value of a building which, as everyone (even in the Internal Revenue Service) knows, is actually appreciating in worth. However, the logic is so screwy that it set a trap for none other than Charles Clore.

In 1960, when British property developers were afloat on easy millions, a lovely, high building in the USA was the most tempting present left for the millionaire who had everything else. Clore's property interest was only one of many broths: he was in shoes, shipbuilding, textile machinery, jewellery, but property in Britain had been among his most successful fields. In buying his Manhattan status symbol, however, he broke the cardinal rule by buying from another tycoon, William Zeckendorf, the then master of compounded debt. The bauble, 40 Wall Street, was seventy storeys high and forty-one years old.

By the time the aged building had been reconstructed, Clore had nearly $20 million invested in Wall Street, a quarter of it his own cash, and the final bitter twist came when the owners of the new Pan Am building, towering above Grand Central Station, had to buy up leases in 40 Wall Street to persuade their owners to become Pan Am tenants. By then, after a deal back home, the part-owner of the Pam Am temple was – Charles Clore. According to Oliver Marriott's *The Property Boom*, Clore emerged with a feeble $700,000 profit (feeble, that is, by Clore's standards) and that much only because of a technicality in the foreign exchange transactions.

Every British tycoon who brushed up against Zeckendorf got crushed in his embrace. Those who emerged with profit needed all the strength and skill of Davy Crockett wrestling with a bear: and presumably got small comfort from the fact that the bear-like Mr. Zee eventually crushed himself under a great load of unserviceable debt.

130

Millionaire investors are no more likely to avoid bear-hugs than anybody else. Their double-barrelled safety valve, however, is that, first, they can afford the inconvenience of an error. Looked at in the worst light, "Charlie's bad egg", as 40 Wall Street was known, tied up some $5½ million of his capital in a sterile manner for half-a-dozen years: that might have broken a lesser fortune, but didn't even cause Clore to break stride. And second is the fact that the more pressing considerations drive the tycoon to pastures where the diversifying is likely to be greenest: not only into property, but into US oil, where the tax breaks are worth having even if the drilled hole isn't.

Bing Crosby and Bob Hope have ample reason to sing about the day when a Fort Worth friend put them into 16% of an especially sumptuous deal: after one dry hole, fifty-eight came good and wet in succession. If other Hollywood wallets have been emptied by less benevolent Texans, that's only fair recompense for the terrible damage done to those brave Texan millionaires who have put their silver dollars into Broadway plays and ended up with dirty faces. (The angel, however, isn't truly buying a stream of future income. Like the millionaire customers for Duveen art in the silver age, he is buying cultural respectability, and the prestige is presumably worth the fee.)

There are, however, other soups which confer both kudos and riches: for instance, owning your own *grande luxe* restaurant. William Brock, one of the three founders of Automotive Products, not only owned the Mirabelle in Mayfair, but also a country restaurant near his home in Maidenhead. The Mirabelle's value alone must have exceeded £1 million: a rival London establishment, the Coq d'Or, was reported to have changed hands for a round seven figures. In New York, the great Henri Soulé, who became a millionaire himself as a result, was set up in Le Pavillon by rich men who had enjoyed his cooking at the 1939 World's Fair. It's the most charming of diversifications: quite literally having your food and eating it.

You can drink your bottle and keep it, too. When Lord Cowdray was persuaded to take control of Château Latour, it was a run-down vineyard which only clung to its precious First Growth status by continuing to make great wine – even though the vines and winery were dilapidated. The richest

131

private purse in England repaired the dilapidations with expert local help: by 1970 the stocks held at the château were said in Bordeaux to be worth more than the entire Cowdray outlay, on purchase, maintenance and repair. That was before the atomic price explosion from 1971 onwards. With 1972 first growth clarets selling at £8,750 a barrel, a rise of 50% over 1970, Latour would rank as one of the happiest investments of all time, even if the wine were less than marvellous.

C. Douglas Dillon, investment banker and former Secretary of the US Treasury, can't be any less happy with his possession of Château Haut Brion: as for Baron Philippe de Rothschild, the hundred thousand bottles of rare vintages in his private cellar at Château Mouton must be worth well over a million in their own right – a five-bottle Jeroboam of the 1929, after all, fetched $9,200 at an auction.

Still, viticulture is too technical a game for the armchair investing in which most of the rich prefer to indulge. In some cases, however, the armchair is jet-propelled. Sir Isaac Wolfson devoted most of his energies to building up his mail order and store chain, but on the side he pushed a posse of financial interests into a company separate from his main Great Universal Stores.

On one estimate, although the total amount of family money ever invested in this sideline was no more than £39,000, the Wolfsons emerged from the enterprise with £28 million. A 1951 investment of £1,000 in Drages, a Wolfson vehicle whose corporate passengers remained mysterious for many years, would have been worth over a million (to be precise, £1,080,000) eleven years later.

Wolfson followed an important rule for your outside interests: never dilute your equity. The joy of a good deal – and all sidelines are deals – is greatly lessened if the proceeds must be given away to every Tom, Dick and Hermann who has climbed on the bandwagon.

It doesn't mean that the entire bowl of soup has to be in your private possession: that may be not only impossible but illogical. The lesson is rather to avoid, in financing, anything that will prevent the maximum benefit from accruing to the most important person in the operation – yourself. In a mainline operation, this, while still commendable, may be impracticable. Acquisitions may necessitate cashing in some of your own chips, turning them over to others, and so on.

But since the sideline is on the side, you can afford to wait until the manna is ready to drop from heaven. And very handy it can be, too: as Spyros Skouras no doubt found when, in the wake of the $30 million *Cleopatra* disaster, Darryl Zanuck ousted him from Twentieth Century Fox: at which point Skouras must have been glad that he had succumbed to the ancient Greek temptation of the sea, building up substantial shipping interests on which, presumably, he could continue to float.

If off-the-cuff successes suggest that casualness is the path to extra-mural pelf, they are dangerously misleading. Let the case of Dan Lufkin, who made most of a $35 million fortune from the Wall Street broking house of Donaldson, Lufkin and Jenrette, stand as a warning. A friend, Louis Marx Jr., of the toy family, thought that DLJ was coming in with him on an oil play in Kansas. But the cheque turned out to be from Lufkin personally: his DLJ company had turned the proposition down. According to Marx, Lufkin "really had to dig down for that money" — which in short order came back tenfold and provided the nucleus of Pan Ocean Oil, which has a stake in many deep oil diggings, including the biggest dig of all — the North Sea.

Lufkin made "spur-of-the-moment, almost impetuous commitments . . . on the spot to people he had never met or knew only casually." The trouble with this method is that it tends to balance every hit with a miss: to match Pan Ocean with the Ontario Motor Speedway, a $27 million flop, to offset the hit show *Oh! Calcutta* with the *Saturday Review*, a perfectly good magazine massacred by a pair of assiduous promoters with their marvellous ideas for renovation.

Sidelines should never commit more than sidestakes. It defeats the definition if an extra-mural activity begins to eat up resources. History does, of course, record cases of spin-offs that have either outgrown the original activity or become great economic empires themselves. Thus two founders of American Express, Mr. Wells and Mr. Fargo, set up what has now become the west's fourth largest bank when their Amex partners turned down their proposal to extend the service to the gold of California. In the same state, the Safeway supermarket chain was promoted by Merrill Lynch Pierce Fenner & Smith (né Bean), the world's largest stockbrokers (and very possibly its most prolific spawner of millionaires: when Merrill

Lynch went public in 1971, 175 employees reached that financial status overnight).

The many-soup technique isn't confined to those whose bowls are already brimming over. It can be used in reverse: adding together many mites to make a nice, fat mint. Owning several small businesses is one route, but tends to be hard on the arteries — the scurrying about required is out of proportion to the pay-off, while the chances of one egg in the basket turning horribly bad are just as great when the eggs are small as with the dinosaur-sized dollops of the conglomerates.

A better technique is to have no real commitment to a multitude of businesses, so that it matters not whether they soar like swallows or subside into the swamp. This may sound difficult but the invention of the non-executive director makes the trick exceedingly simple. The only obstacle is getting accepted as a man of good sense, breeding and contacts whose presence would ornament and dignify any board. The difficulty is more social than intellectual. But once the barrier has been crossed, multiplication can begin in earnest.

The odds are that, out of a dozen or so companies, one will prove to be a big winner. The betting is fair that in most such cases the holdings are not purchased out of the pennies saved from the wise man's salary; although a fee of £5,000 multiplied twenty times does work out at a more than useful pittance.

Those who provide the pittance are unaware of the obvious fact that the main reason which makes their multiple man a catch in their eyes — the fact that he sits on so many portentous boards — greatly reduces his value. The more jobs a man has, the less he can contribute to each: yet, by some strange reversal of logic, the more he is sought after, and the more money gets thrust into his hands by the clients.

The multiple director, however, is not in the same league as the rich collector of broths, either financially or in the one essential respect which should govern diversifying. The non-executive never actually has to like anything about the businesses which employ him, except the money. In contrast, nobody who already has the latter should put it into a side enterprise unless it's partly for a kind of loving. The pleasure he derives from, say, owning Château Latour enhances the chances that, even though he has only a fraction of his mind to devote to the property, he will tend it well.

The pleasure, moreover, is a useful antidote when soups

134

curdle, as they often will, even for more careful investors than Dan Lufkin. Take the Chicago financier Colonel Henry Crown. His involvement with General Dynamics, whose bad habits included losing $450 million on the Convair jetliner and running through presidents like a paper-shredder, must have been soothed by other, more hospitable interests, like the Hilton hotel chain, and, still more, the Empire State Building. Owning that landmark should have been a matter of pride as much as property – like a Parisian buying the Eiffel Tower or a Londoner landing Buckingham Palace. Whether or not his ego was well massaged, the Colonel eventually sold his sideline in the sky to the Prudential insurance company – and massaged his wallet with a profit of $50 million.

SCENE 3

THE GOLD IN GAMBLING

or

The One-Horse Race

In which we discover how to turn gambling into certainty, which is by removing uncertainty ... with some thoughts on the Company Raid Gambit Declined, the Inside Straight and other popular means of fixing the race without bribing the jockey (or with, if preferred).

The man who hasn't got everything suffers a fatal disadvantage in the effort to get rich the easiest way, which is in return for nothing, otherwise known as gambling. Apart from the British football pools or national lotteries in Latin countries, there are hardly any opportunities for sudden, lightning conversion of the poor.

The sad truth is that, if a thousand to one shot comes home with £10 on its nose, you only pocket £10,000: whereas if you can afford £1,000, the proceeds are a whole, round million. It is even sadder that thousand to one shots rarely return to the fireside, a fact of which those who can afford £1,000 bets are fully aware. Which is why the rich prefer to speculate only on stone-cold certs: this has the advantage that they can never lose.

The richer you are, the easier it becomes to arrange the necessary degree of certainty. At the extreme the best way of profiting from gambling is to run it, as the Mafia long ago discovered. However, the techniques which piled up an alleged $150 million for the pursued waif Meyer Lansky have as much to do with banking as with gaming. Like banks the Mafia parts the masses from their cash and makes sure that, before any of the loot is actually paid out, the mob collects its unfair share. It's the latter-day version of Robin Hood: taking from the poor in order to give to the rich. (The gambit is far safer than fixing fights or horse races, where the fixed contestant can always defraud you by having a heart attack.)

The organizers of the Irish Sweepstake, the world's single greatest horse betting exercise, may have taken the same lesson to their bosoms. According to the finds of an enterprising journalist, the lion's share of the many millions taken by the sweep may not get paid out to the beneficiaries. A nourishing chunk he claimed, went into a variety of pockets, the deepest being those of the McGrath family, which for years organized the event on behalf of the Irish hospitals, the supposed beneficiaries, and was alleged to collect £3 million a year for its trouble.

Behind every mass gamble there stands a small family with a large fortune – even if it does no more than allow the odds to work in its favour. The essence of any book or gaming table is that, no matter what combination of winners comes in, the house comes out ahead. In running a book on horses, an element of risk remains: on a football pool, however, the promoter can never lose, since he only pays out a fixed proportion of what comes in.

The take had always been terrific. William Crockford, whose gaming club was the birthplace of London's post-war gambling renaissance, died in 1844 worth the equivalent of £5 million. By 1961, on the *Saturday Evening Post*'s figures, profits from gambling in the Las Vegas area had topped £100 million. The mob's pay-offs – $2 million a year in police protection from one Philadelphia ring – give some indication of the profit margins being protected.

In the legitimate end of the business, the losses are paradoxically a measure of the mighty sums made. William Hill, Britain's most successful bookie, plunged heavily into fixed odds betting on football matches, a pastime later ended by a kill-joy government. One week he paid out £850,000 on winning bets. "That's not what we call a bad week," he said. "It only worked out at 9:8 against us on the stake." What Hill hailed as a good week must have been quite something.

On the other side of the odds the bettor too can turn speculation into certainty if his stakes are high enough. Exact calculation of the odds, plus a deep bank, enabled the so-called Greek syndicate (actually three Greeks, one Frenchman and one Armenian) to win consistent fortunes from baccarat over many decades of parting stupid American tycoons from their teeth. They chose baccarat because the bank has a slight mathematical advantage and can stop play whenever it fancies.

An even more enterprising Frenchman succeeded in rigging the national, state-backed betting game in his certain favour by careful and massive placing of bets around the country. All these operations appear to be perfectly within the law, which cannot be said for the gang of Britons who substituted a horse in a minor race, suddenly inundated off-course bookmakers with bets on this "ringer", and defeated the anguished bookies' efforts to lay off their bets on the course by cutting the telephone wires. But even here an element of chance existed. The substituted horse, the "ringer", might have fallen over its own feet.

Pure business offers the perfect solid state, the only sporting contest in which you can back all the horses and still win. As with most millionaire ploys, the mysterious absurdity of the stock market contains the formula: witness the Company Raid Gambit Declined.

As everybody knows, Wall Street, London and similar emporia of shares are risky casinos: what goes up always comes down, and you never know when or by how much. But everybody is wrong. In this stratagem the player knows when the share is rising and himself determines how far it is going to rise – and even when the rise will stop.

The first move is to assemble a sizeable quantity of shares in the selected victim. This is accomplished through a variety of dummy companies, nominee companies (conveniently organized by banks for the protection and benefit of their clients), obliging friends, trust funds and what have you. There was even a halcyon period in Britain when the amasser could build up a stake of any size he liked in sublime secrecy: now he has to reveal all when the nibble has become a 10% bite. That, however, compares very favourably with 15% in the USA, and is perfectly adequate for the launching of the next move, which is to make a bid for the rest of the company's shares – pitched well above the current market price and even further above the average cost of your collection.

On the "heads I win, tails you lose" principle, the bid must be realistic (i.e. cheap), so that, if by any chance it succeeds, you have a bargain on your hands. But since it is cheap, the odds are that the stunned directors, reeling from one hastily arranged board meeting to another, will fight to the death in defence of their company's beloved freedom (not to mention their own jobs). This fight for liberty more often than not takes the form of finding some other bidder to deprive them of the same priceless possession, but never mind. (One victimized company, threatened with absorption by the octopus-like Litton Industries, defended itself more skilfully by buying a furniture company: since Litton also made furniture, that killed the bid on anti-trust grounds.)

The gambit player welcomes the appearance of a rival bidder, or the arrival of anything else — a scrumptious profit forecast, a swift revaluation of properties — which forces up the victim's shares. True, he may have to raise his own bid: but that costs nothing, whereas the market rise in his previously purchased shares is money in the bank, all the way to which he is going to laugh.

If the bid succeeds, he pockets the company: if it fails, he pockets the capital gain. An early demonstration of this beautiful truth came in the battle for the Savoy Hotel, that chromium-plated pride of London. Attacked by a mystery bidder, it also attracted the attention of Charles Clore, who in the days before his knighthood (and his construction of the London Hilton) was regarded by the Establishment much as Philip of Spain fancied Captain Blood; in the face of this onslaught the Savoy board closed ranks with such adamant fervour that Clore and the mystery bidder, revealed as Sir Harold Samuel, must have come out of the fracas with over half a million between them.

There's no shortage of other targets. Oliver Jessel, an ebullient descendant of the Samuel millions (oil of the Shell variety and banking of the merchant blend) made a determined foray for an oil distributor, Wm Cory. Jessel lost the war, but won one prize — a brisk, substantial capital gain, which lent still more conviction to his saying, after some years of forward and downward struggle, that "at last my business is making more than my private income." The business making a raid may even be smaller than its intended victim. That fact contains two important principles of business chess. In this type of gambit, relative smallness is an asset, making it easier for the raider to maintain a sky-high value for his own shares. (A common double move in the game is to get a friend or friends to buy your own shares during the vital manoeuvres, thus keeping up their price.)

The bigness of the target also has rich implications. Not only are large companies the ones most likely to stuff their cupboards with under-realized assets and their executive suites with managerial dodos; there also will be enormous numbers of shares around the place, thus making it possible for cloak and dagger merchants to buy them in relative secrecy. F. W. Woolworth had 378 million shares on the market in Britain, while A & P in the USA has 24.8 million little pieces of paper: the once great A & P chain was thus a sitting duck for the gambit essayed by Charles Bluhdorn of Gulf & Western.

After a blistering attack on A & P's grocery price tactics (in truth, inane enough) by a Bluhdorn pal, Bluhdorn steadily bought shares in the sagging supermarket chain. It had sagged to a $50 million loss in nine months, on rising sales, by the infallible expedient of giving away its goods to customers at less than true cost. Market purchases of a million-odd shares by G & W were followed by a tender offer to buy another 3.75 million at $20 – a price usefully higher than the $16 at which they stood at the start of Bluhdorn's gambit. The existence of his interest in itself supported the A & P price; and in this situation the player can always expect his opponent to work his hide off to repel the raid.

The ultimate beauty of such gambits is that the purchase money can easily be borrowed from some friendly neighbourhood bank. The dealing creates automatically collateral for the loan, in the shape of the bought shares; and the bank gets what bankers love best of all, fast turnover of their money and, if it's an investment bank, a nice slice of the action.

For the extremely rich, however, a little cash can go a wonderfully long way. One past master at this art can stimulate enthusiasm for a share by picking up a few and allowing word to get around that he might splurge on many more shares; that he might inject some of his own interests; that he might make the company the vehicle for any future empires he might choose to build.

As the shares bound up this master takes his first profit: he next sells short, and the word gets around that none of the deals will materialize: the maestro then takes his second profit, and so on, until no more flesh is left on the picked over bones.

In another variation, the deal was actually consummated. The tycoon concerned took shares in exchange for one of his

140

companies, amid scenes of great rejoicing. With those shares in hand, he proceeded to control the market, mounting a bear raid of swift and stunning success. The very word that he proposed to off-load his newly acquired shares sent shudders down the collective spine of the stock market: and if you can move markets by a word, money is only a useful secondary tool. The combination of word and wealth is utterly irresistible.

But the essence of the Company Raid Gambit Declined and its variations is that the same player cannot make the move more than once every few years: otherwise he loses the essential element of credibility. That would break a prime rule of making millions, which is that what people believe to be real is more important than reality itself.

Playing the market this way has the virtue of being completely honest, or (to be more accurate) entirely legal. However, the players are in a minefield of rules and temptations, any of which can blow up in their faces. The first of the USA's post-war company raiders, Louis E. Wolfson, who assaulted the heaving mail order bulk of Montgomery Ward, had some $210 million of assets under his control at one point, but ended up in prison uniform.

The same risks of falling foul of the law are run in another millionaire-generating game: the Inside Straight, in which the moves come straight from the horse's mouth. In theory, no insider of a public company is supposed to profit personally from information which has been kept from the shareholders at large. In practice, insiders are fixing themselves with this dope all the time – and their crime, being difficult to detect, is seldom punished with anything save money.

The fatal error is greed. The more shares insiders buy in a stock that is heading for Cloud Nine, the more likely it is that some interfering busybody will notice. The more shares insiders off-load in a company which is heading for the tomb, the higher the chance that somebody will compare before-and-after holdings in the shares. Once upon a time, indeed until very recently in Britain, directors were under no obligation to reveal their interests: they still don't have to in most of the continent.

Even today in the UK well over a year can elapse between a sale or purchase and its revelation – by which time the insider can have closed the deal and taken his profit, without anybody being wiser or sadder. Once again, however, the leverage of

141

money is needed to make real money. The insider may know that a bid is coming at double the market price: but to reap a million from his coup, he needs a million first – and raising that kind of loot renders the necessary concealment even harder.

When the stakes are warming enough, however, caution gives way to avarice. Back in the early 1960s, an observant Canadian living in a hick town called Timmins in Ontario noticed that a certain aircraft used by a US company was flying the same route every day to a prospecting site. Being shrewd as well as long-sighted, he bought any land he could find in the area, which proved to bear silver, zinc, lead and other gew-gaws in delectable quantities.

Back at the ranch, however, the Americans who controlled the exploration, executives of Texas Gulf Sulphur, had far more precise information than the plane-spotter, and far earlier. Their public statements played down the value of the finds while their private dealings built up their stakes in a stock which was bound to multiply gloriously. When the true glory was finally unveiled, Timmins was swamped by a minor gold rush – and the Texas Gulf Sulphur insiders reached for their piggy-banks.

After due delay, alas, the sheriffs of the Securities and Exchange Commission reached for their guns and hauled the insiders off to the courts. They had offended, not simply by getting caught, but by being too obvious.

Time and again before a bid is announced or a company crashes the shares mysteriously either rise or fall in due season. The stock exchange duly investigates for the leak: only to find, time and again, that the plug has been so neatly inserted that not a trace remains. Actually, you don't even need a leak. The safest honest way of making money known to man is to buy shares in elephantine companies at the receiving end of bids from raiders who are determined to succeed. The bidder is invariably forced to raise his offer, and the gap between opening shot and closing salvo can be huge. Watney Mann, trying to defend its brewing empire from Maxwell Joseph's Grand Metropolitan Hotels, saw its share price nearly treble before the day was narrowly lost. The outsider gets a free ride on the insider's back. Max Joseph is a grandmaster in the art of sure things. For example, at the time of the 1964 election he put a massive bet on a Labour victory,

142

not because of any loyalty to the party, but on grounds of impeccable logic. If the Conservatives won, all his shareholdings would soar. If Labour won (as it did), he stood to collect a tax-free fortune on the bet. Joseph also showed that he had the correct idea about gambling by putting his money on the best chip of all: he bought up casinos.

The right side of the tables had always been where they keep the money. But the casinos of England have received a rich extra lining of plush from the unwitting munificence of the government. After gaming was legalized, clubs proliferated to an extent that bothered the puritans and affronted the police. And the Mafia regarded it as only proper that its members should take their share of this expanding market.

No doubt, no person in the entire apparatus of British Government foresaw that gaming controls would inevitably create gaming goldmines. Few bureaucrats or politicians in central government do foresee the private results of their public decisions, which often require superhuman efforts of self-control from insiders. There's the famous incident of Lord Kindersley, who as a director of the Bank of England knew that a "swingeing" rise in interest rates was on the way. By selling gilt-edged government stock, his bank (Lazards) could make or avoid losing great fortunes. An unwitting bank colleague, at this untimely juncture, approached Kindersley for his views on selling gilts: at which the latter looked "extremely po-faced".

A later government, by a decision on gilt-edged stock, made it easy for anybody with access to millions to make still more. The introduction of capital gains tax in 1965 applied to these securities: but some had been sold to the long-suffering public, in the days before the tax, at prices well below par. It was pointed out to the politicians that this was sharp practice, denying the purchasers part of a reward which had, in effect, been guaranteed by Her Majesty's government.

So the bonds concerned were exempted from the tax, with the following unintended result. You buy £1 million of bonds, borrowing the money at 10%: the security, gilt-edged stock, is watertight; the interest can all be offset against investment income, which is taxed at rates of up to 90% and more. The stock stands at eighty but in a couple of years must be redeemed at a hundred, thus yielding £250,000 for the outlay of less than £10,000 a year.

As usual, it was mainly the already rich who reaped the fruits, although one socialist millionaire, among the first to spot the wholesome opportunity created by his colleagues, used the chance to set up his old professors and friends with some extra nest-eggs It isn't the only way in which the socialists made money for millionaires. Their addiction to defending the pound sterling created wonderful openings for international currency speculators.

At one point, on a careful estimate, the official regulations had created eighty-nine varieties of sterling, a profusion which offered endless opportunities for switching profitably from one to another. What the politicians damned as speculation, and attributed to people unpleasantly nicknamed "gnomes of Zurich", was actually intelligent action on reasoned anticipation of inevitable events. The pound's devaluation was made certain by the incompetent financial policies of Her Majesty's ministers, not by the machinations of astute men playing the international money market.

Harold Wilson was constantly boasting how these friends would get their fingers burnt. In truth, those fingers were tastefully licked as the speculators cashed in on the fact that sterling's ability to rise (its upside potential) was limited by international agreement to a small percentage shift, while its downside potential was of mouth-watering size. In the event, the price slumped from $2.80 to $2.40, a killing only matched by the final slaughter of the even longer American defence of the dollar.

In the one month of February 1973 at least $600 million was cleaned up entirely by those who were betting on D-marks by two weeks' heavy speculation on the fact that the dollar had nowhere to go except down. Probably the majority of this take was cleared by corporations, but a goodly number of clever individuals went along for a free ride, which was financed by others and entailed (like all good speculation) a minimal degree of risk.

In mythology, risk is the way to millions, on the general assumption that "the higher the risk, the higher the potential reward". But this is an inaccurate analogy from what is a true statement about investment: that "the higher the interest, the higher the risk". Between interest (which is income) and a dealing profit (which is a capital gain) there is a great canyon fixed. Where the odds are a hundred to one, it's because the chances of the bet succeeding are small. The true speculator, however, is concerned not with the percentage of his pay-off, but with its degree of certainty. The surer the thing, the more heavily he invests. True and high risks are for the suckers — for those, in other words, from whom the true speculator makes his true rewards.

SCENE 4

THE BLISS OF BACKING

or

You Can Count on Me

A good old military man turns $70,000 into a quarter of
a billion in eleven years . . . the fine old firm of Harriman,
Warburg and Strauss strikes polarized gold . . . an IBM
heir makes semi-conductor magic — all by picking one
good apple from a barrelful of bad choices.

Once upon a time, in a real-life fairy story, there was a wise
old general who spotted a bright little computer engineer and
gave him both blessing and backing. Within eleven years that
good old military man had seen his investment multiply to a
quarter of a billion dollars.

Compared to that golden windfall, the general's initial
backing was no more expensive than the winning ticket in the
Irish Sweepstake. He bought just $70,000 of the computer's
prodigy's shares, which then proceeded to multiply down the
years like a family of particularly sexy minks. The investor
was General Doriot, whose American Research and Development became an international byword for the astute backing of
advanced technology. Backing successful outsiders is as rare
in business as on the track, but picking winners in advanced
scientific wonder gadgets is approximately as easy as drawing
a royal flush at poker.

Doriot's record in this esoteric field was exceptionally good,
even without his wonder-investment in Ken Olsen's Digital
Equipment. But exceptional achievement in this minefield
means very little more than avoiding detonation. While ARD
made some other lucky pricks with the general's educated pin,
none compared with the DE goldmine. And the net result,
when ARD was finally sold out to the Textron conglomerate,

was not the kind of capital gain to make a mutual fund manager cry with jealous shame.

Doriot would have done better to place every egg in the DE basket – if only, that is, he could have foreseen its future. This is one variety of foresight not given to man, even to man of such surpassing shrewdness as the general. A possibly apocryphal story tells of the general's being offered an ingenious plan for selling hardwood trees and bringing the valuable timber down river to the sawmills below. The general listened carefully to the details, the extrapolations of hardwood demand, the behaviour of prices in the key markets, the increasing proportion of expensive veneers in furniture, and what not. He then killed the project stone-dead with one simple question: will the logs float?

Successful backers need to ask log-floating questions. This demands some instinct about where the project is most liable to sink. The instincts of laymen confronted with technologists, especially technologists of advanced breed, are unreliable and tend to be suppressed by false (or risky) modesty. Backers of technological wonders usually come unstuck, not because of failure to understand quantum theory or the significance of the Second Law of Thermodynamics, but because, hornswoggled by the bewildering magic of the unknown, they ignore the simple rules that they should know by heart and by common sense.

If an inventor fails to keep a watchful eye on how his money is being spent, or to force his pet technologists to give him meaningful progress reports on the latest wonder of the world, he only has himself to blame when the logs sink (as, in such circumstances, they always do). One set of bemused bankers allowed their technical playboys to pile up monstrous extravagances on complex equipment like Rolls-Royce motor cars and interior decoration, completely ignoring the fact, which the simplest of checks would have unveiled, that there were hardly any customers in the whole wide world (only one finally turned up) for the particular magic being peddled.

In contrast, the potential clients for an instant camera were numbered in the multi-millions: and it is a law of wealth that the bigger the market, the greater the chances of achieving financial greatness. The early backers of Dr. Edwin Land can congratulate themselves on following this elementary rule with conspicuous reward: they were, as it happens, a conspicuous

147

group, financially and socially. Averell Harriman, James P. Warburg and Lewis Strauss put up $375,000: family wealth never sowed more fertile seed.

The small sum of $1,000 invested in Polaroid in 1938 would have been worth $4 million within a quarter of a century. Plainly, backing will more often than not come from the rich — after all, they have the money. But it does not follow that rich killings, the creation of the new fortunes of Polaroid dimensions, will inevitably also fall to the wealthy. If you have twice as many shots as the next man, you have twice his chance of hitting the target, and striking in the centre (or the gold, as archers appropriately call it). But the man with fewer shots may still strike gold with his first aim, and the annals of golden backing contain many proofs of this satisfying truth.

John James is a Bristol millionaire who began to build up a chain of radio and TV shops on the strength of a post-war service gratuity. While rising to the giddy heights of three hundred outlets in fourteen years, James had trouble getting sets supplied by the orthodox, established manufacturers. He was forced to look elsewhere, and his gaze lighted on Radio and Allied, whose fortunes were in the tight grip of the then unknown Arnold Weinstock.

James ended up as the largest investor in Radio and Allied outside Weinstock's family. When Weinstock led his company into GEC, James became one of that company's biggest holders, too: when Weinstock led GEC into Valhalla, James cashed in on the richest transformation ever wrought on a major European company. His stake in GEC became worth a lusty sum, even compared to the £6 million which he made by selling his store chain. (His first chain, that is: in a second incarnation, James made some less inspired moves, including the financial support of a chain of furniture discount stores of quite spectacular lack of viability.)

Where Weinstock is (or was) a lean and hungry man, the disappointing furniture king was heavy on the hoof, which is a useful, though not invariable, guide for off-track betters. There are exceptions of course, in both directions. But men who are big, fat and sleep o'nights seem in general to lack the well-placed energy, insatiable drive and self-made success of the true tycoon. In the latter class tend rather to be short, thick-set, small men like David Sarnoff, the genius of RCA, or Lord Marks, the creator of the modern Marks & Spencer. Samuel I.

Newhouse checks out at five feet three inches, at least $300 million, twenty-two newspapers, seven TV stations, twenty magazines: Meyer Lansky, the Jewish Mafioso, is five feet one inch. Neither Sir Isaac Wolfson, the British mail order king, nor Sir Jules Thorn, the British Sarnoff, would be much use, physically speaking, in a basketball team.

In contrast, the truly disastrous receptacles for other people's cash often float high in water – like the salad-oil swindler, Tino de Angelis, who, while only five feet five inches, weighed in at 240 lbs: like John King, the would-be ruler of IOS, or William Zeckendorf, Sr., the real estate tycoon who took several of Britain's over-ambitious property men for a ride around the city centres of the Americas; or Marion Harper, the advertising man who created both the biggest and the brokest group of advertising agencies in the world.

Most such men are terrific talkers, which is another uneasy augury. One clearly identifiable characteristic of the super-manager is that he talks as little as possible, especially in public. This is partly because words waste time, and most men of true action are deeply, instinctively conscious of the way in which time, which is also money, runs through the fingers. They are also acutely aware that the more you say, the more you are liable to commit yourself – and commitment, unless you are exceedingly careful, also costs money. As in poker, so in business, part of the art is to keep the opposition guessing, because, like everybody else in the world, they will more often guess wrong than right.

Preference for the short, strong and silent is a good start along the critical road to making a personal assessment. In the end this is the nature of the backing decision. No matter how developed the nose for a good idea, no matter how careful the checking to ensure that the logs will float, no matter how quick and comprehensive the financial controls over the loved one, in the end everything comes down to the man himself.

There is no such thing, however, as the right man in the wrong opportunity: if you are backing somebody in ventures like tuna fishing, de-veined shrimp and frozen apple juice (to name three of General Doriot's failed brainwaves) you by definition have the wrong man. The right one, like Ken Olsen, at DE, does the right thing: and usually, like Olsen, has eccentric characteristics which stamp him as an unusual creature, a man unlikely to get diverted from the important business of making your money grow at the most urgent possible speed.

In 1972, when worth some £90 million, Olsen still worked out of a deserted woollen mill in Maynard, Massachusetts. He still had a paramount interest in the pure, unadulterated beauty of computer circuits. "I still keep my hand in at engineering," he said once, "for fear that I might one day be out of a job. I do it some Saturday mornings." Between 1965 and 1972 the sales presided over by this curiously indifferent capitalist shot up from $15 million to $180 million as Olsen survived a ghastly catalogue of errors in shipping out the PDP-6 computer. That, maybe, is the hardest thing to predict about an entrepreneur: how he will react in the all but inevitable crisis. Toughness alone won't see the man through: he requires, over and above courage, the ability to stick like a leech to the essentials of his job – which, in Olsen's case, was to produce ingenious small computers which actually worked: like the PDP-8, which promptly sold over ten thousand copies.

Among several moments of painful truth, the most agonizing for Henry Ford I was the year the Model T, thrashed by the ritzier models of Chevrolet, ran out of road. Ford closed the plants for a year, came out with the Model A, and drove on to a greater fortune than ever. This, admittedly, was an eccentric procedure. But Ford conformed so perfectly to the entrepreneurial stereotype as to define it: secretive, taciturn, passionate about engineering, eccentric to the point of lunacy, but crazy (most of the time) like a fox.

No backers of talent in history ever reaped what they sowed more richly than the few who climbed on to Ford's running board. When Ford bought them out there was one little old lady whose $100 had come back to her 3,550-fold: $95,000 in dividends and $260,000 in the final pay-off. Another, bigger Ford backer cleaned up $17.4 million tax-free on an initial stake of $5,000. The surpassing loveliness of such returns is that they involve little or no effort on the part of the backer, while the backed one works himself to somewhere near the bone – a fact, no doubt, which inspired Ford's burning desire to regain all of the equity.

General Doriot, in fact, got 60% of Ken Olsen's equity for his $70,000: and although the General's firm provided a lesser amount in loan capital, along with doubtless excellent advice on money matters, there is a certain disproportion in the rewards of the backer (whose bundle was worth $350 million at the apogee) and the backed (even though $90 million, the Olsen stake, is enough to keep a Siberia full of wolves from the door for several generations).

In most cases it is dangerous policy for the backer to control the stock – otherwise he may get to think of it as a subsidiary and interfere with the management; or for the backed entrepreneur to hold the thin end – otherwise he may get miffed and move to plusher pastures. When a South African, Mark Weinberg, spotted that the British life assurance industry was stuck in its selling methods at around the year 1817, he also saw with perfect clarity how to exploit the delicious opportunity which they had left wide open. Weinberg got backing from two American combines, Georgia-Pacific and the ubiquitous ITT, selling his own stake for what proved, in hindsight, to be peanuts. When ITT bought out its partner, the deal cost $38 million: Weinberg's take had been in the thousands, and it surprised nobody when he promptly stepped off to open a rival shop dealing in much the same line of goods.

The odds are heavily stacked against finding a trusty who is vigorous and self-assertive enough to deliver a big bundle of goods and yet sufficiently mild to tolerate interference from on high. Preferably, high partners should sleep: and the entrepreneur should let sleeping partners lie, unless, that is, he needs their help. Rich, well-connected and self-interested men make excellent advisers: what's more, their counsel comes free.

The disadvantages of the partner who is awake, or thinks he is, can be seen in the saga of Fairchild Camera. Sherman M. Fairchild's inheritance of several noggins of IBM stock, and his enjoyment of the good things of life thereby financed, did not stop him for showing a marvellous eye for an opportunity. The discovery of a semi-conductor group working out of a garage in Palo Alto was perfectly handled. (Another demonstration of the fact that truly rewarding enterprises have an affinity for beginning life in garages, lofts and workshops in the garden.) Fairchild financed the electronic pioneers, led by William Noyce, to the modest extent which they required, taking an option on their locks, stocks and barrels. When Noyce's team delivered the semi-conducting goods, Fairchild took up its option for $3.5 million – one of the decade's most outright bargains. In just the first of the good, soft years

Fairchild earned as much as $8.4 million from Noyce's inventions.

But under Fairchild in person, as chairman of the board, the growing pains of the semi-conductor market were compounded by the upheavals in Fairchild management. The stock gyrated, the managerial wonder boys came and went. Although Texas Instruments had its full share of the market troubles, its rise in the same fiendishly clever trade worked out far more impressively. The Texans whose little instrument company found itself sitting on a fortune in silicon chips allowed it to develop its own life. The net result was that every worthy connected with TI, the two original partners, the executive who ran their show and the Texan watchers who spotted the electronic oilwell, eventually sported fortunes worthy of the Spindletop gusher.

The hyperactive partner, along with getting in the way, is prone to the most debilitating disease of the off-track bettor: impatience. The full, fair and fine reward takes time to mature, like a benign Burgundy. If you try to uncork your Romanée-Conti 1961 too soon, you will miss the ultimate splendour of its bouquet and body. The Ford beneficiaries had to wait sixteen years before the last round-up. Even the great General Doriot's company hung fire for three years at its start, pottered along on a higher plateau for seven more years, spent another decade on a more elevated plateau still, and only then achieved its summit (with a jump from $93 million of net asset value in 1966 to $349 million the next year), as DE delivered the goods.

Backing isn't subject to the same laws as stock exchange investment: on the market, one share is never unique: there is always an alternative. The backer, in contrast, is on the hunt for a Unique Buying Proposition, and if a return of DE proportions (360,000%, no less) is the object of the chase, the hunter can afford time. What he can seldom afford is to raise his stake continually when the hopeful provider returns for more. All good development projects cost more than their developers estimate. But the UBP must not run up so steep a bill as to remove its own ripest attraction — which is the modest size of stake in relation to potential.

The well and truly chosen human receptacle of your cash will detest over-spending no less than you. The spendthrift, whose initial request is in the millions and who spends all seven figures in the first few months, is like the locusts of Africa: let him thrive, and he will strip you bare. The backer is in two hazardous activities simultaneously: deciding on the merits and staying power of a business which he doesn't understand, and judging the ability of a particular individual, almost certainly with no achievement behind him, to develop that business into a screaming success.

He needs the combined genius of a brilliant investment banker (a rare animal in investment banking itself) and a selection consultant of trenchant insight (equally rarely found in selection consultancy). There are men with a Midas touch who instinctively back only winners, but in most cases, the ratio of failure to success is as low as must be expected when playing against the odds. The correct response is to spread the risk, even though this dilutes the profit, and to apply rigorous rules to both the backer's functions.

Most so-called "venture capitalists" do not. The only estimate ever made, by *Time* magazine, is that some six hundred firms exist solely to pump money into other people's ventures. They deploy $3,000 million of assets, according to this report and have pumped in annually as much as $700 million, which would exhaust the kitty in little over four years if nothing came up trumps – and often it doesn't. Some four hundred of the US government-backed Small Business Investment Corporations have died since 1964.

Since they are inclined to plunge into ventures like Sam Snead All American Golf (which dropped over $1 million), women's overcoats, soft-drink bottling, cable television, and ice-cream manufacture, maybe the relative lack of success is no great national or international economic tragedy. Some of the backers, in any event, have little faith in their essential judgment of the venturer. Take a scion of the Phipps steel line, Paul Bancroft III, who says "I do not want the president to have control. If his management is not going to make it, you have to be prepared to remove him." But if his management isn't going to make it, very probably neither is the business, no matter who runs the shop. And the kind of man who for the sake of your wealth accepts your whip is not promising material. Still, at least Bancroft III has a rule to go by – even if it's a bad one. For the best over-riding guide is to stick to your own rules.

The correct lodestar is what, in the past, has worked well for you. If you invariably select men with deep anatomical snuffboxes (there are truly people who believe this wrist formation has some psychological significance), or shun those whose gaze is shifty, or insist on getting a graphologist to give your selection's fine Italian handwriting a going-over, don't break the habit: not because your method means a thing (it doesn't), but because it means something to you, and you are the man whose money is going to have to live with the fellow and his faith.

Unless you as backer share this faith, you shouldn't be backing. Half-hearts lead to full ulcers. But faith must have foundations in fact, not fantasy – and if you can't get the facts you need (and intelligent backing needs plenty), you have the wrong fellow. Not that the business protégé can ever be expected to conform, either to his backer's demands or to convention. But even an eccentric must comply, within reason, with the necessities of economics.

As we have seen, it takes a certain eccentricity to slave for years to enrich somebody else. Great backing demands eccentricity too. But taking your eye off the balance sheet, the market reports, the cash flow, the budgets and all other information which should be gratefully received – that isn't eccentricity, it's financial Kamikaze.

ENTR'ACTE

THE COLLAPSE OF UNCONTROL

or

Look Ma, No Hands

In which we read how minginess, the occupational disease of the millionaire, leads him to keep tight control of the money and thus the business ... and how lack of control helps the man who doesn't mind the pounds to run completely out of pence.

Minginess is an occupational disease of the millionaire. Money in the global sense has long ceased to have any meaning. Figures are simply statistics with the noughts left off the big sums in conversation: thus does familiarity breed respect. But the man to whom "two fifty" means a quarter of a million dollars is likely to be obsessional about $2.50 or even a quarter: as if those twenty-five cents were all that stood between him and the workhouse door.

Psychoanalysts have speculated about the infantile origins of this miserliness. If some of the theorists are to be believed, the best course for any poor mother who wants to have a rich old age is to give her little boy hell on the potty. Unfortunately, cause and effect don't work out so obligingly. Even if all or most millionaires did acquire their retentive habits at stool, it by no means follows that all men with anal problems are worth a million.

A more confident assertion, however, is that the more retentive the Midas is, the more canny, suspicious, super-cautious and self-centred, the more likely he is to last out the long run and to bequeath an intact and inviolate fortune. The historian of wealth must be impressed by the similarities between Gulbenkian, Rockefeller, Getty, Ford and Hughes: secretive, taciturn men whose grip on their businesses was or is only matched by a firm hold on their privy purses.

The tight way of the wealthy with their own young is another strange expression of this psychological compulsion. The eldest Rockefeller's heir wanted just over a million to snatch J. Pierpont Morgan's Chinese porcelains from the hands of Frick and Widener: Rockefeller didn't happen to have a million in cash handy (the very rich often get into such scrapes), applied to his father for a loan and was turned down. Rather than lose the beautiful objects, Rockefeller, a man of forty-one, wrote a begging letter to his father which, even after the passage of half a century, has a pathetic ring.

He told his father that "I have never squandered money on horses, yachts, automobiles or other foolish extravagances." Collecting porcelains ("the only thing on which I care to spend money") was a costly hobby but "quiet and unostentatious and not sensational." Having softened up the old buzzard, John D. II then delivered the knock-out. "The money put into these porcelains ... is all there, and while not income-producing, I have every reason to believe that ... a sale under ordinary circumstances would certainly realize their full cost value, and, as the years go by, more. ..." He got his million — as a gift, not a loan.

A public relations genius, Ivy Lee, converted this vice of Rockefeller's into a virtue by instituting the giving away of dimes by his narrow-fisted employer. Whatever John D. thought about this prodigality, stories about Getty (with his pay telephone kiosk installed at Sutton Place for the benefit of his visitors) and of the first Ford, show them adhering to the same sound maxim: "Don't look after the pennies, and the pounds won't look after themselves."

Another art story, told by S. N. Behrman, recounts the rare collaboration of the leading New York art dealers, including Duveen, to offer Henry Ford I, the last untapped billionaire in the world (it was during the Depression, and they were desperate), the choicest items from their combined stock. They produced a sumptuous catalogue, which the grand duke of Dearborn received with much gratitude. They then tentatively suggested that Ford might like to purchase the items he was admiring. "But gentlemen" asked Ford, "what would I want with the original pictures when the ones right here in these books are so beautiful?"

Men with deep collective experience of the excessively rich should perhaps have known better. Their success, especially

156

Duveen's in persuading equally close men, like Frick and Andrew Mellon, to pay astronomical sums for the priceless and for its housing (Frick's palazzo on Fifth Avenue and Mellon's marble National Gallery in Washington, thanks to Duveen, are the costliest monuments of the epoch) blinded them to the equal tendency of the rich to grasp free hand-outs with the avidity of a drowning man hunting straws.

One transatlantic emigrant to Britain, although rich enough to eat a hundred dinners a day at the Mirabelle or Savoy Grill, was constitutionally incapable of refusing an invitation to a free meal. Nubar Gulbenkian, the free-spending, chatty son of the tight-fisted, close-mouthed Calouste, was another one who found free food all but irresistible — even though he could and did afford to have Lucullan repasts delivered from his favourite Caprice during the intervals of a particular enjoyable legal action in London. Nubar was the author of the perceptive remark that "not knowing how to spend a lot of money is the least of life's problems"; although, since his father Calouste kept Nubar on a tight financial rein, getting a lot of money to spend was Nubar's own major anxiety.

To be fair, and generous, possibly the rich feel easier about accepting gifts because there is no prospect of their being bribed. But whatever the cause, they can never resist the lure of something for nothing, any more than, when offered a deal, they can spurn a profit of several hundred per cent. The liking for free samples and free dinners is part and parcel of the acquisitive urge, a lust which they conceal behind standard *non sequiturs*, such as the immortal line that millions mean nothing to them, because they can only eat three meals a day. Or, as one Francis Leo Cappaert put it, "I don't care how big you are. You can only drive a Cadillac, you can only drink champagne."

To that, the discourteous retort is that, if nature would allow, many millionaires would eat many times more, drive many Cadillacs and corner the entire supply of Bollinger '69. As it is, they indulge other appetites where satiation point is further removed. Even the Rockefeller-type recluse always has some diversion on which he spends inordinately.

But the I-dotting, T-crossing, punctilious, meticulous, introverted recluse even spends — like John D. II — in an organized, controlled manner. In business, if not in enjoyment of life, he has a clear edge over the extravagant extrovert who uses his money and the company's with merry abandon. One give-away of the con company, in fact, is the give-away itself. The firm which lavishes free liquour, free flights to faraway places and free entertainment on journalists and other contacts, or whose executive living standards are lush beyond reason, is rightly suspect on those counts alone. There was no greater cornucopia of goodies for all than Bernie Cornfeld's IOS, just as Mr Nixon's CREEP election committee had many a lavish creep on its secret books.

By the opposite token, stinginess with company money is an encouraging sign, and for good reason. The excellent manager knows in his finger bones that a pound, dollar, mark, franc, lira or yen spent represents, not only an outflow of the aforenamed currencies, but the disbursement of the yield, profit or return from several pounds, dollars, marks, francs and lire of hard-won business. To the professional miser the ideal situation is one in which he spends nothing at all. That being impossible, he concentrates ferociously on spending only when inevitability strikes – which to him means when there is some measureable return from the expenditure.

Among the west's richest private accumulators is an eccentric whose septuagenarian hand will not allow executives to travel abroad unless they can prove that their journey is of direct financial value to the company. Such nit-picking is silly, and possibly self-defeating: executives quickly become adept at shifting spending from a banned area to an allowable zone, for one thing; and, for another, nobody ever measures the loss a company may have suffered from hoarding its money unwisely.

But certain benefits flow from the nit-picking mentality. He who stamps on all unnecessary spending must have some system of identifying and measuring what is necessary. He who forbids spending on this, that or the other frivolity must have some system of checking what is actually spent, by whom and on what. In other words, he must have control; and effective control, especially of the purse, is the heartbeat of all sustained business successes.

A would-be last of the big spenders, in contrast, has very little idea of who is spending what, when and why – sometimes even how. This lack of control is a concomitant of the big spending. If somebody is actually counting the outflow of cash, somebody else is liable to break out in a nervous rash at the sums. If nobody is counting, nobody cares.

In the palmy days of IOS, when Cornfeld could still pose as a kind of Messiah of people's capitalism, his acolytes were wont to hymn the praises of the unique IOS management system. The uniqueness lay solely in the fact that nobody at headquarters had the feeblest notion of the company's financial condition – even when it was sick unto death. The $52 million raised by the IOS public offering disappeared in five months; in fact, the kitty was down to $1 million on the day this cheque arrived.

By the time anybody had diagnosed that the world-wide cash flow, instead of running at $100 million a month, as Cornfeld claimed, was strikingly negative, the haemorrhage of money had reached fatal proportions; a $30 million projected profit was heading down first to $25 million, then to $17.9 million, then to $10.3 million, at which point it meant no profit on normal business at all. The company had spent, in six months, $25 million on buying its own stock: $6.3 million to shore up IOS banks: $15 million on loans to outside companies: and $28.7 million on loans to assorted insiders, including $4.9 million for Cornfeld's very own BAC III jet.

A moving passage in Andrew Tobias' account of National Student Marketing Corp, another star example of the get-rich-quick-get-poor-even-quicker company, spells out the meaning of lack of control. NSMC laid out $750,000 a year on renting its Park Avenue offices, in which it stayed one year, but on which it spent $400,000 for furnishings. It maintained offices to a similar standard in five other metropolitan centres; and ran up $1 million a year on a loss-making force of campus representatives.

The annual report, Tobias says, cost $150,000, or roughly $10 a shareholder. A good rule of thumb is that, the glossier the annual report, in appearance and literary flavour, the more suspect the company. When Litton Industries started venturing into the higher realms of western philosophy in its report to shareholders, *mene mene tekel upharsin* was written on its wall as surely as it had been on Nebuchadnezzar's. Nobody who cares about money hires PR boys (known as "flacks" in the trade) to waffle about Aristotle and Spinoza.

Other items on the wrong side of NSMC's ledger included $100,000 fees for company-wide audits, an expensive management consultancy effort at producing an inoperative company organization chart, and a 278-page proxy statement. On the latter question, it's another not-so-incidental point that the take-over game, to which growth companies are incurably addicted, is an appalling expense. When ICI made an abortive stab at the Courtaulds textile giant, the futile cost in stamp duty on the shares acquired came to a million — and that takes no account of the fees paid to merchant banks, to newspapers for advertising space, to the PR geniuses and so on.

When Maxwell Joseph won the Watney brewing business for Grand Metropolitan Hotels, he inherited a vast bankers' bill, rung up by Watneys in its own defence, to add to the fortune that Grand Met had spent on its own account. Even if the big spending wheeler-dealer doesn't overspend for his acquisitions, as most do, the bill for the technical consummation of the deals amounts to a generous slice of the corporate overhead.

Tobias concludes that NSMC's overhead was actually rising faster than its earnings as the company moved smartly towards nemesis (little items like a $720,000 Lear executive jet helped fly it along the way). It thus followed that, unless the company made acquisitions, its earnings would decline. But it also followed that, if it made more buys, the overhead would rise faster still. Nor is it only buys that cripple the big spender's accounts — it's also new ventures.

Because the business which is out of control never counts its costs, new ventures aren't counted either: whatever's spent, after all, is bound to come back a thousandfold. Cortes Wesley Randell, who, at the height of NSMC's fortunes, had some $60 million of its stock, a $600,000 castle in Virginia, a hydrofoil, a New York hotel suite, and a fifty-five-foot yacht, was an ace at new ventures as well as new companies. The cost of his forays was allowed to swan out of sight — hence items like $533,000 in "deferred new product development and start-up costs" in the 1969 accounts.

The theory behind such entries is that tomorrow this expenditure from yesterday will be covered by the profits it has generated: so today you boost the accounts by $533,000 which haven't actually been earned. This, too, bespeaks lack of control: the venturer is running up costs he can't afford, so he pretends that they haven't really been incurred.

Less assiduous overspenders than Randell have one good

excuse. Few businesses, even small firms, have perfect systems of control: they have systems which are adequate (or inadequate) for their present purposes and present manipulators. While a business pours forth cash, whatever system its creator uses is safely hidden under the Niagara Falls of wealth. But if a dry period comes, and the creator is as slapdash as most big spenders, an awful sequence of events automatically follows.

First, he (like the world) finds out about the horror too late. Second, because of the lack of system, he doesn't find out its full extent. Third, the lack of control which allowed the catastrophe to start also means that there's no mechanism to stop the disaster from developing: the vehicle lacks brakes as well as steering.

The Du Pont family, which should have picked up a thing or two about business methods over the years, provides a case in sharp point: an unusual diversification, started in 1931, a brokerage firm called F.I. Du Pont. The second generation nurtured this house into a position of high respect on Wall Street. When Wall Street as a whole stumbled and bumbled into the most appalling débâcle since the Great Crash, a crazy pavement of paperwork and book-keeping failures, the Du Ponts were in the van. They had to be bailed out, of all indignities, by the Johnny-come-lately Texan computer billionaire, H. Ross Perot (who failed no less miserably himself, so great was the shambles).

The initial bail was set at $70 million. The Texas rangers discovered among other mind-boggling facts, that this venerable house settled its books not every day, not every week, not even every month – but once a year. Small wonder that staggering sums were missing and couldn't be traced. Before its collapse, Du Pont had hastily merged with Glore Forgan, whose Russell Forgan once observed sagely that "Wall Street firms pay a lot of attention to how companies run their businesses. But we don't pay enough attention to managing our own firms." The catch is that Forgan said this, not after the event, but in 1963, long before first his firm and then the merged operation with Du Pont went down the mismanagement drain.

The elementary controls on Wall Street, the nerve centre of modern capitalism, were so weak that at least $500 million of customers' securities seem to have disappeared by simple theft. One reason for this monumental incompetence was the highly personal nature of Wall Street's organization. The firms are dominated by their partners, who in turn are dominated by the senior members among them, men who have often either inherited their wealth or made it the easy way by moving along some inside track.

John Thackray has calculated that for $300,000, which used to be the price of a seat on the New York Stock Exchange (in 1973 it shrank to $72,000 compared to a high of $515,000 in 1958), a richly structured, none too bright gentleman could in four hours of leisurely work do well enough by selling stock to himself, his rich relatives and wealthy friends to pick up $200,000 a year: or twice the standard income for a millionaire. With such easy money floating around, its recipients couldn't be bothered with mundane matters of financial and management control.

On top of the thefts, they therefore collectively lost at least another $500 million through rotten book-keeping: the NYSE alone had to shell out $100 million to pacify the customers of crashed brokers. These crashes, near-crashes and terrible frights all had a direct effect on family fortunes, because a brokerage business is much nearer than most to the personal affairs of its participants.

In contrast, the limited liability company, which has now appeared on Wall Street, can effectively insulate a rich man from what, in all justice, should be the loss of his riches. The company goes bankrupt, the value of the stock thuds down to nil – but if the owner has taken proper precautions, the wolf can be kept, as far away from his door, and his wife's.

Many a crashed tycoon benefits from the non-coincidental fact that his wife had enough in hand to make substantial contributions to a lavish family budget. "The wife's name" is one of the oldest techniques of financial self-preservation in the book; like many ancient devices, it has been carried to a fine pitch in modern times.

Even if you can avoid, by this or some other device, the extreme penalty of failure, there is fearful pain in a comedown, a heartache which no amount of millions can wholly ease. For the likes of Jimmy Ling, the fact that his once proud flagship is now under other admirals and has become a bad business and management joke is liable to hurt even more than the loss of personal status symbols, like $2 million palaces in Texas.

For the Douglas family, once owners of the world's leading manufacturers of civil aircraft, the loss of their loss-making company to James McDonnell, a highly controlled maker of fighter planes, isn't the kind of penalty that money alone could assuage. Their problem stemmed basically from too much success. The wonderful sales of the DC-9 ran away beyond the company's ability to produce: major bits and pieces had to be put out to other manufacturers: the programme rapidly got out of financial control; and the crash duly followed.

Rapid expansion, in fact, provides the harshest test of a businessman's calibre. In the days when the packaged tour game first shipped Britons off to European sunshine in their thousands, few of the operators who battened off the results needed many overheads. But they expanded so rapidly that the overhead problem, for men who didn't realize that such a thing could exist, became overwhelming.

Vladimir Raitz was an ex-Reuter's journalist, who got into the racket by trying to find customers for Russian friends who had a tented holiday camp in Corsica. He sold three hundred holidays in his first year, 1950, and four hundred the next year. By 1952, the total was seven hundred, which produced a profit: in 1959, it was fifteen thousand: three times that six years later: and Raitz's Horizon Holidays was handling four hundred thousand trips by 1972. The pressures of coping with physical expansion on this kind of scale were compounded for Raitz and many of his competitors by the fervent drive for growth itself.

The new rich of European travel became obsessed, like many quick rich before and since, by the urge to expand volume. Prices of holiday packages were slashed, while overhead costs burgeoned. Whole jetliners and hotels were booked up in advance, intensifying the pressure on the operators to find somebody, anybody, to fill the expensive holes. In the haste and confusion, travellers got booked in to non-existent or unfinished hotels, advertised as near to beaches which in reality were a hearty hike away under the blazing Spanish sun.

As the profit on a £50 holiday slumped to 75p (if all, that is, went according to the scrambled plans), operators slid into loss. The biggest, Clarksons, lost £6.5 million in two years, as 1,800 initial tourists shipped to the bulb fields of Holland swelled to eight hundred thousand. In the final stages of its débâcle, Clarksons even managed to mislay £900,000 on its computer (the money was largely found again, after some difficulty) but that didn't help Clarksons, which suffered the final indignity of being sold off for one peanut to a company, Court Line, which then torpedoed itself by buying Horizon, too.

The mechanics of control, in fact, have nothing to do with its effectiveness. Many of the Wall Street firms which bit the dust had computers attempting to do their clerking: some computer software houses, stacked to the eyebrows with electronic data processing aces, fell flat on their faces over their own over-ambitious plans – like a scheme for automating grocery movement which died after $15 million had dribbled down the drain, still $5 million short of the amount needed to bring it to realization.

Few no-hands stories are sadder than a tragedy in toyland, where Ruth and Elliot Handler, parents of the Barbie doll, had to surrender executive control of Mattel, the company which they created – and where they held 30% of the stock. When Ruth Handler resigned as president (to share the chair with her husband) the company had just been forced to suspend its quarterly dividends after one loss-making year ($29.9 million of red ink) was followed by another, and its stock slumped by three-quarters.

The story sprang in part – and ironically – from one of the Handler's great hits, Hot Wheels diecast toy cars. Hot Wheels in turn appeared to have triumphed over the British competitor, Lesney products, which had virtually created the market for cheap diecast cars but had paid the penalty for many sins of omission: lack of technical development (Mattel's thin axles made a vital difference to the speed of the pushed car); lack of merchandising skills; shallow management; excessive factory space; undiversified product lines – and several of the other ills which two ex-servicemen, waxing suddenly rich on a business built on a post-war gratuity, developed as they became older, over-stretched and more careless.

But while Lesney's two proprietors buckled down to repairing their sins, Mattel grew more careless still – spending disproportionately on advertising and failing to recognize that Lesney, although clobbered to its knees, had one basic strength: it could produce its little cars far more cheaply. As Lesney fought back, Hot Wheels lost its market dominance:

but uncontrolled promotion wasn't the only area where the Handlers' hands were off the handlebars.

A vice president acquired from Litton Industries had been acquiring in the good old Litton manner: playground equipment, magnetic tapes, a circus (Ringling Bros), metal frames. The latter offshoot, in a typical diversifiers' disaster, failed to spot the trend to frameless home aquaria, and made heavy losses – as did a new venture into electric music making, with a machine called, none too euphoniously, the Optigan. While all this was going on, proper financial control wasn't. Accounts receivable trebled in three years, and Elliott Handler was still able to predict a profit eighteen days before the significant 1972–73 loss had to be unveiled to jaundiced shareholders – some of whom promptly sued Mattel's management, including Ruth Handler, for selling around a million of stock while still making optimistic noises.

The stupidity is that gaining control and keeping it are the basic administrative arts: anybody can buy them. The rich man needs simply to realize that control problems not only may exist, but almost certainly do.

Take a big, famous publicly owned company like Boeing, source of many of the millionaires around Seattle. The Boeing hits with the 707, 727, and 747 had snatched the civil palm from the faltering Douglas kin (and, doubtless, intensified the pressure on the latter to grab something back with the DC-9). The Seattle company was the wonder of the aerospace world: yet, when recession struck, it was revealed by its own internal admissions to be poorly controlled and inadequately managed.

When orders fell sharply, it took the Boeing brass over a year to realize the implications. When the fall inevitably hit the production line, the brass, desperate for economies, found that operations were woefully inefficient, that two separate divisions making the 707 and 727 were warring pointlessly with each other, that the 727, in one version, had the range but didn't have the economics; while in another guise, it made money, but couldn't reach its destination.

So the tale of woe unfolded in a company which, after a previous loss of profits, had already undergone far-reaching overhaul of its methods. When the managerial experts can falter so fatally, the surprise is rather that more self-raising entrepreneurs, having risen to millions, don't slide back into the slough. Probably the fact that the money is all, or mostly, theirs tends to concentrate the mind no less intensely than a sentence of death.

The knowledge, or illusion, that the money is entirely their own may, by a different token, make them indifferent to sloppiness and prodigal of expenditure: but that same factor is liable, in the end, to bring them sharply back to reality – if not in time to save the ship and the crew, at least in time to rescue the captain and as much of his gear as the lifeboat will carry. It's not only rats that leave a sinking ship with full bellies.

ACT IV

On the Sense of Safety First
or
A Bird in the Bush is
Worth Two in the Hand

SCENE 1

THE VALUE OF FINANCE

or

Always a Borrower and a Lender Be

Containing many rules, and some examples, concerning
the raising of money, including ways in which it may be
obtained for nothing: descriptions of usury and other
prudential enhancements of millions, in which the wily
lender may entrap the unwary borrower.

Many sound rules of management are hollow counsels for
would-be millionaires. Those boring words of Polonius to his
son Laertes: "neither a lender nor a borrower be", should be
engraved on the hearts of the innumerable big, middle and
small-time managements which have lumbered their companies with deadweights of debt; thus imposing a high wall of
interest payments which must be climbed before the firm can
earn a penny for its shareholders.

One of the highest common factors of millionaires, however, *is* their high level of indebtedness. That too sounds like a
paradox – if you're as rich as Croesus, how come you need
other people's money? But the wealthy use wealth belonging to
others, first, because it costs little or nothing to borrow,
second, because the borrowing enables them to achieve a far
higher equity profit, third, because it enables them to employ
their entire capital in the way they like best, which is gainfully,
and fourth, because anyway people are dying to lend them
money.

There are odd exceptions, like the booster of Midland,
Texas, who paid for its first hotel with a $1 million cheque and
financed its extension in the same simple way. Another Texas
oil man, stating that "I worked for Mr Interest long enough",
displays an ignorance of financial process that is often no
impediment to financial progress. Far more millionaires would

subscribe to the sentiments of yet a third Texan, Clint Murchison, who observed succinctly that "cash makes a man careless". Henry Ford, notoriously simple in these matters, thought that you should "get yourself $400 or $500 million in cash, tuck it away and forget about it. It will come in handy some time for a rainy day."

Garfield Weston's Canadian-based food empire, now ranging from Loblaw's supermarkets to Fortnum & Mason, enabled him to tuck away so much that he could actually afford to make the RAF a present of some Spitfire fighters in the Second World War. Nevertheless, Weston used to claim in later days that he never had any money in the bank, just debts. He might have added, an empire worth $1,300 million under his personal control.

In constructing these edifices, debt usually plays either a central or a critical ancillary role. The cash-tucker Henry Ford put not a cent into his original company. The most numerous post-war crop of millionaires – the property developers of London – burgeoned from loaned money which ultimately belonged to the mass-owners of insurance policies.

The borrowing paradox can be resolved by a truly homely example. In most countries in the post-war world, the shrewdest stratagem open to anybody, rich or relatively humble, was to buy his own house in some established and improving area beloved of the middle to upper classes; then to mortgage that house to the hilt of his financial ability.

The mortgage arithmetic is irresistible. Suppose the family bought a £10,000 house and borrowed £8,000 from a home loans company at x% (the actual rate of interest doesn't matter, for reasons to be explained). Over twenty years, say, the loan must be repaid, but in steadily depreciating banknotes. For example, in a case where the entire loan is repaid only at the end of the twenty years (which can easily be arranged), a mortgage of £8,000 paid off in 1972 equals a payment of £4,000 in 1952 currency.

All this time, the loan has been safely secured by the house – provided that its value has risen, the borrower can always clear his debt and still come out ahead. The post-war period has staged few exceptions to the inexorable rise in property prices. After twenty years, if the house has managed to rise by 7% per annum (many have far outstripped this pace), it will be worth £40,000.

Remember that only £2,000 of the borrower's own money went into the house. So in twenty years he has made a profit of £38,000, or 16% per annum at compound interest. That profit is equal to a simple interest on the £8,000 loan of 24% a year — handsomely higher than any rate of interest conceivably charged: and that's the indisputable reason why the actual interest rate doesn't much matter. Another is that the interest is deductible against tax: if the top slice of income is taxable at 50%, the net cost of £8,000 for twenty years at 10% is not £16,000, but £8,000: at 5% interest, the net cost works out at £4,000.

Multiply the key figures by ten, and you get a £380,000 profit on a £100,000 house: a man who would have paid that much in 1952 might well have occupied the 90% upper tax reaches. His net cost of borrowing £80,000 for two decades would have been exactly £12,000 at $7\frac{1}{2}$%. That's some millstone. The higher the debt, the greater the return on the equity. If every pound or dollar you deploy can be made into ten by borrowing, and you make only one currency unit clear on every tranche of cash, you double your money every time.

The trick is either to get the loot advanced in the security of the treasure you want to buy — as in house purchase — or to manage matters magically so that the money is loaned on no security at all. Either way, the borrower can take profitable action that would otherwise have been barred by lack of funds.

Borrowing against existing collateral has the same effect — but with the disadvantage that you need such collateral in the first place. Many of London's property millionaires were once in no such happy position, but knew how to make do. One future financier was markedly short of currency when a beautiful vision, a site behind Fleet Street, swam before his eyes. He hastily purchased a month's option, and rushed round to his bank to procure a short-term loan, secured by the option: he then ran even faster to an insurance company and persuaded the insurers to promise the construction and site purchase money if he could find a tenant: he then sped fastest of all to a company looking for new premises and let them the entire future building — the tenant, of course, was impressed by the insurance company's backing.

At this point the developer, who had so far not even paid his architect, had a guaranteed profit on an outlay of nothing but his time and shoe leather which came to a clear million. In

171

those days, however, British insurance companies were a more innocent bunch. Latterly they have come to demand a piece of the action themselves, which has somewhat reduced the charm of such operations.

The reduction was nothing like so great, however, as that accomplished by the property men themselves. Thrilled to pieces by the availability of floods of money under Edward Heath's Conservatives, they put every penny they could borrow into buildings — and were thus caught, hopelessly over-borrowed, when the Heathites meanly smacked property developers between the eyes, fiscally speaking.

The craziest force of nature ever to hit the New York property scene, a stout party named William Zeckendorf, demonstrated the risks with a spectacular failure. The amounts which he could borrow in orthodox ways failed to satisfy his wayward genius. So he sliced up his buildings like so much boiled ham, into tiers of convoluted debt; even the debts had debts.

This offended the golden rule of borrowing, which is never to borrow more than you could recover in full by some practicable form of selling up. If this rule is broken, the borrower is in the uncomfortable position known as "over-extended" — or, as the unfortunate victims of the Spanish Inquisition knew it — "on the rack". The less you need money, the more easily it can be borrowed: the more urgent your need, the harder it is to borrow — and the higher the interest charges soar.

It isn't merely a question of ensuring that assets cover debts (or, to use the rightly ominous technical word, liabilities). The assets must be reasonably quick: you must be able to realize them in an emergency, such as a sudden voracious demand by the lender for his money back. If you can't deliver, he will devour and you will be dead. In this context, Zeckendorf's words, "I prefer to stay alive at eighteen per cent than to be dead at the prime rate", have a ghoulish ring.

At the less gentlemanly levels of commerce, many an over-extended entrepreneur has found his fixed interest lender pocketing the entire business with the same reluctance with which the Walrus and the Carpenter consumed their little oyster associates. In a bankruptcy, the equity even in a flourishing business suddenly becomes so much dross: the first come, the secured lenders, are the first served — and usually the last, since they swallow the lot. That is why the truly clever borrower aims for the perfect situation: where he borrows at nil interest, where the loan is not secured on any of his assets, and where he doesn't even have to repay it.

Who, you may ask, lends at nil interest? Governments habitually do so: major industrial corporations have been known to, in pursuance of what they fondly imagine to be their real interest – the mighty ICI, the leading chemical company in Europe, lent millions for nothing at a time when its own borrowing costs were 8%. The secret is to offer the giant the one thing for which, above all others, it slavers: guaranteed sales of its products.

Provided that the supplier avoids getting screwed on price, he puts the giant in a tactically impossible fix. To keep the trade, on which it may be earning miserable profit margins, it must keep the supplier's business alive – even if that means largely financing the operation. The executives concerned seldom reflect, even in this sad event, that they might as well have started the operation themselves and kept the whole bundle in company hands – sales, equity profits and all.

Kaye Metrebian briskly turned himself into a multi-millionaire by exploiting the various reaches of trade credit. He was about to accept a menial job in Lindy's Restaurant on Broadway, after failing to sell the USA on the somewhat specialized virtues of Cypriot wines, when $2,000 turned up out of the blue. Three years of subsequent diligent cloth-selling on Seventh Avenue ended when he lost his partner and money simultaneously. Not until 1958, after an up and down career in Italy, did Metrebian hit on Britain, on the idea of selling nylon sheets, and on the beauties of unsecured credit.

He drove to his selected fabric supplier in a large blue Cadillac, parked outside the offices, slammed his hand on the horn and pretended it was stuck until everybody in the building, including the managing director, had looked out. Metrebian was not asked for bank references: the only question was whether he wanted credit for thirty days or sixty. Metrebian's next borrowing was a more orthodox affair. A bank lent him 90% of the £210,000 needed to buy a factory.

But the real take-off lay in Metrebian's deal with British Enkalon, a subsidiary of a Dutch giant desperate to crack a UK market dominated by ICI. Metrebian in short order got a cheap price for nylon, ninety days credit (equal to at least £1

173

million) and a loan of £1 million, which carried a rate of interest so low that it ashamed even the Dutch. The Armenian borrower didn't mind. His 1973 turnover was £27 million and the putative value of the wholly-owned Armenian equity was some £25 million: that of British Enkalon was actually £8 million.

In the USA, the two promoters who spawned Holiday Inns have made equally constructive use of debt. Kemmons Wilson loves to say that he never wanted to own a million dollars, but to owe it. Significantly enough, both he and his partner, Wallace E. Johnson, started on their milky ways in house-building, homes being the easiest security for loans. By 1965 Wilson and Johnson were paying interest on their debts which amounted to $10,000 a day – a comforting situation, if you can meet the interest, but nothing like so comfortable as the formula which founded Holiday Inns.

The first few hotels were built from whatever resources Wilson himself could muster. But once he met Johnson, the pair hit on the marvellous notion of the franchise. They found other men with money or access to money (which comes to the same thing) and generously allowed the latter to build a hotel for the chain, and, what's more, to pay Holiday Inns for the privilege.

The franchisee of a 120-room inn gets a 6–10% return on investment, and supposedly treble that on equity. But he must find at least $1 million, and will pay, among other tolls, $15,000 a year licence fee and a minimum royalty of fifteen cents a night for each room (at 365 nights a year, that comes to $65,700 – not a bad return on $1 million of somebody else's money).

Holiday Inns could never have been built to a four hundred-inn scale, making it the largest hotel chain in the world, without this neat variation of borrowing, at no interest, with no security, and without repayment. The franchisee has to find the borrowed capital, leaving Wilson and Johnson free to pursue the delights of borrowing millions on their own accounts, pocketing the equity profits as they come their way. Those profits came to $65.6 million in 1971: of that golden river, a sizeable stream belongs to Wilson and Johnson whose creation had a stock market value at the end of 1972 of $1,238 million.

The obvious question is how, if borrowing is so beautifully

beneficial to the borrower, lending can be good for lenders. That depends partly on the lender. Sources of money fall into three groups: the rich, the professional usurers and the involuntary money-lenders. The accidental ones are those who had no intention of lending anything to anybody, but ended up that way because they weren't paid.

All trade credit falls roughly into this category. One multi-millionaire chain store tycoon used to be visited once a month by the chairman of a food firm: after some pleasant chat about business, the weather and world affairs, the food boss would raise the subject of the bill for fodder supplied three months previously, the store magnate would write a cheque, and his guest would climb back into his Rolls for the ride back home. When somebody suggested to the manufacturer that this was a wild way for the chairman of a major company to behave, he agreed: but, he said, "if I didn't do it, I wouldn't get paid for six months".

The greatest coup in the history of involuntary financing was pulled off by history's most inventive engineer, Henry Ford I. Henry had made the cardinal error of allowing his debts to mount far above his quick assets, and the Wall Street wolves were closing for the kill. At this point, Ford I turned on his dealers: he shipped out every car in the inventory and demanded payment on the nose. By this inspired device, Henry routed the bankers and tapped a whole new source of free finance: the money-raising problem was passed on to Ford dealers, whose own survival depended on maintaining a flood flow of Model Ts. Up to that point, of course, Ford had been involuntarily backing his dealers: he merely reversed the position, thus confirming the law that, like water finding its own level, money always eventually flows from the weak to the strong.

This does not mean from the poor to the rich. It's perfectly possible to be both wealthy and weak, especially if the loot is inherited. Many an heir has been a soft touch for the plausible borrower who has no earthly hope of tapping any harder source. Generally speaking, however, the rich are mean – and if they part with their means, they do so at the highest interest which money can fetch and on the most stringent conditions.

One borrower, a millionaire himself, emerged from a borrowing brush with a still richer man, intact but gasping. "The old man does love his rate of interest", he noted – and it is that love which distinguishes the successful lender from the professional sucker: and most professional, corporate lenders sooner or later fit, or get fitted, into the latter category.

American pros have long shown greater awareness of the cardinal truism that, in lending, profit equals the margin between the price you pay for money and the price at which you sell it, less the costs of collection and disbursement. Money can be obtained free, by banks accepting ordinary deposits: otherwise its price of purchase is more or less fixed by circumstances outside the lender's control. To a great extent, so is the price of re-sale: but with one vital difference. Interest is only paid by pro lenders on the actual sums deposited with them. On borrowings, however, if they contrive to charge interest on the entire sum lent, regardless of how much has been repaid, they can achieve wonders of usury — and the benighted customer probably won't even notice.

Instalment loans thus enable financiers to borrow at 9% and lend at 18%: the double mark-up may look the same as borrowing at 3% and lending at 6%, but don't you believe it. With a million out on loan, the gross profit in the first case is $90,000: in the second only $30,000. The fastest-growing finance houses in the western world have been those which exploited this simple truth: that the name of the game is the figure on the loan.

By definition the weakest members of the economic system pay the highest rates — the family buying its car and kitchen equipment on an instalment plan, the individual forced into taking a personal loan, the business which is strapped for cash. In 1973 the British Government felt obliged to take action against a whole new army of lenders who had battened onto a special group of the middle class: those whose sole security was their already mortgaged home. The lenders offered, say, "£1,000 for only £2.30 a week". In an actual case, those weeks stretched out for fifteen years. By the time the borrower had finished, his repayments would have totalled £3,000 — a true interest rate of 25%. That pays back the lender's money in roughly three years, after which the money just rolls in free. In one case the rate actually reached 280% in a year.

Every now and again one of the new lenders gets caught in its own web: Billy Sol Estes trapped Walter E. Heller, the shrewdest finance house to emerge from the Mid-West, into lending money on his non-existent grain silos. But more often than not it's the big, respectable pro lender like American Express (the principal victim of the salad-oil swindling of Tino de Angelis) which falls for the pro fraud.

Not that Amex had any great need to maximize its loan rates: like insurance companies, deposit banks and other money engines, Amex contrives to get the use of other people's money for nothing — because of the time lag between selling travellers' cheques to the customers and the point when the cheques are cashed and Amex must turn over the dough. The size of this "float" in 1972 was a cool billion dollars. That's some flotation: and an essential part of the skilful use of borrowing and lending is to ensure that time is always on your side, that you have the maximum use of the money for the maximum time at the minimum cost.

For most borrowers, however, the main problem is to find the money at all. They advanced on the sources of cash diffidently, expecting to be refused, and they pitch their demands at a modest level. This is not only bad finance, it's poor psychology. In the first place, borrowers should always have access to more than they need — partly because they are likely to need more anyway. In the second place, psychology counts: big men are always impressed by big numbers: nobody gets much charge from lending £5,000. But £5 million is another matter — and anybody who wants to borrow that big must (so the idiot reasoning runs) have big ideas and big capacities.

In Britain, an eager venturer named Charles Gordon prised the colossal sum of £50 million for his Spey Investments from a group of institutional backers for depositing in companies of Gordon's choice under Gordon's management (although there was some shortage of proof that the management could cope).

Much of this money was secured on loans which were themselves secured on securities in subsidiary private companies: and what those latter securities were worth was a matter of opinion — and that opinion was worth no more and no less than the judgement of the directors. True, the generous lenders owned part of Spey: but, even more generously, they had left to Gordon voting control and the lion's share of the profits, had there been any.

In fact, this ramshackle edifice ran into losses, and had to be hastily broken up to save the red institutional faces. But pro lenders are in the habit of feeding fortunes to their borrowers without noticing it. The whole miraculous process was encapsulated in the ceremony which surrounded the delivery of the *Globtik Tokyo*, all 480,000 tons of her, on 20 February 1972. The Kashmiri owner, one Ravi Tikkoo, totally unknown a few years previously, handed over a cheque for £17.2 million when accepting the ship from the Japanese builders. As the *Financial Times* observed at the time, this was "largely a paper transaction". Mitsui and Co of Japan had lent four-fifths of the money, at the staggeringly low cost of 6%. British banks had paid the rest. On delivery day, the gap between cost and insurance value was £4.9 million, every penny of which belonged to Tikkoo's very own Globtik Tankers, a £100 company. That's nice work — and you can really get it, if you try.

THE CUSHION OF CORPORATIONS

or

The Company Way is by Me Okay

How stock options and other delights of the corporate
life achieve their sole and perfect purpose, to make
executives as rich as possible in the most painless
possible way ... which is without risk and at the
shareholders' expense.

The balance of economic power (i.e. the place where they keep
the money) has shifted overwhelmingly to the side of the big
corporations, which might, for lovers of the free and rugged
entrepreneur, spell a sad reduction in the individual's ability to
wax exceeding rich. Not to worry: the coming of the corporation has spawned a host of new, easy methods of making
millions – and several of these lush avenues are within
the corporation itself.

For those who lack a rich daddy the safest method is to join
a rich company. After all, with sales of $1,000 million, profits
of $100 million and a stock market value of $2,000 million,
you only need 0.1% of the first, 1% of the second and 0.05% of
the last to pass the seven-figure mark and head off towards the
upper reaches. And if the gambits fail, for reasons of incompetence or accident, the player can still fall back on the
soft cushion of a plump salary and a fat pension.

Minneapolis St. Paul is said to be littered with the millionaires made by 3M, for this salesman's conglomerate, per-
meated through and through by the commercial ethos of the
Mid-West, carries the typical characteristics of the big corporation to extremes.

Its whole system of rewards, from the commissions paid to
salesmen to the dummy stock by which managers get their
profit-linked bonuses to the stock options which grace the top

échelon's safe deposit boxes, is geared to the creation of individual riches.

It is excruciatingly hard, in any country where the taxman knows what he is doing and can't be bribed to do otherwise, to assemble $1 million out of income – let alone £1 million. It's not impossible though. At $200,000 a year, by no means an uncommon US reward, an executive can pile together $4 million in twenty years at the top. If the statistics are right, and no American pays as much as half his income in taxes, that leaves at least $2 million: if he banks half, that gives him $50,000 a year on which to live – plus, presumably, some income and capital gain from the accumulated savings.

As with companies, moreover, a heavy cash flow has uses and charms of its own – why ich, no doubt, is why inordinately wealthy men like Henry Ford II (who resides in his company's salary grade twenty-eight) insist on paying themselves inordinate salaries and bonuses ($878,746 in 1973). The curious fact, however, is that the wealthiest to begin with are by no means shy when it comes to using devices originally invented to enrich the under-privileged executive.

The Watson family of IBM is among the best-heeled in the world, once worth an estimated $400 million in IBM stock: and not counting what is left from the founding Watson's salary, which was running at $1,000 a day back in 1934. Yet Tom Watson Jr, though by no means the most avaricious or self-assertive of tycoons, didn't say, when the stock options were being slung around, "count me out, fellows, I've got enough already". No: he dipped his fingers in the bran tub and came up with a paper profit, on exercising the option – to take one year as an example – of $1.9 million.

That incident, which is duplicated in almost every company with an heir in the executive suite, should give the lie to the otherwise engaging theory that stock options are there to motivate, sustain and finally reward executives for their labours on behalf of the shareholders. On the contrary: the options have one purpose and one purpose only, which is to make the executives as rich as possible and in the most painless possible way, without risk and at the shareholders' expense.

The beneficiary of the shareholders' involuntary largesse usually doesn't have to pay a red cent until he chooses to take up the option – and he only makes that choice, to nobody's surprise, if the shares have risen sharply enough to offer him a pretty piece of immediate profit. In the blessed event, he can finance the payment by borrowing on the collateral – and if the price holds up, can eventually convert his paper profit into the real stuff without having run any risk, or spent any money. If there's no paper profit, being no idiot, he shuns the option.

The cost to the shareholder is wrapped up in mythology and mechanics. The myth is that, without these inducements, the cossetted executives either wouldn't work for the company at all, or wouldn't work as well. There is no proof that executives garlanded with options are any more effective than those who simply work for their livings – and West Germany, whose economy and companies have vastly outperformed the USA, knows these devices not at all.

If options are so effective, anyway, why would a company also need profit-linked bonus schemes? There is no sensible answer: yet most big US corporate nests are feathered in both ways. The object, again, is to maximize, optimize and generally elevate the executives' wealth: and it presumably never occurs to the beneficiaries that every extra $2 million paid to the management cadre is $2 million off the pre-tax profit thus to some extent negating their executives' good work on behalf of themselves as option holders.

The shareholder-robbing mechanics of options are less blatant but still apparent to the discerning eye. Take the Tom Watson Jr case again. He paid $357,000 for his IBM option; where did the $1.9 million difference between that figure and the available selling price arise? At first sight, the money seems to have been created out of thin air: at the most, surely, you could say that it came from the pockets of unknown, mythical investors who might have bought IBM shares at the lower price at the same time and instead are buying them from Watson now (if he sells) at a much inflated figure.

There is however a harder, clearer reality. The effect is exactly the same as if, at the latter date, IBM had sold the same number of shares to the public in a money-raising operation, but had turned over $1.9 million of the proceeds to the chairman and chief executive of the day. It is a straight gift of cash from the shareholders' equity to the executive. The only difference between the option and straight pay is that circumspection demands that the latter be kept within reasonable bounds, while the sky is the limit for the option: and that the gift, if cashed in, pays lower tax (25% in the USA, 30% in the UK when options were legally privileged) than the salary.

The shares, of course, have to appreciate handsomely to make the beneficiaries into instant millionaires: in that case, the shareholders are less likely to complain than in the contrary case, where the company slides to perdition and the options aren't worth a burnt-out match. It used to be said of Litton Industries, a company so red-hot for capital gains that it paid out stock instead of dividends, that Charles B. Thornton and Roy Ash, Litton's inventors, had in a mere decade made themselves millionaires thirty or forty times over and made a score of other executives millionaires along the way.

Unless their fortune reached $10 million or they sold out along the road, none of that happy score are millionaires today – from 1971 onwards, as Litton sunk from decline into fall, piling up horrendous losses, mostly under the impact of its shipbuilding fiascos, the share price slumped to a tenth of its former glory. Options can thus backfire for the executives as well as the shareholder: although that will never stop companies from offering instant millions, as long as the law allows.

There is rough justice in options, in one sense. Running a big corporation is no idle game: it may even be excrutiatingly hard work, executed under a mighty weight of responsibility. General Motors does, after all, employ some seven hundred thousand people around the world, a force which is larger than most armies. Surely, the argument runs, the men with this awesome burden on their shoulders deserve better recompense than the dealer who merely sells and services GM cars. Yet a $200,000 straight-pay executive in Detroit, without financial schemes, would have no capital value outside his pension rights, while a dealer generating $200,000 of net profits (and there are plenty of those) is worth anything from $1 million upwards: one fairly typical Ford dealer in the USA, for instance, had $2 million of net wealth including thirty-three oil wells and real estate.

The share option thus appears merely a rough attempt to redress the balance, before all the guys running GM charge off to open dealerships. But there is, of course, no guarantee that the management magnates either could or would build up a business of their own from scratch. By and large, the man who does possess that drive and talent proves the point in practice. The man who heads for a big corporation has other drives and satisfactions – and it's stretching the argument to suggest that he, alone among all classes of salaried individuals, deserves to share or surpass the rewards (possibly disproportionate anyway) of the true entrepreneur.

The catch with options however, is that the executive actually has to find some capital from somewhere, no matter how easily, before he can exercise his lovable rights. The institution of the cunningly named "performance share" removes even this necessity. Companies like CBS, PepsiCo, Polaroid, General Telephone and Sun Oil decided simply to give executives shares, provided that they met certain pre-determined targets: pre-determined by the executives, that is.

The idea is that these large gifts – one company set aside $16 million for them over ten years – should *supplement*, not substitute for, regular stock options. You can see why an executive like PepsiCo's Donald M. Kendall, good and true friend to Richard M. Nixon, wouldn't want to lose his options. In *Business Week*'s 1973 tabulation Kendall is shown as exercising $3.5 million of options, against $8.1 million the year before. That kind of money beats even campaign contributions, let alone the variety of loot made by most individual entrepreneurs.

Not that big-time corporate managers, and even little ones, never go into business for their own account: this can be a surer and richer route than even the stock option. There is the illuminating case of Ernest R. Breech, saviour of the Ford Motor Company, the man who simultaneously rid the company of Henry I's appalling legacy of company goons and corporate mismanagement and brought Henry II along to super-manager status. Breech seems to have been slow off the mark – initially he refused an offer of thirty thousand Ford shares at $40 a piece, which could have made him a clear million just for starters.

But never mind. He easily made up lost ground with the Dearborn Motors caper. This company was set up solely by active Ford executives to distribute Ford tractors: the most active and the largest stakeholder was Ernie Breech, who got 20% of the action. Setting up Dearborn cost these inside investors $200,000: their employer finally took the encumbrance off the hands for a modest return of $11 million.

The pay-off was invested first in a finance company, then in a securities firm, along which road Breech's original $40,000 was turned into $6 million. By then Breech had recovered from his early false start in other ways: $1.9 million of stock options had been converted into holdings worth $10 million. Although Breech did mighty deeds for Ford, and although there seemed to be an element of bitterness in his parting words, "Henry doesn't need me anymore," nobody can say that Henry Ford left Breech to the mercies of the poorhouse.

Latter-day Breeches, however, have made sure of avoiding that fate before even accepting the job, none to greater effect than one Lester Hogan. He is the outstanding managerial beneficiary of the convulsions which struck the semi-conductor industry in the late 1960s when the prices of these electronic masterpieces slumped from $15,000 a thousand to $750.

In this contest, two scions found themselves eyeball to eyeball: Robert W. Galvin, who had inherited a fifth of Motorola, and Sherman N. Fairchild, who derived heftier financial muscle from a far lighter stake in the company of the century, IBM, but who had Fairchild Camera as his own thing. As the two companies wallowed in a change of fortune akin to that of Pharaoh when the seven fat years ended and the seven lean ensued, Fairchild reached out not only for Hogan, but for seven other members of Motorola's hot semiconductor management.

For agreeing to rescue Fairchild Camera, Hogan accepted in short order, first, a salary rise of a third to $120,000: second, an instant cash bonus of a quarter of a million: third, stock options with a paper value of $5.4 million: and fourth, a loan of $5.4 million, enabling Hogan to purchase the aforesaid options, advanced by the good Sherman free of interest. When the path to the executive suite is carpeted with such goodies, who needs to go into the risky business of business on his own account?

Not content with this largesse, Hogan also got the head office moved from New York to California, where he preferred to live (in a house, what's more, provided by Fairchild).

The final sad word, the final proof that the managerial magic of stock options is strictly in the eyes of the recipient, lies in the Fairchild record after Hogan's arrival: in 1970 it lost $19.3 million, and in 1971 followed that triumph of management with a loss of $7.8 million.

The Hogan deal, which stirred an indignant Motorola to sue

Fairchild, unsuccessfully, for damages, can't have harmed pay-off levels throughout the electronics industry. In 1972 Mark Shepherd Jr, president of the other major semi-conductor force, Texas Instruments, pocketed $2.7 million of options, adding the chips to the pile of $5.9 million set aside the year before. He also gleaned $15,015 and eighty-one shares in incentive compensation, plus $59,875 and 325 shares in deferred incentive compensation: leading the uninitiated to wonder just how much incentive, deferred or otherwise, a manager needs.

To descend from the gee-whiz to the ho-hum, Richard G. Gerstenberg, who at the ripe young age of sixty-three became elevated to the top spot at General Motors, pulled in $551,575 in salary and other payments. With his basic needs thus cared for, the veteran was given $251,550 in bonus payable in stock, making a cool half million in a couple of years. Lest this, too, fail to suffice, he took home $15,000 in company contributions to a stock purchase plan: 921 "stock contingent credits" at $78 a throw: and exercised $297,587 of options, on top of more than half-a-million the previous year, as a further support for his imminent old age.

To the eyes of almost any nationality outside the USA, the fortunes lavished on mediocre men who happen, by dint of long service and noses pressed to the company grindstone, to have reached the ranks of the executive committee, are no less amazing than the fantastic inducements, unmatched since the days of absolute monarchs arranging dynastic marriages, offered to men like Shepherd and Hogan. In Britain, such lavishness would be unthinkable; very few organization men have much of a stake in their companies, partly because the stock option route has only recently become popular; and shareholders – especially in the insurance companies and similar investing institutions, where prim personal standards prevail – would baulk at a package which (like Hogan's) stood to cost the company £4 million or so.

In large concerns, British directors in 1973 would hesitate to offer executives (even themselves) options equal to more than a year's salary – against the level of three to five times annual pay available in US firms. The big fortunes have generally been made the company way outside the major British corporations: but, even by American standards, they are not to be sneezed at.

The example of Rentokil can stand for many. An obscure little company, known as British Ratin, but under Danish ownership, it was given two new leases of life. The first was provided by an Anglo-Dane who developed its business into repelling woodworm, dry-rot, death watch beetle and other afflictions of the unhappy home; the second life-lease was provided by a couple of energetic salesmen who greatly widened the company's attack on its insect foes.

Between 1968 and 1971 the profits doubled to over £3 million. At the beginning of 1971 the estate of the Anglo-Dane owned shares worth more than £15 million at the 1970 peak, while his two successors respectively deployed paper fortunes of not quite £3 million between them. (As for the private Danes who still control half the company, they sat on a pile worth £50 million odd, gathered together from an initial outlay of £5,000 between 1927 and 1930 – no doubt the riches of the British executives appeared in strictly due proportion seen from Denmark.)

Nor are Britons strange to the technique of owning companies which trade with their employer. In one public company take-over, the bidder found that buying the main operation wasn't enough: all the patents on which the business depended were owned by a little private concern which was the sole property of the chairman and founder – so that too had to be purchased, and for a pretty penny.

The weirdest case of a chairman trading with himself was that of Robert Maxwell, MP, the gallant captain whose Pergamon Press profits evaporated first under the scrutiny of America's Leasco, which had bid for the company, and then of some acerbic accountants: the evaporation, which came too late to save Leasco from a $26 million write-off, was partly explained by Pergamon's transactions with Maxwell Scientific International. The normal fear with executive-owned companies is that the bosses will feed their sheep at the expense of the stockholder flock: but under Maxwell's magic touch the reverse happened: the company's profits and hence its share price waxed under the benefaction of timely orders from MSI.

Since Maxwell was the biggest Pergamon shareholder, this curious state of affairs cannot have been entirely to his distaste. But Leasco's Saul Steinberg can be forgiven for wondering if MSI would be quite so helpful to a Pergamon under Leasco control. The whole episode caused much indignation in the City of London — although, as it happens, nobody in the wide world, not even in the stock option executive suites of the USA, is more adept at feathering nests from the inside than your fully-fledged City gentleman.

Behind that immaculate suiting and off-hand manner lies a sharp eye for a passing bank note: and not many pass. The bankers and brokers feed their young and their old from pieces not only of their own action, but of other people's, and in a perfectly legal manner. For instance, suppose that a promising youthful growth business comes a bank's way. In exchange for what is wittily called its financial expertise and for loans of hard cash, the bank picks up for a song perhaps a quarter of the equity that, with growth, will be sold to a fond public at a far higher multiple.

At various points along this route, the bank may choose to cut its executive in on the profits — and may even lend them the cash (à la Sherman Fairchild) to finance the cut. The technique has certain virtues compared to the stock option. First, there is no nasty area of doubt: the capital gain is dead certain. Second, the banks' shareholders never know a thing — and what they don't know can hardly hurt them. Third, the process can be endlessly repeated. The snag is that the game shades over all too easily into the dubious area of insider trading, or buying shares on the basis of knowledge, either fed to the bank in its professional capacity or on the back of deals which the bank can promote or control.

A recent American list of inside enrichment includes kick-backs to a couple of American Airlines executives in connection with printing the in-flight magazine (it's called appropriately enough, the *American Way*): profits made by Kaiser Industries executives from inside dope on a Canadian subsidiary: and some fast moves by Ling-Temco-Vought in the days of Jimmy Ling — like paying Ling and three others $1 million for a ranch later sold for $1.4 million to another L-T-V interest, or selling warrants in a stock to L-T-V insiders which enabled them to treble their money in the most painless manner imaginable.

Even if stock options have not made the executive a millionaire, fringe benefits can enable him to live like one, which is the next best thing, or to die like one (not quite so satisfactory). Retirement benefits are not peanuts. If an Englishman goes out to grass at £100,000 a year, his pension

187

entitlement could be £66,000: but a benevolent law allows him to "commute" a quarter of this sum for lovely, tax-free cash. A standard multiple would be thirteen times £16,500, or halfway to becoming a dollar millionaire, simply for still being alive at the blessed age of retirement.

It's not only corporate executives, and it's not only the capitalist west, which shares such fruits. A well-directed labour leader in the USA can garner a decent harvest: former convict Jimmy Hoffa is said to have a million-dollar pension entitlement, while his successor Frank E. Fitzsimmons, a confidant of President Nixon, not only shared the use of the Teamsters family jet, Lincolns and Cadillacs, but enjoyed $125,000 of salary, a free house and a freely disbursed expense account, one almost worthy of the champions of expensive expense living, the Japanese.

Those industrious easterners are supposed to churn through £5,000 million of expending every year, plunging $1\frac{1}{2}\%$ of the GNP into gross bills for booze and beauty. Activities which in the west are concealed for fear of dismissal, like recording fictitious entertainment of a friend, are a frank part of the Japanese game. Their ingenuity beats even that of W. C. Fields, who once padded his expense account with $25,000, allegedly disbursed on milk for entertainment of newsmen. According to *Time*, there is even a Japanese phrase for it — *shayo tengoku*, or "paradise for the corporate set". But, for some, expense accounts are not enough.

British ex-accountant Wilfred Harvey had built up both a printing company and his salary to considerable heights. In his last year, thanks to a merger which vastly boosted his commission entitlement, Harvey could have taken over a quarter-of-a-million pounds for his pay-cheque. Of that, however, tax would have taken a lion's bite: and it transpired that Harvey, in addition to Rolls-Royces and houses on the good old firm, had conducted some highly satisfactory business deals there-with.

He found, according to the *Sunday Times*, an attractive printing firm which could be had for £36,900 and passed the goodie on to the company (whose board was not in the habit of questioning its master) for £168,819, a price which he maintained was still a bargain. All this strenuous activity was the result of the emergence of British professional managers before the era of options.

188

The corporate bureaucrats of today know about options. Their cash flow is guaranteed by salaries and bonuses of enormous size, even in a recession year like 1970, when Robert B. Walker of American Brands, for instance, pocketed $301,047 in wages and, in case that was insufficient for his needs and deserts, $173,097 in other payments. These extras alone were more than the president of Monsanto got that year for running a company of much the same size, or than Charles B. Thornton of Litton received for managing an even bigger colossus.

For the sake of nostalgic comparison, however, Sir Henri Deterding, the omnipotent between-the-wars boss of Royal Dutch-Shell, pulled down a quarter-of-a-million in the solid sterling currency of those bygone days. The great earners of today — even $800,000-plus men like Gerstenberg, Ford, Geneen of ITT and Philip B. Hofman of Johnson & Johnson, which attaches extraordinary value to powdering the nation's babies, are not truly in the same league as the pre-war emperors, or the post-war Japanese. As far back as 1961, the founding Matsushita pulled in the small matter of £356,000. Even at the old, undepleted exchange rate, Thornton of Litton (left on $200,000 after a sorry run of results) would need to labour for five years to match Matsushita's 1961 stake.

But the company man, in any country, combines to win both ways. With the left hand he dips into the corporate cash flow for the comforts and luxuries of bureaucratic life, all neatly docketed and documented. With his right hand, he dips into the shareholders' pockets for the pleasures, without the pain, of the individual, infallibly successful capitalist.

SCENE 3

THE BEAUTY OF BARGAINING

or

It's a Deal, It's a Steal

J. P. Getty is introduced into the big money with a true,
self-revealing story. A short account of Lord Thomson's
greatest deal, with the difficulties and discouragements
which may attend lesser mortals in the pursuit of buying
— or selling.

"A year later I was offered the Cleaver Lease in Alamitos
Heights by a man who had bought it less than a week earlier. I
knew the property, and felt certain that there was oil on it." J.
P. Getty is describing an incident from his early days as one of
his lessons in *How To Be a Successful Executive.* " 'How
much do you want for the lease?' I asked. 'I paid four
thousand dollars — and I'm satisfied to double my money,'
came the reply."

"I didn't argue — not for a single moment. 'You've just made
a sale,' I grinned, taking out my personal checkbook and
writing a check for $8,000." Then comes the punch line. "The
four wells I drilled on the Cleaver Lease property brought in
almost $800,000 in clear profit during the next twelve years."
This little anecdote tells more about the road to business
success than all the rest of Getty's writings put together.

The text reveals, first, knowledge: Getty was aware, not
only of the property, but of its oil possibilities. Second is
absence of risk, or at least insecurity — he "felt certain". Third
is an absence of any awareness of a higher, or different,
morality than commercial ethics, even if both Getty's account
and his memory are accurate: his attitude would probably
have been just the same if the offer had come from his side.
Caveat vendor is the principle: and if the seller doesn't look
out, that's his look-out. Here Getty was showing, as his vendor

was not, the single most important quality in getting rich: the ability to sense the difference between a buying price and a selling price.

The vendor had clearly recognized that the lease was cheap at $4,000. His error was to suppose that, because 100% is a large and satisfying profit, it must be large enough. The correct price — say, $100,000 — would still have left Getty with the lion's share. In this way do the successful feed off the mistakes of weaker brethren. Getty could have grinned less and paid more: he could even have offered the vendor a share in the eventual proceeds, although to be truthful, this particular man probably couldn't: the chief characteristic of Getty's career has been a passionate drive for total control.

In his dogged pursuit of Tidewater Oil, carried on over several years, Getty never relaxed for a moment in this aim. But it too was a steal of a deal. The first tranche of shares in Tidewater was picked up in the Depression for a song. What cost Getty less than a million dollars must now be worth a billion: which puts the profit on the Cleaver Lease, a mere hundred-fold, in its proper perspective.

He who deals with a master of the difference between selling and buying prices usually ends by giving him a present, sometimes of the whole business. That is one interpretation of the deal by which the visionary Canadian, Roy Thomson, gained control of Kemsley Newspapers and thus embarked on a road that led to gaining a peerage, hob-nobbing with monarchs and presidents of the Presidium, and acquiring ownership of the loss-making *Times* (the kind of expensive hobby to which a formerly shrewd millionaire is entitled in his seventies).

The Kemsley family was ready to sell: it represented one wing of the remarkable Berry clan (divided by waspish tongues into the Goodberries and the Badberries), whose other half owns the *Daily Telegraph et al*. Thomson faced one irritating difficulty in consummating the deal — but not in the process of dealing, which was familiar enough. Starting unusually late in life, Thomson began in Timmins, Alberta, with one radio station, bought to stimulate sales of the radios in which he dealt, and didn't stop buying until he had over a hundred newspapers of various political and intellectual hues, but mostly one economic colour: the pure green of dollar bills.

Kemsley commanded the *Sunday Times* and a powerful

chain of provincial papers; the price after Kemsley came down from £6 to £5 apiece for his own controlling stake, and was plainly right. The difficulty mentioned above was that Thomson couldn't lay his hands on the right price. At that time the master's richest asset in Britain was Scottish Television, the original "licence to print money", in Thomson's own phrase. While the return on capital from the Scottish TV franchise was over 100%, it still wasn't printing enough money to swing the Kemsley deal.

Funnily enough, Kemsley would have faced no problem in buying Thomson. This paradox became the basis of a most ingenious settlement, worked out by Thomson's merchant bankers. In this, Kemsley bought for shares Thomson's controlling shares in Scottish TV: Thomson was then in a position to buy up all the Kemsley interests, thus regaining the Scottish golden goose, by exploiting his now dominant position in Kemsley itself. The Kemsleys went comfortably off to green pastures having, in effect, facilitated their own takeover.

That is the essence of a good dealer's perfect deal. It should be self-liquidating: in other words, having paid for the property, you should still be richer by its full value. One of the earliest practitioners to strike the public eye in Britain was Sir Charles Clore, who long before the days of the hotel and property ventures chronicled earlier, made his first six-figure fortune with the purchase of the South African rights to the film of the first Tunney-Dempsey fight.

A clever London estate agent can claim equal credit for his well-cooked breakthrough. He spotted that the Freeman, Hardy and Willis shoe chain owned freehold properties in virtually every High Street. They were in the balance sheet for little or nothing, but in the right (that is, shrewder) hands, their capital value could be realized by selling the properties to an insurance company and leasing them back again: thus stripping the wealth without stopping the trade.

Clore is said to have cleared £6 million by this elegant footstep. But sale and leaseback in fact proved to have disadvantages for the continuing businesses, since it substituted a commercial rent for a free freehold, doing no good at all to cash flow and reported profitability. So Clore developed a taste for undervalued money: a Scottish motor company, for instance, had millions sitting idly in the bank, and that nest-egg, too, became another contribution gratefully received.

Clore's onslaughts had a catalytic impact on other companies which had grown accustomed to sitting like so many Lord Chancellors on great woolsacks stuffed full of assets. The millions prised loose (or liberated, in the word of a later generation of strippers) not only paid for the purchase itself: they provided the wherewithal to finance a fresh upsurge of assets.

All such deals are founded on the ancient tradition exemplified by Getty's $8,000 transaction. Money measures the difference in knowledge between the weak and the strong. A large part of the billion-dollar fortune amassed by the far right Texas oilman H. L. Hunt measures the distance between his mind and that of C. M. (Dad) Joiner, discoverer of the East Texas oilfield which Hunt exploited, who died broke. Alfred Irénée Du Pont's fortune measured his ability to see, first, that in 1902 the company was worth far more than the $15.36 million for which his relatives were willing to sell, and second, that they wouldn't be so disobliging as to demand any cash – he paid them $12 million of notes plus shares in the new company.

Any of the new brigade of corporate raiders would have been proud of Alfred I's achievement. In the USA, the conglomerate movement finally foundered in the flood of different kinds of security dreamed up by the faster financiers to conceal from the vendors the fact that they weren't actually being paid for their assets. Whoever invented the convertible stock, in fact, deserves some special niche in the Hall of Fame for creators of imaginary wealth.

A convertible is simply a dollar bill or pound note, printed by the issuing company itself: normally, this might be taken as worth less than legal tender: but the recipients commonly believe the engraving is worth more, because it carries with it the right to convert into shares at a later date – sometimes much later. This basic art-form, with all its so-called Chinese-money mutations, turned any number of slick young men into solid financiers on both sides of the Atlantic.

If you can't buy pound notes for nothing, which is the purest form of good deal, you can buy them for imaginary pound notes. In Britain, by the time Charles Clore's crop of successors had cottoned on to both funny money and the Clore technique, the truly rich prizes of his prime had become harder to find. But there were plenty of middling ones around to create more than middling fortunes. One practitioner bought nine drug wholesalers for £1.5 million, wrapped them up in a nice new package, and resold them for £3.3 million in cash and a parcel of shares also saleable for hard currency. Unfortunately, he also bought a mess of pottage when purchasing the remnants of a failed toy business and was lucky to emerge with his hide. Bankrupt stock has always been a dangerous temptation to the greedy. True, it's invariably cheap in absolute terms. But in a deal all that matters is relative cheapness: how the purchase price relates to the business possibilities. If a business goes bankrupt, there's usually a good reason: and the explanation may lie within that discarded pile of old assets in the bargain basement.

Given that the difference between buying and selling levels is critical, how does the dealer work out, for a start, that the price is right? In many cases, perhaps most, he doesn't. The natural man has a feeling in his bones – the Germans locate it in the tips of the fingers and call it *Fingerspitzengefühl*. Just as a knowledgeable musician can recognize an entire symphony from a few stray chords, or a textile expert can identify a cloth by rubbing it between those *Fingerspitzen*, so can a true dealer judge value instinctively from the smell of a proposition.

The dealing instinct was about the only common factor deployed by the property millionaires (108 men and two women, according to a careful business historian) created in Britain between 1945 and 1965. By all odds the shrewdest deal in which they collectively engaged was to off-load shares in their companies on the public. Starting in 1958 at a value of £103 million, property shares on the London stock market had blossomed into £800 million only four years later as the boys (plus the odd girl) took their top slices out of the action.

The company with which Jack Cotton, co-author of the Pan Am Building and a cheerful, flamboyant bottle-lover who worked in erratic fashion from a Dorchester Hotel suite started on his way, was called "Mansion House Chambers". An investment of £1,000 in this receptacle firm, renamed "City Centre Properties", was worth £200,000 by 1964. As Cotton's business methods grew as flamboyant as his manners, his dealing expertise flagged. He made questionable deals for questionable, self-aggrandizing reasons, including the Pan Am venture and the purchase of Charles Clore's property company. Clore, at least, had no doubt where the advantage lay. The delicate question of title was worrying Cotton and delaying the deal: Clore remarked to the associate who bore these tidings, "Douglas, for seventy shillings, I'll be the office boy," according to Oliver Marriott.

There spoke a true dealer. However, Cotton had the last laugh – although it was a chuckle in the great hereafter. The rows in the City Centre boardroom, mostly revolving around Cotton's erratic procedures, grew so severe that a solution had to be sought. Cotton's interests were sold to three parties: Sir Isaac Wolfson, Charles Clore and merchant bankers Hill Samuel. The shares, after Cotton's death, promptly went into a swoon from which they took six years to recover.

When the Hotel Corporation of America was a willing seller of the Carlton Tower in Knightsbridge (then lumbered with the appalling group name of Sonesta Tower) Sir Charles Forte was willing, nay eager, to buy, but he found his colleagues reluctant. Forte who had progressed from milkbars to the George v in Paris by watertight deals, simply reckoned that £4 million had to be cheap for an established hotel in a prime site. The managers who opposed the deal were trained in economic and financial analysis. To them, the Americans' price worked out at too much per room, the industry's standard measure: on that irrelevance, the deal was lost to a sharper bunch of traders.

It often doesn't pay to concentrate on the narrower aspects of a deal. When J. B. Fuqua went into television in Augusta, Georgia, his minority partners were the far richer Martin family. The Martins didn't like the lack of cash dividends, even though they loved the profits: so in 1957 they agreed to take $350,000 for their $130,000 investment of a few years back. Had they not sold, the Martin stake would have had a $10 million paper value in the early 1970s. They had misjudged their partner's potential – an easier trick than it sounds.

The tips of fingers, or pure hunches, are invaluable. But they need to be supplemented by sound factual assessment – and that can only have one basis: perusal and payback. The perusal is needed to ensure that what you think you are buying is actually there. You can't afford, like another young British financier who recently succumbed to the lure of the dollar, to buy four US furniture plants without visiting a single one. The accounts, the stocks, the snags, all need perusing with a suspicious mind. Remember that, whenever you buy, someone else is selling.

The payback, the simplest financial measure of them all, is your golden guideline. Joseph F. Kennedy, one of the most assiduous dealers ever self-made, was reputed never to enter any transaction if he couldn't see his money coming back home in eighteen months. That represents a 50% annual return on capital, the kind of yield big company managers don't even dream of. In a deal, however, it's a perfectly realistic objective: after all, you are never, as purchaser, compelled to complete a deal – the process is entirely optional, and it's nobody's fault but yours if you settle at an unremunerative price.

A high yield in a continuing business means that once your money has come back you have a valuable stream of free and clear income remaining and it also means that the capital can be turned over at a brisk pace. The faster capital moves, the better: it enables the dealer to make more deals, which (barring accidents) means more profit, which means more deals still.

The good dealer would never emulate the mistake of the large British food firm which bought its way into a new sector at the cost of £7 million in cash, every penny of it paid to the owning family. The purchasers had under-estimated the extent to which the business depended on the family management. When the latter, bored with being offered marketing advice by headquarters, abruptly followed their millions out of the company, the purchasers found themselves facing fallen profits and a fifty-six-year pay-back.

The right buying price has nothing to do with the going quotation. If the whole market is grossly overpriced, picking up a deal at 10% below the market carries no compensations. Had a bright real estate speculator picked up a Manhattan cooperative at 10% below going prices at the creamy top of the market, he would still have been weeping his heart out in 1972, when going prices had dropped by 50%. Nor is the right price necessarily the lowest level you can squeeze out by bargaining. Getty, when offered an $800,000 potential for $8,000 didn't, according to his account, try to press the vendor down to $7,000, even though $1,000 means more to Getty than to most.

A British wheeler-dealer still has cause to rue the day when, with terms agreed, he sat down at the conference table to sign the contract for delivery of a whole, beautiful chain of shops. As he raised his pen to sign, he suggested that, as a gesture of goodwill, the price should be reduced by £10,000. His aristocratic counterpart screwed up his gold fountain-pen, gathered his colleagues and departed for the nearest competitor.

Love of bargaining should never be subordinated to the object of the exercise, which is to make a rich deal. S. N. Behrman told a cautionary tale about one of Duveen's customers, an American multi-millionaire, who grew fascinated by the permutations and combinations possible on a lot of rugs carried by one of the itinerant Arab pedlars who adorn the Mediterranean spas. After a glorious passage of "How much for these two?" "How much if I also take this?" "What if I don't have the first one?" the disgusted pedlar thrust the whole pile in his customer's lap. Buying something you don't want cheaply is almost as bad as buying something you want too expensively.

There's another problem with objects for which the would-be purchaster lusts: their availability. If the owner won't sell, it is axiomatic that nobody else can buy. Lord Thomson, after his Kemsley triumph, was once asked by another company chairman, bred in an older school, how one went about the delicate business of finding out if a property is for sale. The Canadian replied simply, "I ask". It's like the old legend of the direct approach to women: you get a lot of refusals, but a surprising amount of sex. By him that seeks, much will often be found.

The great financier William C. Durant, creator of General Motors, once got Henry Ford I to the point of parting with his company for $8 million: the prospect literally gave Ford so bad a stomach-ache that he writhed on the floor and no deal resulted. But Henry I, of course, was no dealer. He belonged to that class of builders who, if not protected by dyspepsia, native caution or good advisers, fall into the hands of men with a better eye for the main chance, and who appreciate the beautiful finality of a signature on a contract.

There are two classes of dealer, however: those who believe that the other man should always be equally happy when the chips are safely gathered in; and those who argue that, if the other man allows you to take his business, house, wife and Mustang Mach I for a bag of old peanuts, that's his problem. The first school always leaves something for the other man, the second school is only interested in maximizing the something which the dealer gets for nothing.

If the Metropolitan Museum is willing to de-access a Rousseau and a Van Gogh which the Marlborough Gallery can promptly sell for a quick double million of profit, one to an art-struck Japanese, the other to a European collection, is it up to the gallery to point out this fact? Those who worry about such problems; those who agonize, on spotting an equestrian Staffordshire figure of Sir Robert Peel in a junk shop for £5, about whether to tell the proprietor that it is worth £1,565; those, alas, may be numbered among the angels in heaven, but they are most unlikely to join the millionaires in the Cloud Club.

This locale, atop the Chrysler building, was where the president of Vick Vaporub gave a class that included William S. Whyte a lesson in the difference between commerce and ethics. As Whyte described it in *The Organization Man*, the Vick king asked what the class would do if a long-time supplier, entirely dependent on the company's business, had his price undercut by a new competitor. Did you give him a chance to meet the new price, or what?

The president, in fact, swept aside all such discussion. Either you were a businessman or you weren't, and if you were, there was only one possible course of action: you axed the old supplier and took on the new. Much the same considerations apply to a deal. If the businessman takes his eye off the deal to consider higher things, like corporate strategy or the effects on the other guy, he won't do as well as the ruthless opportunist to whom weakness equates with loss of money, and who can abide neither.

It's this which gives the lone eagle his advantage over the assembled mass of corporate men. His motivation also gains from the fact that they can hide their mistakes inside billions or millions of other people's assets, while he must personally and painfully feel the pinch. The lonest eagle in legend or fact, Howard Hughes, demonstrated this skill in May 1966, when he off-loaded all his stock in Trans World Airlines, representing three-quarters of the equity, for $546 million, the largest cheque ever made out for an individual's sole benefit. Some of the Wall Streeters who bought the Hughes' shares were presumably among those who flocked to buy his oil-drilling bit company in December 1972 for $150 million: any of them who still held their ex-Hughes TWA stock had lost nearly half their money – it stood at $47, against $82 at sale-time.

Whether Hughes foresaw the collapse of the bull market, or of the transatlantic airfare-structure, or sensed that the new broom management put into TWA by the banks (and busily sueing Hughes) had run out of dust, nobody will ever know. Probably it was a case of *Fingerspitzengefühl* – and even Hughes' fingertips have run out of feel at times. He made a monstrous miscalculation by putting his TWA winnings into Las Vegas, and he also managed, in one deal, to outsmart himself. This was when Hughes, in what looked like a clever tax dodge, put the stock of Hughes Aircraft, then a small company whose title exactly described it, into his own medical foundation. It turned into one of the hotter electronics properties on the West Coast.

But the beauty of deals is the way they change their complexion and their truth. The story goes that long after Andrew Carnegie sold J. P. Morgan his steel interests for $300 million, enough to make all his partners millionaires as well, the two titans met, walking in opposite directions on the promenade deck of an Atlantic liner. "I have been thinking," said Carnegie, "that I should have asked you for $500 million." "I would have paid it," replied Morgan – and passed on down the deck.

SCENE 4

THE BUILDING OF BUSINESSES

or

Great Woods From Little Acorns Grow

In which milk-bars, a £3,883 building firm, a butcher's
shop and numberless other unlikely beginnings grow into
mighty fortunes ... and in which Adolf Hitler becomes
the greatest spawner of wealth in history by unleashing
Middle European immigrants onto the USA and Britain.

Short of inheriting, stealing, printing or finding the stuff, the
millionaire has to work for his apotheosis. And for self-made
millionaires, there is only one method: commercial arbori-
culture. He has to start from the earth, planting one seed,
nursing it to sapling and tree-size, and then encouraging the
good work until he has either a forest or one towering
California redwood.

Any old seed will do: a milkbar in Piccadilly Circus: a
recipe for a bread substitute: a garage in Tokyo: a barrow in
South London. The list can roll on through every avenue of
wealth. These particular fortunes (the Forte hotels and restaurants, Kellogg's cereals, Honda motorbikes and cars, Tesco
supermarkets) have only one thing in common: they began
with one thing.

From that point the laws of geometric progression took
over. The little man who runs one shop or garage well can
probably (but not certainly, so watch it) run two. If he can
operate two successfully, he can with equal likelihood cope
with four ... and thus his progress continues until he comes up
against the sound barrier, created either by his own competence (or incompetence), by competitive conditions, or by
the nature of his market.

For most little men the exact speed at which they either pass through the barrier or stay permanently subsonic is academic. The overwhelming mass of small business ventures remain single, small and unadventurous. On one estimate, ten thousand enterprises fail for every one that climbs or multiplies out of sight. Although in the golden glow of hindsight, the tycoon's advance from doing his one thing seems inexorable, almost pre-ordained, that transformation is a rare event, something like spotting a four-leafed clover in a cabbage patch.

To start with, running one small business efficiently is less easy than it sounds. The activity isn't especially demanding, but the ability to analyse the shop or sweat-shop, to work out the key ratios on which it depends, to understand instinctively what is good business and what isn't – these are uncommon gifts. Without them, the would-be entrepreneur not only can't exact the maximum toll from his little enterprise, but can't hope to control much more as he sets out on his geometric route.

On his way to becoming Sir Charles, Forte worked out in his little milkbar the set of ratios which was still serving him well in a £250 million empire twenty-five years later. Britain's seaside is festooned by catering emporia operated and owned by various members of the prolific Forte family. But only Uncle Charlie made the big time: and his ratios, together with the quality of business mind which saw their magical relevance, had much to do with his dynastic progression.

The proprietor has to be brilliant at tending his seeds and saplings to have any chance among the great oaks. There are, no doubt, exceptions where astounding fortune, or the advent of a fairy godfather, made a vital difference: and even the brilliant single proprietor needs further propulsion than simple efficiency. He must want, truly and deeply, to aggrandize his business – and this quality is almost as rare as competence.

The fact that he runs one appetizing and successful butchery, owns one monopoly local newspaper, feeds the multitude in one lucrative restaurant, or makes loose garments for a few fat ladies in one lean factory imposes no obligation on him to open more outlets or eateries, or to let out more gussets. Growth is an optional extra. For every butcher like one Raymond Bloye, who now runs a £39 million business called Matthews Holdings, and enjoys a personal worth of some millions, there are hundreds of thousands chopping and carving away who can't, won't and don't want to see beyond a single marble slab.

The world is full of small builders who made it big — construction being one of those delectable industries where, since the main item of expense is labour, and you can start with nothing, and nothing is where most builders end, building being the west's fastest route to bankruptcy. For every Sir Godfrey Mitchell, who bought the George Wimpey business in 1919 for £3,883 and retired at eighty-one with 57% of a property and construction empire worth £180 million, there are hundreds of thousands who, while evading bankruptcy, have also avoided the accumulation of anything more than a financial nubbin.

The bitter truth is that most proprietors who stick with a restricted lot are only capable of a strictly limited amount of success. There is a small shop selling riding gear in London which perfectly epitomizes the true situation. For several years it has sported a notice saying that "owing to pressure of business this shop will stay closed on Mondays". The small businessman grown big never has that lack of energy.

Those whose little acorns grow are often astonishingly fast at performing calculations in their head. One statistically trained boss is supposed to go through complex operational research routines in his head while cruising along in his Rolls: another had total recall of the latest figures, or the old ones for that matter, of every one of over a hundred divisions.

This encyclopaedic knowledge of the firm is in itself a good sign, evidence of both flair and thoroughness. But a specialized computer facility in the head is no substitute for paper work. The headman is also capable of placing his figures where they belong, which is on paper: a location which has the advantage that others can also get at those precious digits. And the fundamental difference between the acorn and the oak, let alone the Birnam Woods of business, is that with greater scale the proprietor needs to deal with greater numbers of those awkward objects known as people.

The methods of managing men employed by the self-propelled proprietor often include arrogant repression, or heavy selection from his own ethnic group — and the small source business often does have an ethnic flavour. A high proportion of little acorn to great oak cases are of immigrant stock. There's even a plausible case for arguing that the super-billionaires of the USA are the supreme exponents of the immigrant drive: after all, a century ago practically everybody in much of the USA was a first or second generation immigrant.

This factor almost certainly explains a great deal about the fervent thrust of the business empires created by men like Andrew Carnegie (whose father was a desperately poor Scot) or the Du Ponts (refugees from France) or the seemingly endless list of German-Jewish merchants and financiers (Belmont, Kress, Guggenheim, Schiff, Altman, *und so weiter, und so weiter*).

The same phenomenon occurred in Britain before the war with the creation of Shell (Samuel) and ICI (three gentlemen named Brunner, Mond and Nobel). The biggest single benefactor of British business, you could assert, was an Austrian whose immigrant thrust destroyed the whole of Germany — Adolf Hitler. The Führer completed the work of Polish and Russian pogrom specialists by exporting to Britain, as well as the USA, families which, having nothing to call their own, proceeded to create prosperity from that nothing.

But the impetus isn't confined to any specific nationality or ethnic set. The immigrant wave included Armenians, Hungarians, Italians, Germans, Persians, Australians, a clutch of Canadians (Thomson, Weston, Beaverbrook) and even Americans (Forrest Mars). It's the transplant, not the root, which is the turning point.

Most immigrants, being broke, have a driving and burning need to achieve economic security. That need strongly reinforces the true businessman's innate expansionary urge, but it isn't the only essential carried to Ellis Island or the East End of London. The newcomer has the golden asset of entering the new culture and its markets free from the latter's values, preconceptions, prejudices, received ideas and general stupidities. This capacity for what a British theorist named Edward de Bono has called "lateral thinking", or not looking for a problem in the obvious way, is the common ground from which most uncommon businesses have grown.

The successful grower usually does the obvious thing — there is nothing, after all, very original in activities like selling people food — but he seldom does it in the obvious way. The outsider (and all immigrants are outsiders) is not blinded by the knowledge that things simply aren't, or can't be, done in the way they want: and that, consequently, is the way in which outsiders win.

Although that combative, competitive urge is invariably part of the do-it-yourself millionaire's kit, the immigrant must win, not only for winning's sake, but to survive. This double urge gives him a thick edge over the Establishment firms, which have all the continuity of Old Man River and Old Father Thames, but have often forgotten quite why they are rolling along.

Rarely does the small man grow in a field which the Establishment hasn't been tilling for generations. Like the two ex-servicemen who seemingly invented, but only improved, the diecast model car, the new boy bursts into a field in which some somnolent giant has been thoughtlessly earning an easy income. In Britain, not one of the large existing food chains caught on to the significance of the supermarket – plain enough to anybody who could afford a plane ticket to the USA, or even a seat in the movies – until their minds and profits had been jogged by a crop of eager newcomers.

Economic motivation, the desire to profit personally from geometric progression up the business scale, is vital: and this, too, has an especially awful and useful clarity for the outsider. To him, managerial success is directly associated with individual wealth. The business empire, the family fortune, the public prestige are all tied together in a bundle of total personal involvement which the professional company manager can scarcely grasp, let alone rival.

Failure of recognition was the key to the extraordinary battle in which the pro management of Trust Houses sought to oust what they regarded as the amateur management of Forte, a company with which an ostensibly amicable merger had just been concluded. The pros failed to note that the seat of the pants and the rule of the thumb were only part of Sir Charles Forte's managerial armoury. The critical difference, however, was that Forte owned a large chunk of the merged business – it was his money, his thing, his maximized milkbar, in a sense that it could never belong to his opponents.

In short order, demonstrating canniness as well as tenacity, Forte plunged most of the many millions on which he could lay his hands into buying more and more shares. He bided his time, let the opposition do all the running and make the risky statements: then struck when the iron was hot by forcing a timely boardroom vote. He repelled not only the internal attackers but a boarding party from the mighty Allied Breweries.

It was a classic display of the true entrepreneurial drive, abetted by many of those tricks of the trade which are best learned the hard way. If the margin between a good and bad decision is personal failure, it wonderfully concentrates the type of mind which is capable of concentration. And that's another essential characteristic. Dragging a shoe business up by its boot-straps, so to speak, takes long years and a deep devotion to footwear: any lag in concentration, any sign of boredom, is an awful omen – one that appears fatally in the big insider firm that has outgrown its outsider origins.

The insiders, however, have always done the outsider one gigantic favour: they exclude him from the large-scale, capital-intensive, respectable, established industries.

Thus do the insiders generously force the immigrants into non-established areas which, by definition, include those (like movies in the first half of the century or electronics post-war) with the most explosive potential. It's reported that the father of Max Pavlevsky, who founded Scientific Data Systems and later sold his computer firm to Xerox, came to the USA from Russia in the erroneous belief that the streets were paved with gold. Once he saw the wonders of SDS's price-earnings ratio (it was sold to Xerox for $900 million and promptly started losing money) father Pavlevsky changed his mind. "Max," he said, "the streets *are* paved with gold."

Disestablishment isn't all. The small man, the immigrant above all, tends to be impoverished. It is therefore incumbent on him to find some racket which needs hardly any capital, or in which others obligingly provide the ready. This delicious category still includes movies and property – even though outsiders now mourn the passing of the glorious heyday, when some Establishment muttonhead would put up all the film or property cash, take all the risk and pocket none of the profit – and it embraces retailing at all times.

This, quite as much as any innate shopkeeping or peddling ability, explains why so high a proportion of the great retailing names have nothing of an Anglo-Saxon ring about them. Gimbel, Saks, Marks, Strauss, Ohrbach, Wolfson – they all demonstrate that if you can peddle from one tray, barrow, or stall, you can peddle from the next step up; and that if you have no money, peddling is the quickest way to get some and to go on turning it over.

Again, the phenomenon isn't peculiarly ethnic. In the Outer Hebrides in 1972 Pakistani peddlers were following the same route which sixty years earlier took Michael Marks from Russia to Leeds (then a magnet to displaced Jews) and to his first stall in his first market. For the outsider, or the beginner seeking commercial lessons, retailing provides still more joy than its most obvious pleasure, which is that of a high profit in relation to capital employed. But there are other joys: suppliers finance you, providing goods on credit while the customers are made to cough up either on the nail, or at stupendous rates of interest. Few enterprises teach more business knowledge more rapidly or familiarize an outsider with new markets at greater speed, or respond more satisfactorily to the laws of geometric progression – or give a more thorough grounding in thievery of all descriptions.

Sensitivity to crooks and crookedness is a talent which the man not made by himself finds it curiously hard to develop. The biggest victims of the great cons, from Kreuger to Estes, have mostly been bred behind their desks, which is no place for developing the seventh sense that protects the not-so-innocent from those who are not innocent at all. Even as Cornfeld's IOS sank slowly in the east, several highly reputable houses actually believed there was great treasure left for honest men to salvage. One even sent a team of bankers over to Geneva to investigate – only to be told by them to tear up his file and forget about it.

The immigrant outsider has an unfair edge, naturally. One Chinese can nearly always spot a Chinese con-man. But to Anglo-Saxons (as some of the barely believable lending fiascos on London and Wall Street have proved) all Chinese look alike. It's a hard truth that, just as an unfair proportion of small men grown big carry exotic names and scanty backgrounds, so do most crooks. There are two paths to wealth open to the outsider – the short cut and the long. A few take the crooked path at the fork: and many stay confused all their lives over which road they are actually on.

This confusion sometimes stems from a powerful psychological force. When you have started with nothing, avarice, the lust to hang on to the something you have grasped, can achieve truly terrible power. To Rockefeller I, a man of upright personal morality, there seemed nothing wrong in offering his victims a choice between takeover and commercial extinction. That wasn't vicious, crude blackmail: it was good business, sensible progress.

This curious ethical distinction crops up in case after case. One self-made entrepreneur sold his chain of shops to a like millionaire, in exchange for shares; the purchaser suggested that since the vendor now had several million he hardly wanted horrible, taxable dividends. The vendor agreed to waive his dividend. Later, when the two failed to get on, he agreed to accept the market price for his shares, but was horrified when this turned out to be a million or so less than he expected. The purchaser gently explained that since the stock had never carried a dividend, it had been listed separately on the stock exchange and had never risen a penny since the day of its issue.

In this case the victim won (at the door of the courtroom). But the sagas of small businesses growing up are littered with tales of immoral advantages obtained and ruthlessly seized. And the annals of big businesses are scarred by stories of moral gentlemen failing to recognize the fundamental amorality of their once-small exploiters.

But nemesis is in store. Even as he outwits and outruns the Establishment, the outsider hankers desperately after its established joys. His biggest risk is the desire to come in from the cold; titles, honorific, time-wasting invitations, and all the corruptions or respectability are highly tempting to somebody whose formative years were spent in Saskatchewan, Stepney, Alice Springs or the Bronx – let alone Lodz. The danger sign isn't only a propensity to lavish money on Tudor manor houses, yachts moored in Florida, Rolls-Royces and diamonds from Cartiers: if you have wealth, after all, you are liable to spend it. The weakness is rather seduction by daydreams that have nothing to do with business.

The great once-small companies all share the common factor that the founder is as passionately, obsessively involved with his game at seventy as he was at seventeen. He not only runs the business on the same motivation: he runs it in much the same way, or tries to. The supermarket chain is the barrow writ large. Tenacity, in a real sense, is the essence of his career.

Although the process of arboreal growth takes less time in business than in a forest, it is still measured in decades rather than years.

From the day when Michael Marks laid out his first stall to the time when his son reigned over a hundred shops took forty years. Even the elapsed time from Thomas Watson's arrival at the future IBM in 1914 to its emergence as a $100 million corporate deal was thirty years. The Protean John D. Rockefeller, true, controlled half a million in assets by the age of thirty — but Rockefeller was one of the earliest and most ruthless amalgamation experts.

In the USA and in Britain, in fact, only the merger and take-over route has been quick enough to produce sudden empires which are significant, at least in size, like Litton Industries and its various imitators. But if the average time-span which a small businessman needs to grow organically into a true king of commerce is thirty-five years or so (roughly the span of a generation), it follows that no business started immediately after the war has yet had enough time to make it organically.

The necessary tenacity, however, is built into the true grower's own fibre. You can see it in sagas like that of the Friedland family, which was originally in wallpapers and paints in Minsk. After the Germans took over in 1917, the Friedlands moved on to Berlin, where they sank the family jewels into a small restaurant: it failed. With the family penniless, one Friedland started making wireless sets in the kitchen, from where the family graduated to success in small transformers. The arrival of Hitler moved the Friedlands once more, this time to London where, after the war, they made such sweet financial music with door-chimes that the family rejoiced in several millions of shares in the publicly quoted Friedland Doggart. Robert Bruce's spider had nothing on the Friedlands when it came to sheer persistence.

The grower is never deterred by anything, even failure (Henry Ford I, after all, failed twice). Possibly, when they look back, growers romanticize their small beginnings. But there is, after all, a romantic quality in sagas like that of Bernard Sunley, who at the age of fourteen (when "I hadn't a penny") hired a horse and cart to move a load of earth — and ended up a generation later selling GM earthmoving equipment so formidably that he was the Goliath's biggest distributor outside the USA. The sense of romance is felt, and forcibly, by the men themselves. Romanticism is part of their dynamic, but heavily interlarded with realism – not so much that of figures, but the realism of whatever trade they have stumbled into.

During the fits and starts of his struggle upwards, the man is palpably learning; usually, however, more about doing business than handling men. This is the Achilles heel, the location of the wound which cuts off many half-fledged empires in mid-growth. Every commercial Napoleon needs his marshals, but few are able to choose their assistants as well as Bonaparte: and nature may not oblige by providing a usable son. Henry Ford I needed Sorenson and Knudsen and suffered when he lost them: his grandson needed Ernest Breech and, after him, a series of men in the Breech managerial mould.

It's probably true that no self-made millionaires who have grown the hard way, by stages from the bottom up, are surrounded by the brilliant teams of which they like to boast. But the final distinction between those who rise like self-raising flour and those who stop, or are cut short, lies in the ability of the survivors to keep enough able men around during the three decades of growth. If you can't keep, breed or inherit good men, you can't in the end build a business even for your own posterity.

ENTR'ACTE

THE PRICE OF PRICINESS

or

Gluttons For Punishment

Thoughts on the repetitive pattern of big spending and
the heavy toll exacted by gracious living, big game,
yachts, women and gambling over the years ... with
reasons why heavy spending, in the Age of the Common
Millionaire, is lighter ... and more common.

The rich man whose lavish employment of his riches brings
nemesis down on his expensively barbered head is an often
cited cautionary example. In the 1950s the world knew no
more conspicuous spenders than the two Dockers; Sir Bernard
was a Midlands industrialist whose family money came from
grubby products like machine tools and motor bikes, but
whose tastes ran to a great white yacht (the *Shemara*), a
zebra-cushioned, gold-plated Daimler (his company, BSA,
made them, too), and a diamond-studded, talkative wife.

This over-conspicuous consumption made Sir Bernard too
conspicuous in the eyes of the boring, grey-suited institutional
investors who held more BSA shares than he did. With the
business turning in a performance which, while indifferent,
was no worse than that of many companies run by chairmen
who had less affection for Monte Carlo, the man from the Pru
voted for Docker's dismissal – and, so many other millionaires
must have thought, serve Sir Bernard right. As Lady Docker
put it later, "They denounced us and sacked my husband
because we had dared to bring some glamour to selling nuts
and bolts."

Not that big spending on personal comforts is inherently
wrong or dangerous. Very few of the exceedingly or even
moderately millioned are parsimonious when it comes to
homes, the contents thereof, transportation, women, the decor-

210

ations thereof, and so on. In the mid 1960s Elvis Presley sported a gold-trimmed Cadillac spray-painted with forty coats of crushed diamonds: a vehicle that makes the Docker Daimlers resemble corporation dust-carts. The Presley management could argue that the Caddy was a business investment of high value, adding to the Elvis aura, building up the adulation and admiration which fed the fortune which financed the car.

Lady Docker claimed the same for her special Daimlers: they were splendid advertising for the cars. "I got a million pounds of free publicity and we always managed to promote the product." Despite this assistance, the *marque*, once to be mentioned in the same sigh as Rolls-Royce, slipped out of public regard and ended up as an appendage to Jaguar. Spending, in other words, is no excuse for neglecting the more fundamental functions of being wealthy: and, if they are being neglected, spending will prove deadly, to corpocrats as well as plutocrats. When John I. Snyder, the builder of US Industries, died of a stroke in 1965, "we were just ahead of the sheriff," said his successor, who had the job of selling off a few of Snyder's purchases: seven aircraft, a 110-foot yacht, a fleet of limousines and a hunting lodge in England.

The expenditure tends to have a certain repetitive pattern — gracious living, big game and yachts, for instance, were blamed for the reduction of the third Duke of Sutherland's estates, from over a million acres, to a mere hundred thousand. Gambling has also exacted a heavy toll in its day. Gordon Selfridge, the American who brought the department store to London, went bankrupt at the noble age of eighty-three through a passion for the tables which, in his case, was coupled with a taste for terribly expensive women. While his beloved Dolly sisters were in the process of losing $8 million over a quarter of a century, Selfridge would console them for their losses, paid by him, by sending them diamonds. He thus compounded his own misfortunes.

The reason why the Michelin tyre family, as frugal a bunch of multi-millionaires as France has to offer, got Citröen cars is partly because of André Citröen's insatiable enthusiasm for, and execrable skill at, the game of baccarat.

After Citröen lost a record $550,000 in one session, he also lost control of the car firm, which he had built up by his genius, to the banks. By 1935, after another crash, the business had passed into Michelin ownership. The second time round, Citröen was accused of gambling foolishly on front-wheel drive, the innovation which, as it proved, sustained the company for the next four decades: his gambling errors were committed strictly at the tables.

An addiction to gaming need not be gruesome in its effects. John W. bet-a-million Gates, who could afford to lose $1 million in a single year of poker after starting as a barbed wire salesman in Texas, lived and died a millionaire. Even for gluttons, easy come doesn't easily go unless there is a death-wish present, a destructive urge for which the wild gambling, like that of Selfridge and Citröen, is only a means of expression.

Gluttony takes other forms: the gluttony for power, for instance. The power glutton surrounds himself with secretaries, official flunkies like chauffeurs, unofficial flunkies in the form of yes-men managers: and is abominably rude to all of them. His greed does no harm to his fortune until that avarice starts to grow: then, like a gambler feverishly raising the stakes to counteract a losing streak, he starts to exaggerate the unpleasant and noxious characteristics that, up to now, have been tolerated by his victims. In these circumstances, victims will put up with anything short of physical torture, and sometimes even with that, so long as some pretence of normality is maintained.

In one case, the last camels which broke the back of the managerial straws concerned, included the tycoon's discovery that one of his far-flung subsidiaries had dared to raise a price without his permission. He summoned all the offending executives from afar for a breakfast-time meeting. They dutifully arrived – to be kept outside the tycoon's office for an entire day before being ushered into the presence. Not long afterwards the tyrant was unceremoniously deposed.

Faced with such eccentricities, the beleaguered underlings assume that the overlord is mad: and so, using the word loosely, he is. The megalomania can assume certifiable proportions. The behaviour of William Randolph Hearst became intolerable enough: that of his nearest British equivalent, Lord Northcliffe, passed the point of no return. As increasingly incoherent messages arrived from the demented Nero ("fire all red-headed men", etc.), his staff had to ignore them and rely on the restraining influence of his medical attendants and family. Yet this power-besotted plutocrat was the self-made genius who invented the popular press and demonstrated an uncanny instinct for the motivation of the masses. The power glutton, more often than not, does possess genius. It's almost as if the extra dimension to his mind, which produces intuitive flashes of which other men are incapable, is acquired at the expense of the more humdrum dimension which keeps other, more ordinary human beings stable.

If you start living like a latter-day Roman emperor, however, you begin to imagine that you really are Julius Caesar, Augustus and Diocletian rolled into one: you forget that you are just as likely to be Nero with a dash of Caligula. Absolute monarchs get brought down by the corruption of their absolutism. Tycoons who persuade others that they can do no wrong are corrupted by the absolutism of their wealth.

One sad example involved a clever manager who must be nameless. By dint of hard work and inspired decisions, he built up for his employer one of Europe's biggest and most efficient businesses in its field. The work, unfortunately, took the good servant into close contact with men who had many millions: he began to live like his associates, with a Rolls-Royce in every port of call, race-horses in his stable, large piles of gambling chips on the table at his favourite casino.

Imitation, however sincere and flattering, is dangerous if the means to sustain it are lacking. As this glutton's expenditure mounted above his income, so his autocratic power over the company swelled. The two gluttonies fed each other: he began cheating the firm of money, and his personal and professional positions collapsed simultaneously. Long afterwards, however, the villain of this piece of gluttony was still to be seen driving in one of the Rolls-Royces; in modern times, the corrupt and the crooked seldom get stripped completely bare.

Very costly hobbies such as cars, jets and speedboats are a characteristic of all millionaires, not just millionaire crooks, for the very obvious reason that, the costlier the hobby, the richer you have to be to enjoy it.

It is possible to make even an ordinary hobby expensive: the Indian prince and cricketer, Ranjitsinjhi, used to hire the finest fast bowler of his day, Tom Richardson, to hurl down thunderbolts in the prince's private nets, thus helping to convert the prince to one of the finest batsmen of all time. But the deep purse is usually attracted to the esoteric sport, where shoulders need only be rubbed with those who are similarly well accoutred. There are certain enterprises which regularly attract wasteful diversions of funds – like forlorn attempts to wrest the Americas Cup from the Americans.

In this game, the prime disadvantage is that the world's best designers of yachts and sails happen to be Americans, on whom any non-American challenger must perforce depend. Sir Thomas Lipton, the tea and grocery tycoon, spent a clear million pre-war pounds in five tries at lifting the cup from the USA. An Australian newspaper magnate, Sir Frank Packer, had no better luck in modern times. Nor did the Bic ballpoint baron, Marcel Bich: he charged his forlorn try to the publicity account. But in Lipton's day this kind of expenditure was pure pocket money, which meant that, if the pocket turned shallow, the player was out of chips.

In times of low taxation, that's how the game was played. But with taxes high, the burden of spending, even on some activities that might be considered pure sport, has been shifted on to the corporation, à la Bich. The box at Ascot, the subscription to the opera, the shooting lodge in Scotland, the racehorses, the ski lodge in Aspen; with luck, good management and an understanding tax inspector, all these can be financed by the revenue.

If the beneficiary is only spending 10% of his own money on each pound or dollar of pleasure, it's far harder to spend himself into bankruptcy than in the good old days, when every cent was actually his own, instead of money that would otherwise go in tax. In the Age of the Common Millionaire, efforts to soak up the resources of the rich have thus enabled them to finance their gluttony at the public expense. A latter-day Gordon Selfridge would probably have had the Dolly Sisters on the books as publicity consultants.

The glutton with truly well-bred financial tastes can have it both ways: tax reliefs and capital gains. If the lavish hobby has a direct financial benefit built in, it can cost less than nothing. Buying fine art, especially in the USA, is a notorious example: the purchaser can either choose to reduce his tax liability and build up credit in heaven by giving his art purchases away, or he can hang on to the pictures for his private enjoyment and watch the capital gains built up in an effortless manner.

Stocking a large cellar with fine wines, a game with similar advantages, was among the most lucrative activities which the 1960s had to offer. Collecting of any kind, apart from its aesthetic joys, offers constant prospects for this kind of double pleasure. You can control it by buying your own art gallery (Armand Hammer of Occidental Petroleum finances Knoedlers), but unless your appetite for bad art and high prices is insatiable, spending yourself into bankruptcy via the auction rooms or the dealers is a difficult feat.

The glutton's worst danger is either to indulge his tastes at the expense of the time required to run the business effectively: or to engage in a form of gluttony that, like lust for power, ruins the business entirely. Marion Harper's desire to build the biggest ad agency in the world overwhelmed all other considerations, as a prescient Madison Avenue critic, John Orr Young of Young and Rubicam, predicted. "I think Marion *will* make his agency the biggest in the world," said Young, adding after a pause, "for about ten minutes." As Young foresaw, it's this regardless nature of the true glutton that is the danger sign — the reckless spender is the one to beware of, not necessarily the big one.

If spending has become less reckless than in the times of the Whitneys, of Jay Gould, or Diamond Jim Brady, and of the various British and French noblemen who set themselves seriously to the task of destroying their patrimonies, the reasons are in part obvious. First, the necessity to ensure that the spending is in fact going to meet the taxman's approval, or at least not excite his displeasure; second, the fast fading of royalty which, in its hey-day of spending both inherited wealth and the taxpayers' money with equal abandon, set lofty standards for the proletarian nobility of wealth: third, the fact that in the days of high taxation on income, the latter must be turned into capital — and all rich men with any sort of instinct for survival are reluctant to dig into capital.

Fourth is the change in tastes generally with democratization. Parties or estates on the Edwardian scale have fallen out of favour: one peer had his footmen clad in gold livery for a visit by Edward VII. Today, even if you want a private railroad coach, you can't have one (apart from anything else, in the USA there are precious few passenger trains to attach the thing to). The equivalents in the terms of minority transportation are non-starters — a million dollars will buy forty assorted Rolls-Royce, Ferrari and Cadillac cars, which is too many for anybody's comfort.

True, the private jet comes much more expensive, at 1973

prices of $3.5 million for a Grumman Gulfstream II, a couple of million for a Lockheed Jetstar, almost as much for a North American Rockwell Sabre 75A. The truly ambitious giant of commerce can take to the air in a DC-9 with walnut panelling (Kirk Kerkorian, also proud owner of MGM) or round bed and bunnies (Hugh Hefner), for which they could buy several of the above. But it won't be the tycoon who does the shelling – it will be a company plane, tax-deductible and depreciation-attracting all the way along the air corridor.

As the emphasis in status symbols has swung to the air, yachts have slipped down the scale of desirability. President William Tolbert of Liberia moved into the same $15 million mansion which his predecessor, William Vacanarat Shadrach Tubman, built during a twenty-seven-year demonstration of the political route to riches: but Tolbert sold Tubman's $2 million yacht. Very few of today's ocean-going spenders, including men like Stavros Niarchos, who are not apt to worry about being in when the tax collector calls, are up to the spending standards of real yacht-owners like J. Pierpont Morgan, whose *Corsair* could only be rivalled today by the British Royal family's *Britannia*: her six-figure annual cost is paid for by the taxpayer; the ship officially belongs to the Royal Navy, and will presumably come in useful one day if the British Isles are ever attacked by a fleet of sampans.

For all these reasons, sheer gluttony, or eyes bigger than the purse, is unlikely to decimate more than a modest fortune these days. Even Huntingdon Hartford, whose gluttonous projects tended to run into seven figures (like £5 million on his Hog Island Bahamanian resort), didn't succeed in exhausting the lode. For decimation to happen, the surest way is greed for money allied with a high degree of plain old-fashioned stupidity.

No: gluttony must be accompanied by some attendant vice, like egregious folly or paranoia, before full punishment is meted out. Some Puritans believe hopefully that, even if most of the rich run to expensive trappings, the weaker vessels reveal their frailty by talking about it. "I have a taste for gracious living," confessed one well-heeled gentleman who was about to part some fat companies from a silk purse containing £1 million in exchange for a sow's ear of a business. It's true that the type of self-made tycoon who spends $14,000 on one bathtub approaches the idea of living standards entertained by tycoons of the Golden Age.

Eugene Klein of National General planted his Beverly Hills mansion, according to John Brooks, with $1.5 million of modern pictures and antique furniture and bought his Rolls-Royce second-hand (at some removes, be it said) from the Queen of England. But all this spending was still a pale imitation of the devotion decades before of a Henry Clay Frick to the disbursement of his cash. The Frick palazzo on Fifth Avenue cost $17 million – and that was without its indescribably beautiful and precious contents, for which any museum in the world would give its soul.

For every hot, now *passé* conglomerator who made a poor shot at becoming a latter-day Frick (and Frick, although addicted to unpleasant habits like machine-gunning his workers, was a tight and tight-fisted businessman), there were plenty of others whose life styles, if not Puritanical, certainly showed no trace of Texan or Californian flim-flam and flamboyance. Maybe Toots Shor, the Broadway restaurateur, had the right idea: "I don't want to be a millionaire," he said, "I just want to live like one" – and in recent times, that hasn't been too difficult.

The taste for gracious living has spread inexorably. Financial writers in New York knowledgeably sip their Clos Vougeot. Managers from Hamburg cavort in Adriatic resorts where once only yachts carrying the like of Edward, Prince of Wales, could penetrate. Expense account executives monopolize the expensive tables of Lasserre. Some 2,850 people every year take delivery of a new Rolls-Royce (or rather, their companies do). In such sad times for the exclusivity of exclusive spending, it may not only be safer to be like Alte Yebsen, the Norwegian shipowner (fifty vessels) and industrialist, who drives to work in a battered station wagon, and the small number of other truly frugal millionaires: in this age of lesser gluttons, such frugality may even come to be the new smartness.

ACT V

On the Availability of Presents
or
Trust the Greeks When
They Bring You Gifts

SCENE 1

THE GRAFT IN GOVERNMENT

or

This Mess in Washington

The principles of legitimately separating the tax-payer from his taxes for private benefit, with the willing and innocent assistance of politicians and civil servants ... and why plebian politicos, adoring the company of the self-made rich, make them far richer.

Corruption in government excites almost as much scorn in the ranks of business as does the government's bureaucratic proliferation and constipation. For big business can teach even the civil service a knot or three when it comes to red tape, protocol and waste of money — like the German oil firm which kept one quarter of a car park empty because it backed on to the summit offices, whose bureaucrats didn't want to have either their slumber or their deliberations disturbed by the shutting of proletarian car doors.

Big business also knows no peers when it comes to exploiting for its unique benefit the mess in Washington, London, Paris, Bonn, Caracas — or wherever in the world some unstable mixture of politicians and career officials tries ineptly to manage an economy which is swimming with financial sharks.

Straight corruption, of course, exists, and flourishes like a dirty green bay tree. The bulk of the bezzle (bribery offered and taken is nothing but an indirect embezzlement of the public's hard-earned bread) lies in bribes. An unpleasant odour was exuded, even before Watergate, by US campaign contributions. (The Nixonian acceptance of £80,000 in bills from Robert Vesco, the alleged picker-over of the IOS carcass, was no nastier than the unpunished and much larger amounts with which the US dairy lobby greased its way to higher price supports.)

221

In the same category lie, or lurk, the fat jobs offered to former officials; the largesse scattered around useful contacts, as by the British architect John Poulson who offered jobs, loans and holidays to those with contracts in their influence; the obligatory payment concealed in tenders submitted to Latin American bureaucracies.

In the latter method, at its most methodical, bank notes of ascending denomination are interleaved in the tender, enabling each succeeding official in the hierarchy to take his appropriate cut as the contract wends its way to the top. It's the same principle that governed between-wars tipping in restaurants in gay Vienna: customers left piles of coins for each rank of waiter spaced round the edge of the table, the principle being that whatever the horny hand of the head waiter could span was his alone.

But the criminal bezzle is as nothing compared to the legitimate take. Even if you throw in the depredations of Latin dictatorships like the Trujillos or Perez Jimenez (who is supposed to have taken the Venezuelans for $250 million, or more than Meyer Lansky, father of the modern Mafia, purportedly put in his poke), the grand total is still only a drop in the ocean of legislated transfer of funds from the taxpayer to the pockets of the rich.

The largest, most splendiferous flow of money in the world is tax: no other industry comes near tax-collecting in efficacy or profitability, millions of money pouring in daily for negligible costs of collection. If predatory pairs of hands can seize a modest smidgen of one day's flow, all financial problems evaporate with sublime ease. The funny fact is that other, perfectly clean hands will be equally eager to give it to them.

The natural law of taxation is that spending rises to surpass the revenue earned, from which the corollary is that those in charge of the public purse are always searching for outlets for its contents. Businessmen therefore do their utmost to encourage the politician's natural desire to live well and die (or lose office) in dignified economic circumstances.

In the USA, because of the spiralling cost of elections and the clear relation of expenditure to electoral chances, the tendency is for politicos to make their moolah before plunging into the fray: in the 1960 election, out of all the candidates for nomination, only Hubert Humphrey and Richard Nixon were not millionaires. Any candidates who are not provided for prior to their election have a strong chance of being well looked after subsequently. Wealthy to start with, George Washington died worth $530,000 in 1799: Dwight Eisenhower benefited from special tax legislation which made him a million. While "resting" (as actors put it), Richard Nixon was converted from a poor boy to a well-heeled ex-corporation lawyer with real estate in choice locations on both sides of the USA.

Similarly, Edward Heath's time in the City, where he was employed as a merchant banker, while being the leading light of Her Majesty's Opposition, presumably helped him to enter 10, Downing Street better than empty-handed. Indeed, Heath could by then afford costly racing yachts and private madrigal concerts. He is unlikely to have been a banker of brilliant success, given the small amount of time which politics can have left for banking; presumably fortune favoured the politically brave.

In an earlier generation, Lord Beaverbrook made it his business to see that ill-luck never ran the way of his political friends. He would buy choice investments on their behalf and present them with the profits when he sold. (If, by some savage quirk of fate, the investment fell, there are no prizes for guessing who stood the loss.) But nothing which Beaverbrook contrived for his favourite prime minister, Bonar Law, can match the accumulative feats of the poor young Congressman from Texas, Lyndon Baines Johnson, who ended up, not only as the most powerful senator in Washington, and the most arm-twisting president, but as the owner of broadcasting stations, land, securities and other odds and ends which the *Wall Street Journal*, back in 1964, assessed at $9 million to $14 million.

Yet this is picayune compared to the amounts accrued by LBJ cronies such as oil tycoon Sid Richardson, and it doesn't rank particularly high in relation to the estate of a relatively minor state official, the former speaker of the Illinois House of Representatives. He died in 1970 worth $3 million, of which $175,000 was found in notes in a shoebox in his hotel room. The accidental revelation of the Powell hoard, a consequence of sudden, ill-planned death, coincidentally reveals just how much swan's down must have stuck to the nests of politicians at all levels of the US system.

The billion-dollar burglary of the public purse arises, not from mutual back-scratching, but from the ineluctable nature of economic forces. These can be visualized as a mighty torrent, fed by innumerable tributaries. As it surges down the river bed, events threaten – a village swept away here, a cornfield ruined there – which no responsible government can allow.

So the torrent is blocked in one place, diverted in another, by measures which are economic in effect but political in motivation. So long as their interference meets the political requirements (or appears to), the politicos are indifferent to the economic effects. These, however, are gigantic – not only directly, but indirectly. For the force of the torrent is in no way lessened by a blockage or diversion. Narrow the stream in one place, and you must enormously increase the force of the flow somewhere else: someone will be waiting there to drink.

The classic examples include the US farm-price supports, which even made men rich for agreeing not to farm their land (under Ike they got $100 an acre) and also troubled industries like ship-building the whole world over. In Britain at one point the Labour Government was innocently offering cash grants to non-British shipowners who were building ships in foreign yards for operation by non-British crews under the non-British flags-of-convenience (the convenience in the case being no tax).

All that the lucky Greeks needed was a plaque on the door of a London office. Some £60 million is supposed to have plopped into Greek and other foreign pockets before the civil servants of Whitehall, as ever reluctant to spoil the perfect symmetry of a scheme by correcting a ludicrous error (it never occurred to them that London shipping firms weren't necessarily British), were persuaded to block the drain. The Labour minister, a businessman himself, who spotted and ultimately scotched this boon-doogle, was convinced that the drain only failed to gurgle more because most of the Greeks simply didn't believe that even in bureaucratic Britain, Santa Claus had been so miraculously reborn.

"Greeks" is now a misnomer. Mountainous new shipping fortunes have been assembled by a Taipan (Y. K. Pao), a Japanese (Sanko), a pair of Israelis (Brener and Meridor), and a Kashmiri (Tikkoo). The scale of their fleets (Pao's 1975 plans envisage 13.3 million tons; the Israelis owned $450 million of ships in 1973 at cost price) is no more amazing than the tininess of their equity stakes.

At the time when Brener and Meridor offered to order $500 million of ships from British yards, the shareholders' equity in Maritime Fruit was just $31.4 million. Ravi Tikkoo, the prize orderer of super-giant tankers, shares just £1,000 of ordinary capital in Tokyo Tankers. On his forecast, each mighty vessel will yield Tikkoo a £3 million operating profit during its life – yet the British government gave the happy Kashmiri a cash present of £4.3 million to have the monster *Globtik Tokyo* built in Kure, Japan. Even larger presents were to be handed over in various forms to Maritime Fruit, the object being simply to keep Britain's Tyneside yards in business.

Over in Belfast, in an even more bizarre situation, the government was busily pouring £50 million more into a shipyard, one with a notorious appetite for cash, which it didn't even own. Half the benefit of this enormous State expenditure will go to the outside shareholders, of whom by far the largest is a conspicuously non-needy Greek, Aristotle Onassis. With legitimate gifts like this floating about, who needs graft?

Nor are shipbuilders and shipowners the only beneficiaries of the insatiable desire of governments to make millionaires, or to make millionaires richer still. Economic development, in much of its operation, represents less a boon to backward masses in the neglected corners of the world than a means of creating instant private fortunes out of public funds. In country after country, the government will lend (cheaply) or give you the capital to build a factory, charge you no tax whatsoever (or very little tax) for several years, and impose no restriction on your right to divert the profits to anywhere you have in mind.

Cement plants in Trinidad, engineering or textile factories in Northern Ireland, electronics plants in Scotland, all will do nicely. As for the *Mezzogiorno* of Southern Italy, the mind boggles at the possibilities, given the generosity of Italian politicians and tax-collectors to businessmen all over the country.

Any entrepreneurs who start their enterprises in a British development area (a euphemism which means that the district suffers from above-average unemployment) can spell out some seductive arithmetic. The capitalist is eligible for the extra large investment grants provided in such areas; the local authorities may even provide the site at no rent, or rent a previously built factory to the entrepreneur, who can write off all plant and machinery costs against the first year's profits. One local authority in Lanarkshire advertised its charms under the headline, "How to Make £378,000"; that was the whopping total value of "Tax Benefits and Grants" on a £1 million investment, "in Year One Alone".

Many men of absorbing wealth have been made wholly or partly by the government's desire for their technological hauteur. Georges Dassault is one of the richest men in Europe thanks to the Mirage and Mystère fighters whose development was allegedly 60% financed by the French Government. In this case, it could be argued that defence capability had to be preserved: its preservation, however, also ensures the safe keeping of the riches of its owners.

If a company like Lockheed heads into bankruptcy as a result of egregious management errors (mainly on a civil project at that), a politician like Richard Nixon will always bail it out, not only because of its vital defence capacities, and powerful political pull, but also because of the jobs at stake. The curious, or not-so-curious, fact, however, is that (with exceptions like James H. McDonnell) the defence fortunes enshrined within big corporations have tended to suffer severely from the effects of monstrous mismanagement.

By and large the financial results of major US defence contractors are awful, which takes some achieving, given that the government, first, provides plant and factories for them, *gratis*, second, advances working capital, and third, always ends up by paying vastly more than the originally agreed price. Any civilian in the same happy fix – a building contractor, say – would clean up millions in a trice. Yet defence contractors like Lockheed or General Dynamics have the utmost difficulty in keeping their shareholders' bodies and souls together.

What an efficient contractor can manage was shown by two British cases. In that of Bristol-Siddeley, the company was found to have made an excess profit of many millions on merely repairing aircraft engines. In the even more celebrated Ferranti affair, the profits from making the Bloodhound missile came to so much more than the government was prepared to stomach that, even though this profit would have been pleasant for the Ferranti family, who owned all the shares, the political recoil forced a hefty refund.

Many a pile of similarly shining profit must be concealed beneath contractors' bushels. But true lack of profit reflects in part the tendency of main contractors to share the mindless extravagance of government. Take Concorde: as that misbegotten project moved inexorably towards £1,000 million of spending, many hands must have plunged into the till, if not for negotiable cash, at least for costly facilities, all wholly paid for by the taxpayer.

At all times the British Aircraft Corporation was reluctant to explain, even to interested members of parliament, exactly how it was possible to spend £1 million a day on a single project, even a supersonic one. The case of the pilot's chair explained how easily the spending materializes. Seats for Concorde's crew were originally ordered at a development cost of £54,000. Dissatisfied with the results, BAC as prime contractor upped the ante first to £216,000, then to £409,000. At this point even the civil servants in the act grew queasy. After a probe they finally approved £351,000 – still over six times the original estimate. If the wizards can achieve such marvels with mere seats, it's no wonder that they can provide such bottomless pits for tax money with entire aircraft.

To get rich from public contracts, however, the privateer has to tread a narrow tightrope between being efficient and being too efficient – that is, becoming careless enough to let the profitable results of super-efficiency show. The other guideline is the same as for borrowing: aim high, think extravagantly, and press the moneybags on whatever is currently their most sensitive point.

The aluminium companies, when being pressed to erect smelters in Britain to save foreign exchange, played this game to perfection. They got multi-million loans at favourable rates of interest, cheap electricity (a subsidy which had the extra convenience of being incalculable), plus all the normal investment grants (i.e. cash presents) and tax breaks. The beneficiaries of this bounty included such poverty-stricken companies as Alcoa, embodying the aluminium interest of the omnipresent Mellon family.

Politicians, like big company managers themselves, are victims of the paper number game. Harold Macmillan (a publishing millionaire by inheritance) airily observed that alerting the forces early in the Suez crisis cost "only £10 million". Now, the professional millionaire knows to the depths of his being that £10 million, or £1 million, or even £1,000 is never "only". But paper number players simply forget that the game isn't Monopoly: the resources are for real.

Governments deal with such elongated paper numbers that small sums, like the £25 million which Britain pumped into the Upper Clyde shipbuilding fiasco, seem piddling. In the even more amazing Rolls-Royce affair, the politicians kidded themselves that because the original loans for the RB-211 engine were limited to a mere £50 million they had in some tough way restricted the risk.

But governments are equally benign in circumstances in which they are not actually called upon to disburse coin. The flood principle of economic affairs also applies with physical controls, such as licences and quotas; hence the huge fees commanded by the lobbyists who cluster around the regulatory agencies of Washington. That city, in the shape of the oil import quota, produced the perfect pork barrel of its day, which lasted throughout the 1960s – at one and the same time protecting domestic prices and profits, and presenting oilmen with valuable, completely free, marketable assets, saleable at $1.25 a barrel.

British governments, not to be outdone, produced the triumph of television licensing (which generated profits so embarrassing that special levies had to be clamped on).

Often politicians would be best advised to let things be and to stop monkeying about with economic tides which neither they nor anybody else truly understands. The praiseworthy idea of redistributing wealth by taxing high incomes to the hilt, for instance, has had the paradoxical effect of making the rich still more wealthy. It has very possibly increased, rather than diminished, the inequalities of wealth.

The main explanations are twofold: first, the high-tax principle has put a premium on converting income into capital at all times and in all possible ways: second, the use of the devices by which capital is created (borrowing and investment) has been made wondrously cheap, and the higher the tax rate rises, the cheaper it becomes. For a man taxed at a marginal rate of 90%, an interest charge of 10% comes down to 1%: where a completely untaxed pauper would over twenty years pay 200% of the capital in interest, the millionaire coughs up only 20%.

As for investment, any plunge that is tax-deductible is subject to the same pain-killing effect. It costs the millionaire only £100,000 to make a million pound investment, and that investment will be subject to all the delectable, automatic rewards by which governments seek to conjure up the genie of economic expansion. If the million of investment yields a modest 10%, that profit will be offset for ten years by tax allowances, including depreciation: in a decade, the already rich investor thus makes a further clear million on, effectively, a risk of only £100,000.

If he invests in the special situations which governments adore, the returns become still more astronomical. The British Government even gave special assistance at £1,000 a room, for the benefit of the tourist trade and hence of the country's beloved balance of payments, for the construction of luxury hotels in London. The Government's generosity, naturally, resulted in an over-supply, not only of hotel rooms, but of excrescences on the London skyline.

The danger which Eisenhower warned the USA against in his valedictory address was the military-industrial complex. But there is a far more insidious conspiracy of which the Pentagon capers form only a part: the Old Boy net of rich men, who finance and flatter the would-be statesmen, batten off their economic ignorance and work their way into political favours by natural means.

The American habit of blatantly selling embassies in return for campaign contributions has long been a source of wonderment to more sophisticated machinists in this shady area where politics and plutocracy overlap. A little embassy like Luxembourg, purchased by Mrs. Ruth L. Farkas in the Watergate election, fetched $300,000. The *New York Times* suggested that the $254,000 Nixon contribution advanced by Walter H. Annenberg (who could afford it, having sold the family newspapers for $55 million) could be regarded as the renewal of the lease on the London embassy – the plum in Nixon's ambassadorial pudding.

As Watergate revealed so horrendously, however, the exchange of American plums is private as well as public. Richard Nixon expressed no qualms in reporting, although under intense pressure, that the aerosol king, Robert Abplanalp, had helpfully lent him $625,000 to finance the purchase of San Clemente, and, even more kindly, had relieved the President of his surplus Californian acreage for a nice price. It must help a millionaire to have an indebted friend wearing the crown. But there is more to the courtship of the rich by the powerful than sheer greed for possessions and their enjoyment.

It's no accident that plebeian politicians, Eisenhower, Johnson, Nixon, Wilson, Heath, have chosen favoured sidekicks who are among the self-made rich. Those who don't have big money are fascinated by those who do. But there is one ever-present danger in rich sidekicks: the threat of rich kickbacks, if not at the top, somewhere down the receiving line.

SCENE 2

THE LOGIC OF LUCK

or

Someone Up There Loves Me

Containing the true essence of good fortune, which consists, not merely of holding the right cards, but of playing them ... and including the truth about bad luck, which, more often than not, is nothing but appalling professional judgement.

If the good fairy ever offers an aspiring businessman one wish, there's no question what he should ask for: luck. Good fortune is the essence of all fortunes, but it is the prime factor that few of the rich, *nouveaux* or otherwise, are honest enough to acknowledge. Maybe Julius Rosenwald of Sears Roebuck was exaggerating when he attributed as much as 95% of business success to luck, leaving only a twentieth to aptitude and application. It is still no exaggeration to say that, without luck, all the other virtues are only slightly more useful than a bridge player who consistently draws bad cards.

Fortune presents the opportunity at the time when the opportunist can exploit it: cometh the man, cometh the moment. And fortune has to attend most subsequent actions if the man and the moment are to combine in satisfactory monetary terms. A goodly, if not particularly godly, crop of London's property millionaires owe their wealth to the blind workings of chance. For a start, it was precious fortune to be in, or even near, the property business at the time when building restrictions were removed by the Conservative Government of the day. The crop thus blessed included solicitors, estate agents in fair number, surveyors, the odd architect, property developers of the old school – and several business-men who merely happened to have a piece of London where the action started.

One such was Max Rayne, now Sir Max, and chairman of the National Theatre: artistic, social and financial prestige have an engaging habit of marching hand in hand. Rayne first got interested in property when, finding that his father's business didn't need all its modest premises, he arranged a sublet and discovered that renting was far more profitable than making clothes.

Encouraged by this tiny start, Max Rayne moved on to mightier things. A fat and none too bright company which owned Selfridges in Oxford Street, allowed him to develop the site at the rear of its store. At this point, Rayne owed thanks to fortune twice: for the initial discovery of property and for the folly of Selfridges' owners. His third stroke of luck must have seemed Heaven's brightest gift: Marks & Spencer, the bluest chain store chip in the land, intimated that it would lease Rayne's new building.

Enter calamity: Lord Marks decided on another site to the north, leaving Rayne apparently stranded like Sailor Kelly up his flagpole. Rayne scurried about, obtained additional backing in the property world, and went ahead. By the time of his building's delayed completion, rents and hence its value had soared far beyond the terms abandoned by Marks & Spencer; Rayne was most of the way to his first million – and he had as tenants IBM and 3M, which must have eased any lingering pain from the loss of Marks.

The story, with variations of time and place, was repeated many times in the property hey-day. The men who made the most of these chances had to display acumen, persistence and initiative: but fortune kept on dealing the right cards. Sometimes the cards are so apposite, with a royal flush appearing at the very moment of truth, that the less god-given factors are blotted out from sight.

Charles W. Bluhdorn, the founder of Gulf + Western (the plus sign is his own invention) was once a Wall Street wonder boy. He was then infested by the bubonic plague which hit nearly all conglomerates. His shares fell in a series of plunges reminiscent of so many F-IIIs crashing over Vietnam. Behind Bluhdorn's share slump lay the usual conglomerate hang-up. As sales continued to pile up, operating income first took a sharp tumble and then resolutely refused to grow. Among his acquisitions was Paramount Studios, picked up, so report had it, as much for its real estate potential as for any money in the allegedly moribund movie game. As it turned out, Hollywood, old-style, came to the rescue of the new-style front office. When the shares plunged to just $9\frac{1}{2}$, compared to $64\frac{1}{4}$ at their brightest and best, Bluhdorn's boys must have been grateful for the $80 million of mush-money from *Love Story*, one of the hot properties in Paramount's can.

However, this success didn't generate great front office fervour at Paramount for another best-seller — who was interested in a gangster movie these days? Although the disappointing returns from another gangland epic supported the point, *The Godfather* was allowed, not only to proceed, but to devour a $6 million budget, and the results, an expected gross of $120 million, will gladden Gulf + Western's lucky balance sheet for years to come.

In fact, everybody is lucky in some degree or dosage. The luck may not be readily translatable into capital: the lucky one may studiously or stupidly fail to recognize his good fortune: or he may make the elementary error of thinking that luck is the sole ingredient of success, whereas in truth nobody, apart from the winner of a football pool, a lottery or a surprise inheritance, ever has wealth poured on his head without the need for effort.

Consider the case of Zographas, one of the two Greeks who gave their national name to the Greek five-man syndicate. Nobody can survive in big-time professional gambling without being luckier than average, even with the mathematical advantages of baccarat, the Greek pastime. For all that, one disastrous week in 1926 Zographas lost the equivalent of $672,000 in play at Cannes. On the last night he risked a further million francs and won everything back. The romantic would call this pure chance. The realist, the Greek himself, knew the odds exactly, knew that their failure to work in his favour before was unlikely to be repeated, knew himself, knew the game and judged his decision accordingly.

The pure gambler, unless the table or cards are impure, loses a great deal of the time. Nicholas Andrea Dandolos, alias Nick the Greek, is said to have seen $500 million pass through his hands (including $6.4 million of winnings at stud poker) as he passed between the opposite poles of wealth and penury seventy-three times. That is because ultimately the run of the cards is something which the gambler cannot influence. This fact, paradoxically, makes it bad luck that gaming should be their profession.

There are those who, with similar varieties of flair and equal application, stumble into fields where the cards are more closely under their own control – and that fluke start, part of the perennial mythology of capitalism, is where luck truly comes into its own. Starts don't come much flukier than in the case of Dr. Osman Khalil Osman, now a Sudanese of many millions, who originally set up shop in Kuwait as a veterinary surgeon. In this capacity, Osman treated and cured a cow which was the prize milk producer of the then crown prince.

In his gratitude Sheik Saba al Salem, the present ruler of the richest country on earth, helped to set Osman up in a business career which is a combination of textiles and courtship of the appropriate rulers. Being called to that particular cow's bedside was (if the story hasn't been embroidered over the years) pure luck: curing it was skill; gaining the Sheik's business confidence required visible talent capitalizing on that confidence, and recognizing that in the underdeveloped world politics is where the pay-off is, demanded lesser assistance from fortune; but by far the greatest contribution came from the talents of the world's most moneyed cow doctor himself.

Now that the vet is rich, the odds of fortune that favour the well-stacked can come freely into play. But the dividing line between the luck and the hard work of the wealthy is a fine one. For instance, it was a misfortune for the McAlpine family, though a common enough catastrophe in the building trade, that the clients for whom they were putting up the Dorchester Hotel in Park Lane ran out of ready cash in the Depression. But the McAlpines owed their own financial security, which enabled them to take over the hotel, to their own Scot's diligence and prudence: Sir Robert had begun as a Glaswegian bricklayer: there are few starts more basic or less blessed. In 1962, the family was offered £6 million for the hotel, which they very properly refused: its present-day value must be nearer £20 million.

The McAlpines can't originally have known much about hotels, except how to stay in them. But knowledge can be bought. The courage to seize a chance opportunity can't be acquired. Like sex appeal, either you have it or you don't.

But if an investment which turns unluckily sour is in a security about which the investor is profoundly ignorant, that isn't unlucky at all: it's incompetent. Take the sad case (or the sad cases, millions of them) of Scotch whisky. A cheerfully gloomy distiller warned in early 1973 that up to two hundred million gallons of grain whisky (the stuff that is mixed with malts to produce the blended booze) might have to be poured down the drain. Most had been bought by over-sold, over-eager Americans, some of whom in the mid-1960s paid up to $3 a gallon for whisky that in 1973 couldn't even be sold at the nominal price of fifty cents – for the blunt reason that nobody wanted it.

The price of folly can't be described as misfortune, so the reward of shrewdness cannot be perfectly described as luck. Take the case of Colin Forsyth, an Oxford man who was learning the investment trade on Wall Street when, with time hanging on his hands, he found Hampton Gold Mining Areas in a London stock exchange reference book. The shares, four million in all, were selling at $1\frac{1}{2}$d apiece. But this unconsidered trifle owned freehold land in Australia: dividing the market value by the acreage, Forsyth worked out that land anywhere in the whole wide world, the Sahara and odd tundra excepted, must be worth more. He told his broker to buy any shares that came up at $1\frac{1}{4}$d to 3d, and from 1962 to 1964, collected a bundle thereof.

Forsyth went out to Australia for a general look, which confirmed his particular view on Hampton. He formed a noble scheme to sell land to Americans as an investment for their grandchildren – the Trans-Australian Highway was due to pass by Hampton's land, and the Hampton board, which big shareholder Forsyth had now joined, didn't mind. But the land scheme ran into political difficulties; and Hampton was still hanging fire when, around 1966, Western Mining found nickel on adjoining land. Those once unconsidered Hampton shares burst into flame after the Western miners negotiated an excellent deal with the company to allow drilling, and hence discovery, on its land. At the peak this ardent enthusiasm took the Hampton shares to £6: representing, on an investment of $1\frac{1}{2}$d, a profit of 95,900%: and on 3d, a gain of 47,900%.

You could, if you wished, attribute this to the purest fortune. But Forsyth was looking for his luck, by studying the form, in the first place: he followed not hunch but judgement in working out that the company must be worth more than its market value, even though he had no idea of how much: he

235

took the trouble to inspect what he had bought: and he was conveniently placed, by his own initiative, in the cockpit when the Hampton jet took off into the blue skies beyond. The luck, a colossal stroke of the stuff, came in the unsuspected presence of nickel. But chance, as Pasteur once said, favours the prepared mind.

Commander Eugene McDonald, the quality fanatic of Zenith, lost the hearing in one ear as the result of a car crash in 1940. Forced to buy a hearing aid, he was so shocked by its price that he ordered his designers to come up with a cheaper model. They succeeded, and Zenith went on to become the biggest force in the market. The bash from fate was converted into a touch from Midas not by luck alone, but by McDonald's habit of acting on observation, by his possession of a competent design team, and of the finance to underwrite both the designer's work and the production.

A somewhat different illustration of the conversion of ill-luck into good cash appeared during the awful moment between the wars when salt water appeared in the oil being extracted from the Mexican Eagles concession originally discovered by the first Lord Cowdray (and exploited by him in partnership with the most forceful man in world oil, Sir Henri Deterding of Royal Dutch, and the wiliest, Calouste Gulbenkian).

The initial find, like so many in oil, had been a matter of fortune. (One of the fattest Texan cats, Sid Richardson, liked to tell the tale of how his take-off depended on a choice between two drilling sites: the one he chose, at random, was a fabulous West Texas pool, the other, when he got round to it later, proved dry.) Cowdray, then plain Weetman Pearson, had built his fortune largely by building railways all over Latin America, and had obtained the Mexican oil rights during the course of his worthy work. Many millions of shares had been sold to the public before the fatal traces of salt-water appeared and ruined the company for keeps.

As some counter-blow from fate, Cowdray's heirs, many decades later, decided to dispose of a little-loved painting which had long hung in their Whitehall offices. It fetched a few thousand and was resold by a deliriously happy purchaser as a Rubens for the best part of a quarter of a million. The common truth, that bad luck is often poor judgement, afflicts rich and poor alike – the difference being that the rich can afford it. The various British property men who tangled with Wild Bill

Zeckendorf all survived the psychological and financial shock – even the directors of Second Covent Garden, who found themselves plunged into a mare's nest of good money disappearing after good.

One who escaped with profit and honour was none other than Sir Max Rayne, who managed to extricate himself from Mr. Zeckendorf's toils and end up with what is now the General Motors building. Rayne's good fortune was to come late in the series of British suckers. Since forewarned is forearmed, at least to the canny, Rayne covered himself in time. But the directors of Second Covent Garden also had warning: their mistake was to suppose that their forearming was adequate.

In fact, none of the British property argosies into the USA produced a lasting business empire. The Britons, by and large, misread the prevailing conditions in the USA and also misunderstood themselves. Their fortunes owed their genesis to the lucky combination of their being alive and well and interested in property at the time when the property boom took off. The beneficiaries concluded, however, that they were developers of great genius: ignoring the fact that in the conditions which had enriched them, even developers of substantial stupidity could clean up at least once.

The lasting empire requires more permanent talents. For instance, the Vestey meat-packing empire would be lucrative, but less all-embracing, but for the mishap of its founder in meeting shipping difficulties out of the Argentine. Reacting to misfortune in the born manner of the entrepreneur, he built his own shipping line.

That decision amply cushioned his major mishap – failure over eight long years of hard trying to establish a meatpacking industry in Australia. The net result of the founder's luck and labour (he started as a stripling of seventeen) was that his descendants in the 1970s presided over what was probably the second biggest private empire based on Britain – the latest accounts of their Western United Investment showed £333 million of sales, all on a nominal £5 million of capital employed.

Chance, just as mythology says, does play a critical role in establishing a major business. It was chance that led Lord Rank, as an ardent Methodist, to make his religious film *The Rising of the Sun* and, on being unable to secure distribution, to buy into movies, which took him into the optical industry, which led to a tie-up with the US camera firm Bell and Howell, which culminated in the epic saga of Rank Xerox.

It was chance, you could say, that forced so many émigrés out of Hitler's Europe into an industrially backward Britain where their talents, especially in modern industries like chemicals and plastics, were at a premium. They virtually created whole galaxies of growth industries as a result. One, Sir Frank Schon, began unpromisingly by making firelighters out of sawdust. When he moved on to the indispensable ingredient for the new synthetic wonder-detergents, Schon happened to build his factory on top of a thick seam of the essential anhydrite rock. This golden stroke was like building a steelworks and finding that the thing is sitting on a solid deposit of iron ore.

Schon sold out his £1,000 company for £2 million and stayed aboard to manage it for the purchasing chemical conglomerate. He quit in a considerable huff years later when the chemical colleagues, against his advice, insisted on putting up a giant phosphorous plant in Newfoundland. It proved to be an unmitigated disaster, haunted by what the uninitiated call bad luck, like a leakage which poisoned the local aquatic fauna, but which the *cognoscenti* recognize as the invariable price of bad decisions.

Much the same line of thought applies to the lucky men who catch a tycoon's eyes early in their careers. The cow-curing Osman isn't the only multi-millionaire who can thank an encounter with the superlatively rich. Cyrus Eaton was a seventeen-year-old office boy when he came to the attention of John D. Rockefeller I. That Rockefeller background taught him how to tackle the Morgan interests in head-on conflict. But mutual admiration was not the only characteristic which Eaton and John D. shared. They had the greatest good fortune of all – living to a great age.

Those whom the gods love don't die young: they die old and rich, and the older they are, the richer they get. The magic of compound growth, on which all great accumulations of wealth depend, works under their control, saved from the depredations of inept heirs and unwise stewards. The man who dies at seventy loses two and a half decades of compounding, compared to a John D. Rockefeller I, who died at ninety-four: and Rockefeller II proceeded to live to eighty-six.

Survival to these heights of antiquity is not altogether chance. The ability to purchase the finest and most concentrated medical attention available (although it killed off several rulers and rich in an earlier stage of medical ignorance) has preserved many tycoons beyond what nature intended to be their natural span. One American insurance millionaire has been walking and working for over fifteen years with an interior constructed mostly of plastic tubes. The exceedingly rich, like all potentates, can take their personal physicians with them on trips (President Nixon even took his osteopath to Russia).

If long life is a business boon, it follows that a long career also helps. Many rich men of the past, like Eaton or Rockefeller himself, started at an early hour of life because no other option was available. Fate decreed a start which today might be delayed by school, college, possibly even business school.

This wasn't what John D. I meant when he uttered the sanctimonious judgement: "the poor boy is in a position of impregnable advantage. He is better off than the son of the rich man ...", but it is possibly the only sense in which that persuasive phrase is actually true. What Rockefeller meant is that the poor boy has the sovereign impetus of wishing to escape from his poverty, which is true. But, as we have seen, the exercise of that magic motivation, the unsparing expenditure of that abundant talent and effort, merely lands the ex-pauper in the same situation which the rich boy achieved painlessly by the mere accident of birth.

Some of the once-poor rich have arrived in that category by the mere accident of time and place and money. The last-mentioned chance is often crucial: the accidental availability of cash when needed has made many careers. Money does tend, in a mysterious manner, to stick to the fingers of certain men in the same way that certain great cricketers need only to stick out a hand for a ball to fly into it.

The general reaction to money-catchers, to men with a modernized Midas-touch, is to attribute their acquisition to luck, in the sense that all natural talent is God-given, they are lucky. The curious fact is that the very rich often do talk of their success in terms of acts of God rather than acts of themselves – Julius Rosenwald's attribution of success to 95% good fortune is echoed by Big Al Abplanalp, Nixon's pal, who believes that genius is "2% inspiration, 8% work and 90%

luck" — and leading luminaries in oil's hall of fame seem to think likewise.

H. L. Hunt declared that "you have to be lucky"; Sid Richardson that "luck has helped me every day of my life, and I'd rather be lucky than smart, because a lot of smart people ain't eatin' regular": R. E. (Bob) Smith that "my West Texas oilfield was solely luck. It has thirty-eight million barrels in reserve and cost me $5 an acre. The lesson you learn as you get older is that it's luck." In oil, no doubt, the good luck story is truer than in most contexts — although the fact that the great discoveries were made by men who died broke demands some explanation. In truth, the emphasis on luck is a variation on the theme of false modesty, the opposite of whistling to keep your spirits up — moaning, so to speak, to keep your guilt down.

Close analysis of a brilliant player of any game, including the oil and money ones, always shows that behind the success lie application, method and motivation that anybody can imitate: the difference being that mastering the mechanics of Arnold Palmer's swing won't turn anybody into Arnold Palmer. The distinction is exemplified by the bad, black day of one publisher who turned down Joseph Heller's *Catch-22* in the morning and Joy Adamson's lioness saga, *Born Free*, in the afternoon — the latter being on the grounds that he didn't publish animal books. Bad luck, you might say: thus unwittingly condoning what was truly poor professional judgement.

Not that making million-dollar mistakes is in itself a condemnation of the professional concerned: being wrong, sometimes, is a corollary of often being right. The Midas millionaire simply has a surer instinct for when to be right, when to be wrong, and when to get out before a mistake exacts its penalty. Luck has merely an ancillary role in this connection. It's said that George Gershwin, travelling across the USA in the days of luxury trains, looked down from his upper berth at his wonderful pianist, Oscar Levant, and said, "you know what this represents, Oscar? The difference between talent and genius."

Rightly Gershwin didn't mention luck: and the would-be millionaire who blames his failures on bad luck deserves his unlucky fate.

THE BOUNTY OF BIGNESS

or

Inside Every Fat Company

In which we read how some computer men made bigger
fortunes outside IBM than inside ... how two brothers
outwitted United Fruit over the humble banana ... and
other ways in which fat companies, confronting lean
entrepreneurs, get the fuzzy end of the lollipop.

Inside every fat company there is a lean entrepreneur screaming to get out. Some of them make their escape, armed with all
the experience, contacts and other equipment which a fat
company can provide, but free of the main impediment to that
company's freedom of movement, which is its lard. The large
unwilling parent may be efficient, like IBM, or merely prolific
in hiring, equipping and losing managers, like Litton Industries in its heyday as a star conglomerate. Whatever the
parent's powers, however, baby often outdoes big daddy when
it comes to the main point, which is the creation of personal
wealth.

No firm has spawned as many profitable breakaways as
IBM: it is perhaps the only company which has accidentally
created so much of its own competition. That is the inevitable
price of being a scandalously rich monopoly in a hotly
attractive market: anybody who has worked for you literally
has a price on his head. At one point the only two computer
companies making money, apart from IBM, which was all but
printing the stuff, were both breakaways from fat computer
firms — Max Pavlevsky's Scientific Data Systems and Ken
Norris' Control Data Corporation. They were joined in the
money-spinning game by Kenneth H. Olsen's Digital Equipment.

Combined sales of these three before SDS went back into

the fat company matrix by selling out to Xerox were a long way short of the mighty $11,000 million of IBM, daddy of them all, but still generated fortunes worthy of the IBM Watson clan. Since IBM's Tom Watson Sr was himself a breakaway from National Cash (forced out by a megalomaniac master) there may be rough justice here. But all three made their mark by competing in areas where the corporate father of all computer men, for all his big talk, was surprisingly ineffective: in very large, complex computers and in small specialized ones. (IBM's fat company competitors, like GE and RCA, both now defunct in this line, made the mistake of competing in-between, or just where IBM bulged with muscle.)

Nor was it only making computers that extracted riches from IBM's groaning table. There, fighting equally hard for the meats, were the leanest and hungriest of the salesmen on whom the great company has always depended for its penetration, the assault troops whose dominance largely explained the invincible resistance of IBM to its fat company foes. The most energetic soldiers in these ranks also spotted chinks in IBM's armour – like the fact that it over-charged on rentals, if a less conservative view of depreciation was taken; or that the company's customers, while happy to shower millions on the leasing, care and maintenance of the computer and its servants, had only the faintest idea how to use either.

The first vision gave birth to the leasing game, which for its brief, butterfly time in the sun, spread fortunes like wings and with no more difficulty. The second vision produced the computer service concept, which, while it needed harder work (unlike leasing, which involved no work at all) proved longer lasting in the hands of clever men.

The cleverness of one ex-salesman, H. Ross Perot, deserves its legend. The computer company thought highly of Perot, as well it might: as the ace of the Texas territory, Perot was chalking up terrific sales for IBM, and terrifying amounts of commission for himself – that is, they terrified the bureaucrats at head office, who couldn't bear the idea of a salesman earning more than the chairman.

Head office, reacting in the way of all fat companies since organizational time began, slammed a ceiling on commissions: nobody could earn more than $250,000 of commission in a year. So Perot walked out onto the streets of Dallas, made his maximum in a couple of weeks – and quit. He put a tiny fraction of his quarter-of-a-million (the standard, legendary $1,000) into a company called Electronic Data Services, which would make computers actually work for the people to whom he had sold them. By 1972 EDS was earning $16.5 million, which, since profits the previous year had been $14 million, was valued by the investing public at a growth (or lofty) price-earnings multiple that made Perot's company worth a warm $645 million at the end of 1972 before the paper value of his stock continued to crumple away.

Another Texan, Sam Wyly of Universal Computing Corporation, now renamed after its progenitor, was behind in the paper gold stakes – but his fortune from UCC was still worth several hundred million pounds in 1968; a fine feat of multiplication, given that UCC's profits that year were a mere $8.5 million. Wyly, ex-IBM and ex-Honeywell to boot, had also started with only that magic $1,000.

These crumbs from IBM's cake were worth even more than the stakes of the pioneers behind CDC, SDS, and DE, who actually made computers, as opposed to nurse-maiding the machines and their users.

Big corporations, just like big governments, have a penchant for accidentally scattering largesse about them. They contrive to share their fat in all manner of ways. They lend money at low interest, sometimes for nothing at all. They go into partnership with lean men on terms which give the latter all the butter (if any). They buy out lean men at gross prices. Above all, they hold up umbrellas which keep off the rain while the leanies, dry and comfortable, dig their goldmines underneath. This is because the fat company, like any bureaucracy, likes to do things in the way in which it has always done them. It objects to changing its fixed practices or its fixed ideas – and if a leanie spots that the rigidity has provided an opportunity to make a killing, the fatty takes an unconscionably long, bureaucratic time about recognizing that it is being taken for a Chicago-style ride.

Saul Steinberg's fat company formula is a textbook model. He noted that IBM depreciated its computers over a period of between four and five years. The boy wonder observed in his undergraduate thesis at the Wharton Business School that this exceedingly conservative approach made it cheaper to buy an IBM computer than to rent one. If the buyer then took a more realistic eight to ten year depreciation, he could undercut

243

IBM's own leasing terms by 10% to 20%, while relying on the obliging fat company to go on servicing and supporting the machine free of charge.

If, moreover, this shrewd undercutter borrowed the purchase price of the computer, he had the greatest prize of all: instant money. A million-dollar computer, financed almost entirely by a bank loan, would rent for $225,000, say, against $251,000 from IBM (of which some $200,000 would have been IBM's depreciation). After paying his lower depreciation and his interest charges, the Steinberg-type wizard ended up with $64,000 net profit. Not only would this return his entire equity investment in a year; but the stock market was then prepared to value leasing companies at up to thirty-five times earnings.

Now, thirty-five times $64,000 equals $2.2 million. Thus, if the formula worked out perfectly, as it sometimes did, the leasing genius made a clear, untrammelled million the minute the lease was signed. Small wonder that Steinberg and family, even after an abortive stab at buying the Chemical Bank, a lamentably successful bid for the sorrowful Pergamon Press, and a collapse in the leasing market was still worth $100 million in Leasco stock.

The whistle was blown on leasing by the fat computer companies, which finally got wise to the fortunes being made on their backs and revised their leasing terms. They screwed the leasers so painfully that in 1969 Leasco gave up the activity which had taken Steinberg most of the distance from a borrowed $25,000 and a loft in Brooklyn. A year before that traumatic event, however, Steinberg had ensured Leasco's and his own financial survival by buying an insurance company. In exchange for some paper, Steinberg bought $550 million of real-life assets in the Reliance Insurance Company, dropped the Leasco name in Reliance's favour and lived, if not happily, at least ever after.

The money company move, or the Steinberg-Geneen Defence, has been played in time of trouble not only by Leasco and ITT, but by the biggest of the computer breakaways, CDC. The Defence is made possible by the highly developed adipose tissues of money companies which are prone to pile up wealth by unglamorous methods like collecting premiums, breaking even (if lucky) on the insurance, and making profits by investing the cash in the stock market.

244

Their time horizons are so distant that, even with the usual inexpert handling of the funds, capital gains accrue. But investors are unlikely to get excited over so humdrum a kettle of fish as an insurance company – and that makes the insurers easy prey for corporate anglers who, in contrast, can offer highly valued paper. The fat company hands over its accumulated cash and cashable investments to the skinny man, who thus rescues himself from the main difficulty of the lean: lack of ready, fat cash.

CDC bought a finance company, Commercial Credit, three times CDC's size and so desperate to escape from the arms of Loews that the deal, worth $600 million, went through in seven weeks. CDC's Norris had broken out in 1957 from the Univac division of Sperry Rand. A group of Univac conspirators asked Norris, the head of the division, to lead them away like a modern Moses to set up their very own computer factory.

The team quit *en bloc*, and inside two years marketed the first brainchild of its big computer design genius, Seymour Cray: his big baby sold for half the price of the comparable IBM machine and actually made a profit. By 1964 Cray's team at tiny Chippewa Falls, Wisconsin, had given birth to the mammoth CDC 6600, six feet tall, seven tons heavy. In that fiscal year sales all but doubled, and profits rose six times. In the first eleven years of its life, CDC had grown from seven men sitting on a capitalization of $600,000 into a two billion dollar company, making Norris a millionaire fifty times over.

So much for Univac. But Norris and Co were so successful, in fact, that the fattest competitor of them all, IBM, felt seriously threatened and retaliated savagely – and another fight developed between the fat and the lean. In 1965 IBM announced that its 360/90 would be better than the 6600 ("IBM is out to get us," Norris told the *Wall Street Journal*, "and you can print that."): the 6600, which let itself down by some poor performance in the field, was stopped cold in its tracks – and Norris wasn't a bit pleased when the 360/90, like other IBM giants before it, disappeared from the market and from sight.

Norris took an unprecedented step against his fat foe: he filed a private anti-trust suit. Four years later CDC had its reward in an out-of-court settlement. IBM sold Norris its computer service bureaux, worth an estimated $60 million, for

$16 million, and paid off CDC's legal bill, which came to $15 million more.

Computers, because of the rapid growth of the market in all directions and because the market was dominated by one super-large firm, with only other fatties competing, was the ideal postwar set-up for little outsiders, or for insiders moving outside. But the governing factors are identical in less highly-charged and high-flown situations.

These dominants are the sheer size and strength of the giant, which encourage it to believe that small intruders or extruders can be ignored, and that, in any event, the latter are highly unlikely to spot or snatch any opportunity which the big managers have missed, and that, in the final sweet analysis, they can always crush the attacker, or buy him (a device which, once the small company is in the fat one's embrace, often has the same effect as crushing).

Conceit, apathy, and ignorance are not the best ingredients of a commercial brew. The United Fruit octopus, for instance, although its banana-like tentacles reached to every corner of the globe, refused, in its lordly and ignorant way, to believe that bananas could be grown in the Windward Islands. Two brothers named Geest, who knew nothing much about bananas, but had deep lore about growing, acquired from early days in the Dutch bulb-fields, saw no objection to the islands, duly planted their bananas, and reaped a harvest which gave them half the British market, raising the profits of their entirely private operation to £2 million a year – at which level the family business was worth a minimum £50 million.

Even when a marbled company shares a lean vision of a market, the fatty somehow often manages to get what Marilyn Monroe in *Some Like It Hot* called the fuzzy end of the lollipop – as when the British Printing Corporation, paving the way for Saul Steinberg, fell in love with Pergamon's Robert Maxwell. The biggest printer in Europe had originally ventured into encyclopaedias for a very common big company reason: a customer, in this case a publisher, owed it money. By sharing Maxwell's vision of a world brimming with encyclopaedias, and forming a joint company, the printers cleverly thought they were exchanging a liability (a £300,000 after-tax loss) for a golden future.

One of the oldest precepts in commerce, which is to compare your prospective gains with your prospective risks, was ignored; so was an equally aged maxim, which is what you don't control, you don't dare to trust. In its first eighteen months the grandiosely named International Learning Systems Corporation was first reported to have made a profit of £806,000: after the auditors got to work, they cut the figure to a draft profit of £40,000: when the accountants had completed their labours, they came up with a slightly different answer still – a loss of £2.6 million, which fell like a thunderclap on BPC's unhappy head.

The innocent may argue that, surely, big companies rarely go into an expensive enterprise without careful investigation, without ensuring that they have adequate control, either managerial or financial, and without limiting their liability. But the ILSC case is no isolated example. When the International Publishing Corporation decided to back two software pioneers in that insidious computer game, it not only paid £600,000 for their nascent company, it accepted their dictum that, since publishers knew nothing about computers, they should have no votes on the board, where their ignorance might upset the experts.

At the end of the day, the publishers' losses had come to at least £3 million; ignorance is seldom bliss. Nor were they alone. A little later a City merchant bank led a group of institutions into backing the same entrepreneurial pair with £6 million cash – it wasn't supposed to be that much, but the two got through the original amount so fast that good money began to flow after the bad. Faced with entrepreneurs who use big numbers, and make rich forecasts, even financiers, although supposed to be able to do sums, lose their senses. Poor, simple managers, who can't add up at all, are utterly lost.

For instance, one modest entrepreneur had fallen into the majority control of a larger company by a series of accidents: the lean man retained an option to buy his big brother out, which proved, in these resolute hands, to be a marvellous asset. The fatty, strapped for cash, decided to sell: and the lean man exercised his option for $2½ million, financed by a group of banks in a deal raising his stake from 40 to 60%. A little later, the fat boss enquired after the health of the lean purchaser and was informed that his condition was excellent, as you would expect after receiving a present of nearly $1 million. The fat boss was astonished: it was gently explained to him that, since

247

the deal valued 60% at $2\frac{1}{2}$ million, the extra fifth was worth over $800,000. Within a couple of years even that assessment was falsified; the profits having risen in the interim, the entrepreneur's stake was worth $15 million, of which $2\frac{1}{2}$ million represented the large company's putative loss.

The bigger the company, the larger the largesse, because big-time managers, like politicians, like to play the paper number game. If the board rejoices in a turnover of £1,500 million, a million isn't even petty cash – unless one of the sub-managers wants to spend it, when the proposal becomes the subject of earnest boardroom deliberations. Even £15 million is only 1% of sales; but if you drop twice that much, as ICI's board did in its vain attempt to finance the British textile industry into prosperity, it offsets the value of many minute examinations of managerial spending plans.

The most spectacular of ICI's exertions involved Joe Hyman, whom ICI's greyer managers correctly saw as the strongest individual force in the industry. So they backed him with a vengeance: ICI took a quarter of the Viyella textile shares which Hyman had revitalized and provided him with £10 million – most of it in the form of an interest-free loan. Within a week Hyman had spent the boodle on buying British Van Heusen. "We like to see things happen fast", said an ICI spokesman lamely. Presumably, the ICI directors could see that they were perfectly capable of buying the shirt company themselves: they probably didn't see that their action made automatic millions for Hyman in person, just as surely as if they had pressed the cash into his hand.

If you have the use of a million free of interest (as Hyman did) it will purchase after-tax earnings of at least £100,000: if that is multiplied by a very average stock exchange multiple of fifteen, the capital value to the equity-holders is £1.5 million, half a million of it pure profit. Hyman, as the largest individual shareholder in Viyella, reaped the harvest sown with ICI's seeds. In 1963 alone his shares shot up two and a half times: at least, in this deal ICI made a profit, which is more than can be said for its other textile forays. Desperate to salvage one wrecked customer, the chemical giant merged it with another, run by an entrepreneurial family whose previous run was of unbroken glory; ICI ended up with the whole profitless caboodle. When relations soured between ICI and Hyman – the corpocrats reluctant to share his entrepreneurial visions,

248

and the entrepreneur eager to tell the corpocrats how to run their corpocracy – the financing arrangement was undone: but ICI still ended up, after yet another of its textile investments had tasted the bread of affliction, by popping Viyella back in its pocket again.

That was also after Hyman's board, in a finale worthy of Shakespeare, had ousted him from his own creation. With his Viyella and other proceeds the tycoon bought control of a woollen textile company in a brief takeover battle in which he seemed infected by the usually fatal desire to win at any price. Within a year or so of this expensive-seeming deal, wool prices soared upwards. The money which Hyman put into J. Crowther appreciated and the shares multiplied almost tenfold in two years.

The record of the involvement of giants with entrepreneur-built companies the world over makes sorry reading, partly because the two sides don't speak the same language, let alone work in the same way. The entrepreneur instinctively relates a proposition to his individual well-being, the manager thinks of it strictly in terms of corporate strategy. Take the strange example of Sylvania and Sir Jules Thorn. Sylvania, later absorbed into General Telephone and Electric, was the largest shareholder in Thorn Electrical after its founder, who had made extensive use of Sylvania technology.

The obvious assumption was that the Americans were biding their time until Thorn, who was no chicken in years, but not easy to pluck, decided to relinquish control. A plump British affiliate would then fall ready-made into the American lap. While this build-up continued, the US part-owner even increased its shareholding, stirring happy speculation in the City of London. As Thorn grew to a height symbolized by its name in lights high above the West End, the fortune which Sir Jules held as closely as he controlled the company grew too.

Thorn's whole career was founded on the lean outsider principle. Coming to Britain as a refugee from Austria and the Nazis, and deciding to sell light-bulbs, he found the market encircled by a manufacturers' ring. This broke, not the law of the time, but the Law of Fat Company Preservation; this lays down that every artificial restriction of a market or price level opens up a natural, protected opportunity for any lean man who is not bound by the restriction.

The outsider cracked the ring, and drove his company on to

a score, at its best levels of 1967, worth £74 million. He then played his master-stroke, by merging, naturally, just before Britain's colour TV boom, with another TV rental giant. At this one stroke, the American stake was reduced to non-strategic proportions; it was subsequently off-loaded, while the Thorn equity marched on to a 1972 best level of £732 million, of which the directors' share (meaning mostly Sir Jules) was £48 million.

The fat company's final defence, buying the lean ones out, has the inevitable effect of turning the latter's paper wealth into the real McCoy, and the undesirable side-effect that the business is often worth less without its lean progenitor – especially as the latter, by instinct or design, tends to get out when the going is good, or, rather, before it gets bad. Xerox paid its $900 million for Pavlevsky's SDS – of which the founder himself pocketed $50 million in Xerox stock – shortly before the bright lights of the computer market and the SDS profits were abruptly switched off.

Another danger is the old switcheroo. When Gillette paid Pat Frawley and his partner $15 million for the Papermate pen business, the razor men sharply insisted that the lean vendors should not compete in the ballpoint market for five years. Frawley promptly took his millions, bought Eversharp, sold its pen side, and concentrated with all the remaining resources on competing with Gillette – with electric razors and razor blades, only desisting from the latter when the government forced the blade company's sale.

ITT under Geneen has made far more cash millionaires by its purchases even than by its stock options, as in the buying of the Levitt building company, creators of Levittowns, for a pay-off of $92 million. British gentlemen conglomerates out on the spree have done likewise: one family got over £26 million for selling out its cosmetic business to a diversifying tobacco giant. In the same beauteous trade, one entrepreneur bought back his firm, previously sold to a mammoth, with one innocent condition lurking in the large print: the vendor was to take the financial responsibility for the old stock.

The purchaser then cruised round his retail outlets, offered to take back all the stock on hand (which rejoiced the retailers' hearts exceedingly and cemented their affection for evermore), and then passed the goods back, with his compliments, and in return for a large cheque, to the big company. This effectively

250

reduced the purchase price by a third: there's no fool like a fat fool.

Yet the normal human reaction, when put in a ring with a heavyweight, is to run for the ropes. In making millions this policy is woefully misguided. The correct course is to search for the weak spot, hit it hard and go on hitting until the heavy either surrenders or buys you out, which comes to the same thing. If the heavy is theoretically on your side, never make a deal which gives you less than, or only what, you want. Aim for the moon – the heavy may give you that planet, because it costs those in charge nothing to give it away; but it costs you plenty to miss the chance of your private Apollo money mission. If you can squeeze the fat out of your friend by seemingly modest deals as Gulbenkian did with his guaranteed 5% of Iraq's oil, do so. (They tried to fob him off with a penny a ton royalty, with no success whatsoever.)

Never repeat the error of Haloid, the little company that became large Xerox. In its youth and innocence, Haloid sold the Rank Organization, for £600,000, half the rights to xerography in the whole world outside the USA. On declared profits alone, that give-away was worth £89.8 million in a decade. Even skinny companies, at times, can have fat heads.

THE AVOIDABILITY OF TAXES

or

The Taxman Cometh Not

Why the taxman, adept at picking off small criminal
evaders, is outwitted by rich mass murderers ... including a map of the Middle East of tax loopholes, as
rich in cash flow as Arabia's oil wells – that being the
handy tax differential between income and capital.

The ordinary income earner the wide world over is a com-
plaining taxpayer. Wriggle how the victim may, the taxman
always succeeds in extracting the full exaction of the law.
Small dodges are practised by most people, such as taking
extra jobs which are not revealed to the official predator. This
moonlighting may be the largest single category of employment in the western world. In the more lax, usually Latin
areas, under-cover, under-the-counter and even under-the-desk
payments play the same rôle.

But when the taxman can't get at your income, he attacks
your spending instead, through the more direct method of
what are therefore known as indirect taxes. One way or
another, like the Mounties, he always gets his man – except,
that is, when the man is really flush with taxable money. It's as
if the Mounties, while adept at picking off petty thieves, were
totally incapable of catching mass-murderers.

This strange situation, that the more tax you are supposed
to pay under the law, the less likely you are to pay it, is most
clearly seen in the careers, not of business moguls, but of
movie stars, telegogues, pulp novelists and the like. An income
of $1 million, even after genuine tax, still leaves a sum that is
beyond the spending powers of all but the most determined
playboy. But the residue, after meeting all expenses, would
take many years to add up to a seven-figure fortune, even with

the aid of shrewd investment. That factor will probably be offset, anyway, by the idiocy to which investing stars are prone (the Beatles' Apple Corps got chewed over by every maggot in town); and by the hugely exorbitant cost of the hangers-on whom show-biz personalities accumulate as rocks gather barnacles.

Yet many super-tax bracket stars put together a million in no time at all: the high marginal rate of taxation doesn't stop a David Frost from hopping across the Atlantic in search of the highest possible marginal income, but nobody in the taxed rabble seems to wonder how these things can be. The solution is far from complex. The rich pay less tax, sometimes even no tax at all, simply because they can afford to employ better accountants, lawyers and other acolytes, and, equally important, can afford to do as the acolytes advise.

The ordinary hen-pecked taxpayer doesn't know that the Republic of Ireland, for some inscrutable Irish reason, levies no tax whatsoever on creative artists. The shrewd creator can not only find this out, even if his creation is as far, culturally speaking from *Juno and the Paycock* as Len Deighton's *The Ipcress File*: he can also buy a castle in Eire to take advantage of the benevolent provision.

A swift change of residence is obviously a prerogative of the rich. Best-selling British authors today head for Malta as earlier generations of American actors and writers sped to Switzerland. That trick isn't open to the average or even above average income-earner. Apart from anything else, your average, even your well above average, man has to live where his work is: whereas the superbly rich can even buy their own island, like Len Matchan, who is Britain's biggest manufacturer of lipstick cases, or Aristotle Onassis (to go from the financially superior to the sublime). The island proprietor can then, with luck, fix his own tax-rate. Nor are the exiled condemned to spend the rest of their lives in Malta.

The over-rich Briton, for instance, flees to Malta on 4 April, just before the new tax year starts. He stays there until 5 April a year thence, at which point he patriotically returns home. Now, all income from self-employment, like all profits from corporations, is taxed one year in arrears. That is, the income of the temporary expatriate for the year of his absence is technically the money earned in the previous year. But since the wandering boy has wandered out of UK residence, he has

253

no tax liability for the income in the wandering year – even though he spent every month in which the loot was actually earned living in Esher, Surrey.

That's not all. During his year of absence, the wanderer is not a UK resident for tax purposes. Therefore the money he receives during those absent months, be it never so large, is not eligible for UK tax – even though during the months when, in other circumstances, the loot would have been taxable, he is safely ensconced once more in the splendours of Esher.

The result of this statagem is that two years' income can be received free of tax: and it takes little further ingenuity to put three years' income, or sometimes even four, into those twelve months by some judicious deferring here and advancing there. Even so, exiles are liable to find the months of exile trying, and to skip back to London for a brief taste of something livelier than Malta, all muffled up in false beards.

The foreign residence loophole has a different shape and mode of access in every country, but it is a defensive gambit which isn't needed if the player has foreign income. Generally, money earned abroad can be taxed either where it's earned, or where its owner lives – or in some neutral spot on the map selected by the earner for the understandable reason that its government levies little or no tax. The Cayman Islands thus came into unwonted prominence in 1973, when it was revealed that former Cabinet Minister Duncan Sandys had money, paid him for consultancy services, delivered into a Cayman account: and that Sandys' company, Lonrho, habitually rewarded its executives, at least in part, in the same home from home.

The saga played no small part in persuading the Labour Government, after Sandys' Conservative friends had been ousted, to clap restrictions on such overseas fiddles – with the unexpected result for squealing expatriate Americans living in London, of abruptly altering their rosy view of Britain's charms.

In countries like Italy tax evasion is almost a second religion. Since no Italian will ever give an honest account of his income (now that torture is illegal) the authorities have been reduced to taxing him on the appearance of wealth. That's why Italians keep private planes at an airfield just inside the Swiss border.

It follows that any foreigner who has income in a land of

eager evaders can benefit from the same rules. Being foreign, moreover, he can keep some of his money outside without let or hindrance – and is not reduced, like an Italian who distrusts the lira, the unions and the Government in equal proportions, to humping suitcases full of currency across the frontier which separates Italy from the Swiss paradise.

Most authorities, while tough on domestic money that wants to emigrate, are kind to overseas earnings that decide to come home. A British star can pop his foreign proceeds into a bank account in the Channel Islands or the Isle of Man, where kindly bankers will invest it anywhere in the world. After a few years, the star can bring all the proceeds back the last few miles across the sea without paying any tax of any variety.

That's one of the ways in which the one-year exiles can get more than two years of income saved from tax. During the year they finish another masterpiece which collects foreign royalties. If the film-script or whatever had been written in Esher, the normal UK tax would have applied. Since it was compiled in sunnier climes, the proceeds can go straight to an off-shore tax haven. Performing artists, of course, never have this problem. Their work takes them legitimately all round the world, and where they choose to be paid (or rather, where their business managers choose for them) is where, if anywhere, their tax is handed over.

Time as well as place is optional. You can defer income over several years, as William Holden deferred his take from *The Bridge Over the River Kwai*, or as the original late-night chat hero, Jack Paar, did with his phenomenal contract. The smaller the annual instalments, the lower the tax liability in each year. In fact the deferred trick can confer more benefit on the employer than the employed. In one case, the interest received by the movie producer on the sum set aside for his deferred star substantially exceeded the payments due each year – so he actually got the super-star's services for less than nothing.

Time and place are thus two dimensions on the side of the heavy (or supposedly heavy) taxpayer. Another is space: the wider a man's sources of income, the more room he has to juggle those flows around, to decide in which of the other two dimensions he will receive the gold. He can even decide not to receive it at all – while still retaining almost as much benefit as if he had. This is not only through the dividend waiver, by which a man forgoes the dividend on his controlling shares in a company, thus hopefully enhancing the value of those shares. That is a relatively crude and blunt instrument, not to be compared with the delicate and flexible touch of the trust.

This device, in its family form, allows papa to "make provision" for his children, which sounds no less innocent than popping coins into their piggy bank. In fact, it exempts the income paid into that trust from any tax until such time as it is paid into the children's hands. The family trust – the Stranahans of Champion Spark Plugs erected thirty of the things – is probably the most heavily worked device in the whole field of tax avoidance, used even by those families which have graduated to the ultimate in trusts, the charitable foundation.

In the American heyday of 1950 foundations were being created at a hundred a month. The donor could give 20% of his income to the foundation without paying tax. If he gave it goodies, like stocks or property, he deducted 20% of the value from gross income; yet in seven years the Moody Foundation, set up by a man who owned half of Galveston, gave away precisely $422,000. Even if the donations are of somewhat nobler proportions the charitable founder is enabled to spend tax-free money on some of his own desires – and supporting the Metropolitan Opera is no less a gratification, even if a worthier one, than owning a yacht.

You can, in fact, get the yacht tax-free, too: if not through the trust route, by the company way. Income earned by a company, although the currency is precisely the same colour, is different from income earned by an individual – although it does not possess the sovereign difference of income received in a trust or foundation, which is total exemption from tax (despite the fact that many studies of US foundations have shown that the Moody money-deposit is not alone in giving away far less than it receives).

Corporate income can have expenses deducted before the taxable amount is computed – so long as the charge is a legitimate business expense. Enter the yacht. Mrs. Bernard Castro, whose fortune is built on convertibles of the sofa rather than the stock market variety, has a small liner at Fort Lauderdale; scattered around among the convertibles (a sofa converting into a bar at one end and a stereo at the other, a chair becoming a hair-dryer cum ironing board) is Castro sales literature. As Mrs. Castro delicately points out, "After all we make this boat tax deductible." Another American taxpayer, manufacturer of footwear, argued that the entire cost of his ocean-going plaything was legitimately deductible, because it afforded the opportunity to study the adhesive performance of various soles on a sloping, slippery surface.

The wealthy taxpayer, indeed, is a sloping and slippery animal. Even three dimensions – place, time and space – don't exhaust his appetite for evasion. There is also the fourth dimension. As opposed to income received by trusts or foundations, which would attract tax if received in any other than the third dimension, income of the fourth degree is income which is identical to every other form of receipt, except for one thing: that it pays no tax.

This category, almost exclusively reserved for the exceedingly rich, includes blessings like US tax-exempt bonds, issued by local authorities with the benediction of Washington, which loses heavily on the deal; Eurobonds, the new international medium, also tax-free, from which all governments suffer, without apparently knowing or caring; the oil depletion allowance in the USA, which allows rich men and richer corporations to deduct against tax, not only the cost of all holes dry and wet, but also $22\frac{1}{2}\%$ against their gross income; depreciation money all round the globe, which allows those with money to build up still larger investments out of untaxed cash.

The classic depreciation cases are not the Texan oil fortunes. No, the strongest depreciation cases, because the industry is not inherently lucrative, are the shipping lines. Ships not only attract depreciation charges, even though they may easily be worth more at the end of the depreciation period than they cost, but in many countries they attract specially generous rates of tax exemption, with subsidies thrown in for afters.

Politicians have a seemingly insatiable desire to foster their merchant marines, lest in some future holocaust their country gets cut off from the high seas (the phobia dates back at least to the days of the Spanish Armada). The net result is that one of Britain's most successful companies, European Ferries, engaged in the vital strategic business of ferrying tourists and their cars to the Continent, earned £20 million and paid not one penny of tax in four years (and then, in the next five, smidgens of 0.2 or 0.3%).

257

This is no mean effort even by the standards of Dallas – and the extraordinary preponderance of shipping as well as oil magnates among the world's new rich is partly explained by the remarkable freedom from tax which they enjoy. Thus Y. K. Pao, estimated to be worth $700–800 million, has two main companies, which in 1972 made profits of $26.8 million: neither paid a penny of tax. Among other fiscal advantages, ships, like pop singers, travel the world about their business: which makes it that much easier for the owner to locate his personal tax base wherever on the surface of the globe he can best ensure that his private income, like his corporate flow, is tax-free.

There are also tax anomalies and oddities, like the first £5,000 paid, and untaxed, as compensation to a big British executive who loses his job. Once upon a time, the whole "golden handshake" was free of tax, meaning that it paid a highly paid man hand over fist to engineer his dismissal.

There was another lost British beauty which allowed retiring barristers to collect tax-free all fees outstanding at the date of their retirement – no matter how often they retired. One or two made almost as many last appearances as Sarah Bernhardt, taking care that, for a year or so before each retirement, no client was encouraged to pay up. Since a goodly proportion of the House of Commons consisted of lawyers, the chances of this loophole being closed were rated about as high as those of a US Congress in which oil interests were the most powerful paymasters doing anything nasty to the depletion allowance. The tax collectors' victory in both cases demonstrates that the life of all loopholes, no matter how gilt-edged, has a limit. But never mind – the ingenuity of moneyed man knows few limits, either, and as soon as one loophole closes, another opens up.

The Middle East of loophole drillers, as rich in cash flow as the oil sands of Arabia, is the differential tax between income and capital. If tax rises as high as 90% on income, but falls as low as 30% on capital gains (25% in the US), there is a profound saving (60p in the pound to be precise) in converting the former into the latter. Since capital, in most countries, is not taxed at all until a gain is realized, the advantage of conversion is even greater than immediately appears.

The simplest and unstoppable way is to become a genuine incorporated, publicly-owned business. In this event, your wealth is no longer your taxable income, it is your income, taxed at the lower corporation tax rate, and multiplied by the price-earnings ratio: £100,000 a year then becomes, say £1 million of capital instead of £30,000 of taxed income. Enterprising Britons set up two companies whose stock-in-trade was to get stars like Tom Jones to exchange their future earnings for shares: another company, Booker Brothers McConnell, better known as a West Indian trader, purchased the future earnings of authors like Agatha Christie and Ian Fleming.

This loophole was among those gummed up by the Inland Revenue, but the principle can still apply. One neat method is the Bahamas partnership, in which the partner, a local lawyer, is well paid simply to sleep. After suitable passage of time, during which the earnings have poured in at the indulgent local rates of taxation, the partnership is liquidated and the profits are paid over as capital increments, and in the previously determined proportions, to the partners.

This is a relatively new wrinkle to an old device, the Liechtenstein or Luxembourg company, in which, again, a local lawyer comes in as the ostensible part (or even majority) owner. Many a rich income finds its way into these safe harbours — but the catch is that a resident in some country with an efficient tax system like Britain's may find it difficult to get his tax-free money back home in the same blissful untaxed condition.

All is less well than it used to be in the grand old sport of tax havenry. Not the least disturbing aspect to the tax evader of the Howard Hughes affair, or rather the non-Howard Hughes affair, was that a Swiss bank dropped the veil of secrecy to the point of total nudity, simply to put Mrs. Edith Irving on the spot.

A tenet of the dedicated tax savers who have deposited billions of foreign money held in Switzerland ($5,000 million is supposed to consist of US tax evasion money alone) was that Swiss banks, no matter if you opened the account in the name of Mickey Mouse, Scarface Al Capone or Nikita S. Krushchev, would protect your secrecy to the death. In this instance, no doubt, the Swiss banks' dislike of helping to perpetrate a particularly blatant fraud, especially on a man with as much money as Hughes, outweighed the racket's traditional respect for the privacy of its numbered accounts.

But however special the circumstances, the Hughes-Irving

incident was another example of the steady erosion of what was once the rich man's inalienable right to keep every red cent he earned. In 1969 the US Congress actually decreed that the wealthy had to pay 10% of their income in taxes, irrespective of the dodges to which they and their advisers had resorted. A senator later turned up the information that in 1972, no less than 276 Americans with income over $100,000 paid not a bean to the Internal Revenue Service. The minimum tax, it transpired, was to be levied on "adjusted gross income" – and after they had finished adjusting via their favourite deductions, these 276 worthies had an adjusted gross income of nothing.

All the same, one by one, stone by stone, the bastions which protected a millionaire's income in his lifetime are, if not coming down, being chipped away: and it follows that his defences against depradations after his death are also being gradually eroded.

For instance, the Disappearing Estate Trick, a gambit as satisfying and mysterious as the Indian rope variety, came to the pained attention of the British authorities. It operated on the fact that works of art, instead of being aggregated together, were charged after death separately – at the rate which applied to the rest of a man's estate. Suppose a millionaire was suddenly informed by his doctor that he only had a week to live. His correct fiscal response was to rush to the nearest friendly banker and borrow another million, then racing on to Bond Street and the nearest equally friendly art dealer. With the borrowed million, he buys some assorted masterpieces, and then dies as promised.

The following equation then applies, to the great joy of his heirs. The estate consists of a million of assets, less a million of debts, which equals nil. The art must be assessed at the same rate as the rest of the inheritance, which also equals nil. This loophole, created by the general and laudable feeling that artistic patronage is to be encouraged, has been plugged: and the US authorities, too, are getting leery about the tax-avoidance uses of *la belle peinture*.

Time was when a rich man could buy a picture for $100,000, give it after a suitable pause for appreciation to a museum and deduct the entire appreciated value from his income tax: while still enjoying full possession of the painting during his lifetime. Today he must hand it over to the museum within four years: but the provision, again eminently laudable in intent, still has the prime effect of allowing the wealthy to hang on to more of their income than the taxman has a right to expect.

The latter's job is like that of Hercules in the Augean stables. The politicians are always creating new ways of keeping fortunes intact – or refusing to repeal old ones. In the USA, half of any estate going to the wife is non-taxable. In Britain, matters can be arranged to pass on the entire family insurance proceeds to the wife at a privileged rate. The results are plain to see: in the USA in 1958, when estates were supposed to carry duty ranging from 69% to 77%, those of $20 million or above actually paid 15.7%. Incomes over a million, by the same token, paid 38% instead of a nominal 87% in tax.

In Britain, estate duty has been called an "optional tax": and those who fail to take advantage of such options are often robbed by their own blindness. One was the first Henry Ford. According to an almost certainly accurate estimate, the crisis forced on Ford by his failure to make suitable provision decimated the family fortune; in the emergency, the old man had to give away to his hastily erected foundation the bulk of his interests.

Far lesser men devote far greater time and ingenuity to the blessed trinity of tax avoidance; to first, achieving the exemption of income from tax, second, obtaining the conversion of taxable income into capital, and third, accomplishing the preservation of capital for inheritance. One honest scion of a noble house, asked what he proposed to do with himself, now he had come into his fortune, remarked frankly, "defend it against the Inland Revenue."

The defenders come both low and high. Katharine Winsor, author of *Forever Amber*, had her income from that work adjudged a capital gain, thus paying a maximum tax of only 25%. At the other end of the scale, literary and otherwise, Winston Churchill's proceeds from his war memoirs are supposed to have been treated as a sale of his archives (a capital gain, then tax-free), not as income from writing a book. Since the great old man got $750,000 from *Life* for the serial rights alone, the scope for savings must have been immense.

The sudden enthusiasm of film stars for forming their own production companies, or taking their fees in cuts from the world-wide take, arose because income derived in this way can

261

be treated as corporate rather than individual. Lucille Ball and Desi Arnaz, by forming Desilu, or Frank Sinatra with Reprise Records, exchange potentially highly taxable income for lower-taxed money: said funds can be retained and invested in a corporation which then becomes a highly saleable capital asset.

In fact, the main wonder, given that so many wonders can be worked by tax advisers, is that anybody should opt for less favoured treatment. But it does happen. Edward Boughton was one of an elderly trio whose Automotive Products, with its chairmanship rotated amongst the three annually (until one died), made three vast fortunes out of Lockheed brakes, Borg and Beck clutches, *et al*. On his death in 1973, Boughton left £2.8 million. Of that nearly £2 million went, voluntarily, to the Exchequer, because the ninety-one-year-old Boughton had not availed himself of "ways and means available to reduce death duty", believing that the tax bite was "just and equitable". If Boughton is right, then the rain of tax-avoidance riches has been falling heavily on the unjust and the unfair.

On the Yields of Achievement

or

If at First You Do Succeed, Try, Try Again

SCENE 1

THE INCOME OF INVENTION

or

The Better Mousetrap Gambit

On the failure of foolish inventors to realize the financial rewards of their invention: and on the success of shrewder men in preserving the fruits of their own inventive genius, or (better still) the fruits stolen from somebody else's tree.

Invention is as famous and heavily trampled a road to fortune as prospecting – but rockier by far even than the deserts of Colorado, more hazardous and less hospitable even than the North Slope of Alaska. Great manufacturing companies are built on technological advance. It may be scientifically sensational, like the germanium dioxide semi-conductor, a mystery to all but the electronic elect; or humdrum, like the moving fly-button, alias the zip-fastener.

The idea may be revolutionary, like the internal combustion engine in its day, or the notion may have been kicking around for years, like television. Whatever the circumstances, if the gimmick meets a real demand, works without need for constant ministration by white-coated specialists, and can be sold at a profitable price, money is there for the making – and the more astounding the innovation, and the greater the technical discontinuity with the past, the richer the prize available to the technological prospector.

Alas, he rarely collects it. Many a brilliant, ineffably creative inventor has seen other men garner his harvest – while he gets a grain or two as total recompense. The case of polyester fibre, an innovation which is literally one of the world record money-spinners, is guaranteed to bring tears to an adamantine eye.

Manufacturers of Terylene and Dacron (the former ICI and

Du Pont near-monopoly), Trevira (Hoechst) and the rest have spun mounting millions of pounds of the stuff in the last decade, which even at the occasional depressed prices, came to a world-wide total of Midas proportions. The two intellects which created this cornucopia, you might think, must have been laden with honours and wealth: you would be wrong.

Their names were J. R. Whinfield and Dr. J. Dickson, and they worked for a company, the Calico Printers Association, which bowed to nobody in its knowledge of printing calico, but was in no fit state to handle the Whinfield-Dickson discovery, made in its labs. In 1947 the bonanza was sold to ICI in return for royalties which kept CPA shareholders in happy ease for many years.

Whinfield went over to ICI with his discovery (which caused its purchasers no end of problems in its early days – the first all-terylene trousers practically stood up by themselves). His booty from one of the century's premier achievements was £600 a year. Dickson wasn't even on the ICI bandwagon – he went to work for a company manufacturing linoleum, a product which the Victorians knew well. While no mean invention in its day, lino was a long journey away from the product of the finest modern polymer chemistry.

The inventor of the jet engine fared well, relatively speaking, but in absolute terms his money fate was much the same: others made millions out of his discovery. He depended, for his main reward, on a government hand-out. Sir Frank Whittle's principal misfortune, perhaps, was that his jet made its slow progress towards realization under the war clouds of the late 1930s. This inevitably made the government intensely interested in his little private company, Power Jets which had originally been financed by City investment bankers.

In the end the Government purchased the entire kit. A few weeks before the historic moment in 1941, when the Gloster Whittle E28 made an unintentional two hundred yard flight during the taxying trials, the total government investment was put at £96,000. Whittle was given £4,000 more than that – or £100,000 tax-free – in 1948: a sum which sinks to its proper proportions before the knowledge that, three years later, the US government alone paid $4 million for the use of the patents.

History is littered with men who similarly made the breakthroughs for others to exploit. The liability of the innocents in these cases is their very innocence. Like the stock character of the absent-minded boffin-brained professor, they truly are an unworldly bunch. Build a better mousetrap, they fondly believe, and the world will beat so many paths to your door that the problem is merely which road to choose.

In fact, when the improved, Mark II, all-electronic mousetrap does appear, the world says it will never work; if you prove that it does, the world (or rather the worldly) will try to steal the drawings. The scepticism and the thievery are in a sense both justified: every year hundreds of thousands of patent applications are made, many by private individuals whose ingenuity is matched only by their incompetence. Of the small minority which does have a worthwhile wonder on its hands, an even tinier minority has digits adroit enough to exploit the opportunity which they have created. If some more capable, cunning fellow doesn't lift the invention from its parent, the chances are that its birth will be still.

The most likely scoffers are, as you have gathered, the giant corporations: partly because it goes against the corporate grain to accept any idea from outside, except on their own initiative: secondly, because the acceptance of the new, the untried, the unknown, must involve the corporation or somebody within it, in time, trouble and expense. It's the unknown, more than any other psychological deterrent, which is most off-putting.

Thus Eastman Kodak listened to the two concert pianists who dreamed up Kodachrome in the bath, because film was its business. It rejected xerography because Chester B. Carlsson's invention had its potential and technology in areas where Kodak didn't, at that time, feel that it belonged.

Kodak's loss was the Haloid Corporation's infinite gain. The executives of that obscure New Jersey operation waxed adequately rich even by the standards of the George Eastman family, and Carlsson, while lagging behind, was financially among the inventing élite: his royalties themselves created a substantial fortune.

That pile, however, was negligible beside that of Charles F. Kettering, inventor of the self-starter and other handy gadgets, who, on his death, left at least $200 million, the proceeds of his long and lucrative association with General Motors and automotive technology. The closer the inventor nestles to business itself, the better-heeled he must become — even if invention itself is his business.

That is the lucrative occupation of a Dane, Karl Kroyer, who is the proud author of such benefactions to humanity as the non-stick frying pan; he also thought up an *ersatz* hosiery elastic during the war, worked out that expanded polystyrene granules could be used to salvage ships, and devised a detector for deathwatch beetles. All this inventive activity is masterminded and promoted through a series of companies: a man with a commercially viable mind should have higher hopes of developing a commercially viable product.

Unfortunately, from the pecuniary angle, the inventor is more often preoccupied with the problem for its own sake. Without that preoccupation, he would never have possessed either the stamina or the concentration to solve his conundrum. When Dr. Jonas Salk was working towards the discovery of polio vaccine, or Dr. Selman Waksman towards streptomycin, their thoughts may conceivably have drifted towards the fortunes which attend all pharmacological breakthroughs: but the imagination finds this notion as hard to encompass as the idea that pharmaceutical companies are the devoted benefactors of mankind that they purport to be.

The profits from genuinely new drugs are probably larger than from any enterprise except a successful bank robbery. According to the industry's standard defence, astronomical profits are required to finance research into the new drugs from which greater medical progress will result. But that progress, as the apologists fail to mention, inevitably goes along with still more nourishing profits.

Some idea of this nutritious take emerged in 1973, when the British Government decided that the world's biggest drug company had been overcharging it by unholy percentages for two tranquillisers, Librium and Valium, both of which are valuable in treating various psychological disorders. The British offshoot of Hoffman La Roche, a Swiss company so secretive that even elementary financial figures have to be prised loose by detective work, was charged by its parent $925 a kilo for Librium supplies and $2,300 for Valium that can't have cost the parent company more than $22.50 and $50 respectively (the prices at which Italian pirates, who make fat livings out of Italy's lack of patent protection for drugs, were willing to supply the same compounds).

In seven years in Britain, according to the investigators, Roche pulled in $55 million, most of it siphoned back to the Swiss parent in the transfer price. Small wonder that Roche was among the pet investments of millionaires. At a mid-1973 cost of 140,000 Swiss francs each, a dozen cost a quarter-of-a-million pounds: the stock has become so heavy that trading has long been conducted in "mini-Roches", worth a tenth of a share apiece.

What the millionaires were buying, in addition to a share whose price kept it beyond the reach of *hoi polloi*, and whose limited supply kept the price perpetually aloft, was an entrance ticket to the inventor's perfect product situation. The sick man is in no position to haggle over price. He isn't the direct customer, anyway: that role is filled by the doctor, who doesn't have to pay a penny. The situation, provided that government can be kept out of the act, is perfect: urgency of demand, total elasticity of price, and floor-level costs of production.

Most inventors design their wonders with no thought for the market's demands, ignore the fundamental importance of price and don't understand that, since profit is the sum of price less cost, if the relationship between the two gets out of hand, their work will go for nothing. The perversion of that essential basic marriage tends to begin at the beginning, with the cost of development.

Anybody who has financed any noble try in research and development sooner or later stumbles over the fact that inventors always grossly underestimate the cost of getting even to a working prototype. Even then, the final 20% of progress towards the crock of gold at the end of the technological rainbow seems to cost as much as the first four-fifths put together – plainly, the process is governed by some inexorable geometric law.

Nobody has ever come up with a sane solution to the problem. Sanity is probably ruled out by the tendency of inventors to come up with something for which they weren't looking at all. This was true of the best businessman who ever made an invention: or, for that matter, the best inventor who ever went into business – Dr. Edwin Land. His original preoccupation with the polarizing of light was founded, wrongly, on the notion that he would create a break-through in car headlights, not with sun goggles.

But the launch of Land's non-glare glasses in 1937 set Land up in a business that, thirty-five years later, was still selling twenty-five million pairs of lenses a year. This supported him through lean times and fat – the leanest coming after the war, when the loss of military business plunged Polaroid into a $2 million loss. In addition to the indispensable tools of a good basic business and luck, however, Land was saved by his high degree of the inventor's highest uncommon denominator: single-minded persistence.

His original experiments took nine years to pay off. The first instant camera, appearing in 1948, had been in the works for five years. Its apotheosis, the SX70, was seven years in the making. As time-scales go, these were probably unusually short. The inventor has to prepare for a long investment of time, which is money: and of money, which is time – the more you have to invest, the quicker the heavy returns must come to produce the desired payback.

In obeying the demands of this iron law, Land by accident or design helped himself mightily by aiming at the top volume end of mass markets. Just as Polaroid sunglasses are extremely expensive but still sell in millions, so the first Polaroid camera was no toy for the poor at a price of $89.75 (nor was it a plaything for the weak – it weighed in at nearly four pounds).

Another law rules with its rod of iron: prices of innovations always fall after the innovatory honeymoon. To Land's eternal credit (and fortune) he recognized the virtue of this necessity. That virtue lies in the constant widening of the market as prices decline: he simultaneously improved the product, with five major developments between 1960 and 1971, so that it kept the up-market cream while it widened into Kodak's mass-market preserves. Even this process, culminating in the $250 million SX70 development, didn't mark the end of Land's business ingenuity – indeed, that quarter of a billion appeared to be a far from inspired investment on its own.

But every buyer of a Polaroid camera is a captive customer for Polaroid film, without which he cannot use his captivating purchase: and buyers of consumable accessories are notoriously indifferent to price. By an interesting coincidence, the culmination of work on the SX70 was accompanied by a Polaroid decision to make its own films, instead of buying from Kodak. Looking for ways to build new and recurring turnover and profits on the initial sales is a neglected avenue to

270

making money: the great prize-winners of invention all have this characteristic – like the usage charges on Xerox machines. The ultimate lesson of Land is that the two approaches – the financial and the technological – are equally important: and that lesser inventors fail because they are one-dimensional.

Land's dual approach extended its bliss to the stock market. At the peak of the excitement over the SX70, the shares were valued at over a hundred times earnings, making the Land family worth some $700 million. The valuation meant, incidentally, that if Polaroid doubled its earnings every three and a half years, the company's earnings were being purchased well into the twenty-first century. Such are the wonders of technological sex appeal (they seldom last: within one more year of the twentieth century, the Land fortune was down to $350 million and still dropping as the SX70 fell behind schedules and into problems).

Not that high, or even new technology is needed to achieve financial appeal. The $150 million fortune which Ewing Kauffman, owner of the Kansas City Royals baseball team, boasted in 1972 was started in 1950 with $5,500 and a pharmaceutical product, Os-Cal, confected from crushed oyster shells. His fortune was made by another wonder of medical science, Pavalid, an opium derivative for dilating blood vessels which had been known since 1848. The proceeds from selling these preparations enabled two of Kauffman's executives and one salesman to retire with a million in their money boxes.

In Britain an immigrant of Greek extraction, Demetrius Comino, scored his millions with a construction device called slotted angle, which worked on exactly the same principle used in the child's building kit known as Meccano. Robert H. Abplanalp, whose wholly private means are estimated at $100 million, made a basic improvement in a common-or-garden product, the aerosol spray-can valve, which cut down its propensity to leak. That one stroke enabled Abplanalp to grab a patent, 60% of the world market, and some notoriety as the financier of San Clemente.

Some better mousetrap makers command neither glamour, headlines nor much notice even in the industry where they earn their bread, butter and cream. The car is the dominant, if not over-dominant product of twentieth-century civilization. Yet it has seen relatively few revolutionary inventions since

Model T days: possibly the can-opener has changed more. Yet those innovations which have penetrated the industry's iron curtain have mostly made it big – from Kettering's self-starter to Dr. Felix Wankel's rotary engine, the rights to which cost General Motors every bit of $50 million. Still the name Hub van Doorne, which sounds like something from a German fairy tale, probably means very little to car *aficionados*, even in Detroit. Yet van Doorne's mousetrap produced £124 million of sales in 1971, three-quarters of which belonged entirely to the inventor's family.

Like all great inventors, van Doorne did not rest his laurels on one trap. Apart from restlessly fiddling with the entire apparatus, a new cheese-holder here, an improved spring here, the true inventor tends to germinate a new idea from the solution of an old one. Just as Land moved from lenses to cameras, so van Doorne progressed from the container transporter in 1936 to the infinitely variable V-belt transmission for cars.

This gadget, operating on a principle completely different from the torque converters used in conventional automatics, made the impossible a reality – launching a range of small cars in the Netherlands, one of the industrialized world's midget markets, and keeping the company viable at an output rate (a hundred thousand cars a year) which any self-respecting maker would spurn contemptuously in this price-bracket. Van Doorne's transmission had its birth-pangs before and after birth – the rubber belts of those early days tended to snap at uncomfortable moments. But his funny little Daf cars had a cheaper, lighter and smoother transmission than the combined motor industries of the USA and Europe could produce.

On that unique selling proposition the most anomalous and eccentric auto company in the west pursued its singular course – even after Hub and his brother Wim, sons of a Limburger village blacksmith, neither with more than five years of elementary education, had handed over to the next generation. But the technical hopes – in particular that of extending Hub's Variomatic idea to heavier cars – at handover time rested heavily on Hub, beavering away in a shed at the bottom of his garden.

For the Daf successors' sake, it was vital for him to find something nice in the woodshed, for genius has one dangerous defect: it is irreplaceable. After all the Edwin Land moves have been analyzed, the moral, depressing for the uninspired, is that none of them, however well-conceived managerially, could have succeeded without his peculiar inventive power — a force that more or less overcame prodigies of unco-ordinated mismanagement as the programme for developing the SX70 lurched about.

Genius is seldom required to see whether a market exists for an unknown but wholly innovatory product. But you do require perverse genius of a different sort to say (as various worthies did) that the automobile, the electric train, and the instant camera would never sell. Again, those with a vested interest in the technological establishment naturally reject a challenge to their sacred and financially consecrated way of life, like the British motorcycle firms who refused to believe that bike engines could rev at the breathtaking speeds which Soichiro Honda developed.

But challenge to established ideas need not mean the pursuit of far-out technology: that chase offends against the well-known rule that the further out you go, the longer it takes to get home. For instance, Honda's "compound vortex controlled combustion" engines for cars sound hideously complex. They are actually much closer to existing engine technology than the contemporary expensive developments for controlling noxious emissions with catalysts, batteries, and so on. Practicality is the trademark of effective inventors. Honda's engine, apparently a demon foe to carbon monoxide, unburned hydrocarbons, oxides and nitrogens, is what the fans would expect from this deskless, workshop-happy multi-millionaire. No good engineer likes to waste precious time on chasing an impossible dream.

Honda, like Land or van Doorne, served a long apprenticeship before becoming a master. That, too, is characteristic of inventors. Their tenacity is bred by their experience, and in a world peopled with far richer prowlers, they need to be as tenacious in business as they are at the bench. Witness the doggedness of Harry Ferguson, who let Henry Ford use his revolutionary tractor principle (the engine drove both tractor and tools) on the strength of a handshake. When Ford abused that handshake, Ferguson filed the heaviest breach of patent suit in history and stuck with it until he won (he collected 9\frac{1}{4}$ million).

This eccentric genius from County Down proved equally

hard to pin down when his Canadian partners decided to buy him out. A powerful delegon Canada found Ferguson willing to talk anything but business — then its leader overheard his host telling the butler that the Canadians could be kept cooling their heels. The Canadian threatened to return home at once unless Ferguson signed; which he did. One queer feature of the case is that Ferguson was not profoundly interested in money: he once lost $1 million to his Canadian partners on the toss of a half-crown — they generously had the million-dollar coin mounted at Asprey's and gave it to Harry as a present.

As it happens, the most inventive artist of the century, Pablo Picasso, exhibited all the traits of the inventing breed: enormous powers of innovation, persistence, instinctive commercial shrewdness (no business manager could have manipulated the market in Picassos more adeptly), and a close-fisted tenacity which made him not just the richest artist in any medium in all history, but possessor of one of the greatest fortunes in Europe.

Would-be Picassos in business need that' self-s of eccentricity combined with deep understanding of the ordinary. Ultimately, the invention has to find its reward and justification in a market place formed by people in the mass; it must find its expression in a business apparatus manned and managed by people who have neither genius nor inspiration. The sad truth is that invention, like most of the admirable qualities in life, is not enough. Salesmanship is essential.

The inventor has to start by selling himself, continue by selling his invention, capitalize by selling the product of his inventiveness, cash in by selling the business which produces the product — and preserve his birthright at all times by refusing to be sold down, up or across the river. At various stages, he can get off the gravy train: but the earlier the exit, by and large, the smaller the spoonful of gravy. Those who want all the rich juices which invention can provide must, like Land and Kettering, stay on to the end of the line.

THE SECRET OF SALESMANSHIP

or

Can *He* Sell Salt?

Concerning the differences between selling something
which is actually better, something which differs not at
all from the competition, and something which is actually worse ... and revealing what the great salesman is
always best at selling – which is himself.

A regrettable necessity of commerce, regretted especially by its
more respectable exponents, is that it rests ultimately on the
disreputable process of selling. Even in the upper realms of
high technology or higher art, selling is the open sesame. The
foot must still get in the door; the pitch must still be delivered;
the sale must still be clinched.

The whole embarrassing process is as important to the
businessman or professional manager as to the door-to-door
huckster. But the god among businessmen pretends otherwise:
he calls selling "marketing", or "customer relations"; he
sometimes severs himself almost completely from the sales
operation, manned by a caste of company untouchables. Most
businesses prefer their customers to buy, thus apparently
removing the disagreeable imperative of selling. From this
weakness, rooted in the same psychological depths as fear of
money, the supreme salesman makes his mint.

An illustrative Jewish fable tells of the grocer whose store
and storerooms are heaped high with cartons of salt. "My
God," says his visitor, "you must sell a lot of salt." The grocer
shakes his head slowly. "I don't," he answers. "But the man
who sells me salt, can *he* sell salt." Salt-sellers rely on their
powers, techniques and tricks to persuade their marks to buy
goods which the marks may not really want or need.

The purchase may be perfectly good value, although the

champion salt-seller also aims to get the highest price which he traffic can bear, even if the customer can't. But the image of the forlorn housewife standing helplessly on her doorstep holding a set of brushes or encyclopaedias which she never intended to buy is what gives salesmanship its bad names — and they even come in Latin. It's the *emptor* who has to beware: nobody ever says *caveat vendor*. Nevertheless, selling is a two-sided relationship, and the bargain can easily work against a seller — as many who have tried selling a family heirloom to a dealer have found to their cost and the dealer's profit. As Marcus Samuel, the first Lord Bearsted, a sea-shell merchant who moved on to higher things and Shell Oil, once remarked succinctly, "the price of an article is exactly what it will fetch".

The greatest salesman on record was a dealer, Lord Duveen. To a substantial extent, he created his market, the transfer of European art treasures to American millionaires. To a substantially higher degree, he created that market's prices by paying exorbitant amounts so that he could charge still more extravagant sums. He stalked his prospects with a whole armoury of blandishments, from bribing their servants to simple acts of friendship, and devoted years to the pursuit of an indispensable target, notably Andrew Mellon, the supreme millionaire of his day.

So long as Duveen lived, he went to remarkable lengths to defend the market which made him rich. For instance, Alfred Erickson of the McCann Erickson advertising agency, bought Rembrandt's *Aristotle Regarding the Bust of Homer* from Duveen for $750,000. Hit by the Great Slump, Erickson sold it back for $500,000. Duveen then stored it for his customer until Erickson could afford to repurchase that noble work (the storage cost him $90,000, but was worth it, from his heirs' point of view: the picture fetched $2.3 million at auction in 1961, when it passed to the Metropolitan Museum).

Duveen made himself the social superior of his customers: spending and living like a prince, acquiring a title (by long, apparently disinterested courtship of Prime Minister Ramsay MacDonald), moving in exalted circles, deploying a considerable scholarship to which the clientele could never aspire. But the whole bravura performance was rooted in the Garden of Eden of all selling: faith. The great art dealer had surpassing faith in himself, bounteous belief in what he sold.

276

Insecurity is the enemy of selling, and insecurity is the normal condition of man. Cross that psychological barrier, and you are in the promised land. The difficulty of making the crossing, however, shouldn't be underestimated. Its hardness and stress explain why so many salesmen, at all levels of the art, hit the bottle with unending percussion. They don't drink to be sociable with their customers: they drink to obliterate the shock to the psyche of overcoming the instinctive urge to hide away in safety.

Selling is no simple activity. It has as many subcultures as the Polynesian islands, each with its own complications. Even the ostensibly simplest form — selling something which is actually better — is complex (and is relatively rare). This problem confronted Procter & Gamble in acute form with Crest, the first fluoride toothpaste. P & G's Cincinnati million-aires had developed to a super-fine art the second main division of the sell: flogging a product or service which differs not at all from the competitor's offering.

This is usually the case when the salesman claims that his goodie is superior; just as, if the fellow boasts that the thing is new, you can bet your trading stamps that it is merely an old offering mildly revamped. With such basic techniques did the boys from Cincinatti make P & G world-famous. Crest, discovered in a university, threw them into mental confusion. It truly was a more effective toothpaste — and P & G, having cried wolf in reverse so often, simply didn't know how to advertise the truth, the whole truth and nothing but the truth.

In the end, Cincinatti was taken off its painful hook by the American Dental Association, which made Crest the first toothpaste it had ever endorsed. Straight ads retailing this fact, with none of the huckster devices which P & G and its agencies had perfected, swiftly turned Crest into the best-selling brand in the USA. But selling the genuinely better product, in addition to such subtle problems, has the more obvious heartache of limited lifespan. Sooner or later, some-body is going to match the new marvel, and its superiority will be lost and gone for ever.

The Randolph family had for years been minding its own genteel business, manufacturing superb swords and good, if clumsy, razors. They then suddenly burst forth with a stainless steel blade that left all other forms of wet stubble remover far behind. As word of mouth spread like stubble, the Randolphs' only difficulty was to produce blades. After the company went public in 1964, the Randolphs' company was worth, at the peak, £28 million.

When the selling had to start, because a flabby, out-of-condition Gillette had finally caught up, Wilkinson Sword was no longer in the position of beatific superiority, even if the aura of advantage lingered on for quite a while. There is only one sure method of maintaining the position known as "company superior" – by eliminating the opposition entirely, by fair means and (inevitably) by very foul.

The father of modern selling, John H. Patterson of National Cash Register, was a devoted adherent of this faith. His techniques, illegal even in their day, included setting up dummy companies to corner the second-hand market and undermine his competitors. The henchman in charge of this department of dirty tricks, Thomas J. Watson Sr, at IBM later passed on to refine both Patterson's ways of objecting to competition and his more orthodox approach to organization of the sales force – including the heavy use of evangelistic commercial theology.

The difference between the sales evangelism of Patterson, Watson, W. Clement Stone (ace inspirer of insurance salesmen), or, for that matter, Billy Graham, is very little in principle. It uses the Group, the Cause, the Leader, the Message, the Slogan and the atmosphere to induce in the subject precisely the reaction which the psychological theory of salesmanship demands: faith, the suspension of insecurity, the elimination of disbelief in oneself, its replacement by belief in the company and the product.

Patterson and Watson worked their wonders in a field, office and shop machinery, where the salesman always makes the running. Most other selling armies, no matter how similar the generalship or inspirational technique, face the logistical difficulty that they cannot penetrate to the ultimate customer. They can use a multitude of methods to get goods on the shelf, but the goods won't move off the shelves unless the mass public buys; and that means advertising.

The distressing truth for ad-hating puritans to confront is that clever ads have translated several modest fortunes to imperial heights: for instance, the celebrated Doyle Dane Bernbach campaign for Levy's Jewish rye bread. These one-shot operations are freaks, however. The big money spent on ads can't be divorced from the intrinsic appeal of the product, the strength of the distribution set-up, the use of other promotion methods. Generally it's an illusion that you can start with nothing and turn yourself via a collection of TV spots into a mini-Rockefeller.

In fact, the more spectacular sellers from a zero base usually rest heavily on other techniques, even if they also use the media. The appeal of two much favoured methods, door-to-door selling and direct mail, lies in eliminating the infuriating gap between buyer and seller. If some worthy citizen will fill in a coupon cut from a publication, or return some junk mail dropped in his letterbox, you have a ready-made mark. The game even has the deceptive charm of being measurable. Replies to coupon ads can be tabulated: the conversion of replies into sales can likewise be measured: offers which fail these statistical tests can be dropped and others substituted.

Then, the tiny percentages required for a successful operation look deeply encouraging. Get 1.5% response to a properly designed mail shot, and you cover your costs. Get 2.5%, and you have a real business on your hands. Get 4%, and you can start counting the cash. Unfortunately, a selling method is no substitute for what is actually being sold. The frenzied efforts of US publishers to boost sales of magazines hit by television succeeded all too well. The circulation of *Life* shot up from six million to eight million, but since the sales were being serviced for substantially more money than the new, expensively purchased subscribers actually paid, the operation merely brought forward, instead of warding off, the evil day.

In Britain, which has fewer doorbells to ring than the USA, a series of door-to-door appliance millionaires have lost their millions through the same basic cause. The number of easy marks who will buy a vacuum cleaner or washing machine over the doorstep is always finite. To maintain sales, the promoter must move on to the harder prospects – and in his efforts to woo these, John Bloom, whose Rolls Razor crash was the most comprehensive of any post-war British growth stock, cleverly succeeded in giving away more in premium gifts, advertising and salesman's commission than he received from the marks.

One of Bloom's imitators, a trained economist trading higher up the market, used his professional knowledge and a computer to match advertising and sales, thus avoiding this particular trap. Alas, the system worked only with minor fluctuations in sales: the logic, if sales plunge, is to stop promoting altogether — in other words, to wind up the business. When the economist proved unable to accept this dictate, exactly the same sad fate as Bloom's overtook him.

The doorstep drawback reflects the fundamental fact that using individual salesmen on commission to sell individual items to individuals is inherently expensive and wasteful. The problem has only been overcome on a consistent long-term basis by the agency gambit and the catalogue caper (which can be combined for best effect). The agent can even be an amateur, like the 450,000 Avon ladies ("independent businesswomen", according to the company) who helped to make their employer the most profitable company in the whole USA. From 1961 to 1970 the eighty-seven-year-old Avon increased sales by 19% annually, earnings by 19% and dividends by 464%. By 1973 its stock was so avidly desired by the big institutional investors that, at $7,910 million, this cosmetic firm was worth more in the stock market than the entire US steel industry.

The psychology of women selling to women in the highly conditioned and conditioning atmosphere of the home is only part of the Avon deal. From a salesmanship angle, the advantage is the low cost of displaying a low-priced article before the dazzled customer — and safely removed from the odious business of price comparison in the shops. Avon and Tupperware, with its macabre twist of coffee parties to display the wares, are rare birds in the annals of modern selling. Their success isn't easy to emulate, and their version of the agency gambit is specialized in its application.

Door-to-door either needs cheap agents and little or no advertising costs, or indecently large profit margins — like those earned on life assurance or encyclopaedias. In contrast, straight mail order, which gets by beautifully on small margins and costly catalogues, has produced more than its fair share of millionaires outside the USA, where the colossal shadow of Sears Roebuck hangs over all. The business built by Julius Rosenwald now turns over more than $30 million every day: the kind of figure which many considerable and rich retail businesses would be glad to produce in a year.

The idea of mail order selling, not to far-flung farmers who couldn't get to town, but to ordinary town and suburban-dwellers who like shopping from a catalogue, with or without the help of Avon-style neighbours, has made many millions in Britain alone, for, among others the Wolfsons, the Ramptons, and the Fattorinis (two separate branches thereof). The high degree of family ownership implies (correctly) that mail order doesn't demand much capital, turns over stock rapidly, is highly controllable and doesn't let the proprietor in for nasty retail necessities like loss leaders, freehold sites and clearance sales.

The neatest variant on mail order is the trading stamp. This is simply catalogue selling to captive customers, whose money has first been converted into stamps which can only be cashed in for the stamp company's goods. Sperry & Hutchinson, the world's stamping giant, is the pride and joy of the Beinecke family, who must be contemplating with some gloom the dismal decadence of the trading stamp age in the USA. In Britain S & H barely got its pink stamps started, thanks to the combined attentions of Lord Sainsbury and Richard Granville Tompkins. The former, combining ownership of his family grocery chain with active Labour politics, organized a boycott of S & H's biggest outlet – the Fine Fare supermarket empire built up by Canadian Garfield Weston.

Weston's misfortune was that he also sold flour and bread to Sainsbury and his retail allies. After a spirited attempt to sell himself out of trouble by exhorting his salesmen to supreme endeavour, Weston surrendered – in what is possibly the last example of a full-bore restraint of trade that Anglo-American business will ever see. As for Tompkins and his Green Shield Company, he had a boycott-proof supermarket-eer, Jack Cohen of Tesco, taking his stamps – a business which was 100% in the hands of its proprietor.

In fourteen years Tompkins has built up a £42 million turnover and £4.5 million profit with no visible sign of either financial strain or undue effort. As for his insistence on keeping this handsome possession entirely within his own bosom, along with a nationwide discount chain and a public furniture business, that's one of the eccentricities to which self-made millionaires are prone – provided always that going public offers them nothing except an extra capital gain. If your post-tax income is high enough (Tompkins paid himself £289,834 in 1972, and collected an estimated £1.4 million in dividends, which is presumably the taxable tip of his particular iceberg), who needs more capital?

High-intensity sellers often fall into this colourful category – especially if they are in a position to conceal from everybody, including the tax-collector, just how much they are paid. Hence the self-evident, but secretive, profits of those in the ancient trade known as export-import. The little-known private fortunes often cluster round this admirable activity – not only the Bunge y Born commodity trading empire, but those of Anton Besse, who made enough out of import-export in Aden, the most God-forsaken spot in the British empire, to found his own post-graduate Atlantic College in Britain: or of Juan March, who made one of Europe's largest piles by bringing tobacco into Franco's Spain: or of a former egg-dealer's son, Count Volpi, whose father's tobacco beat was the trade between the Balkans and the Middle East.

The Count, Mussolini's "financial wizard", was crowned with enormous estates in Libya by his patron, and ended up with a hotel chain, a power company, shipping, resorts in Venice (of which he became uncrowned Doge) and a Palladian villa, equipped with priceless frescoes by Veronese, not far from Bassano. The export-importer buys in one place and ultimately sells in another, often far removed in time and space, and after a series of barters and other deals which totally obscure (except in his computer-like brain) precisely where the profit was made – and there usually is a profit.

Since the export-importer seeks to buy where his commodity is in surplus and sell where it is short, the profits may well be high beyond the dreams of usury. But so long as he stays in line with prices prevailing locally, nobody is likely to notice, still less care. It's the position into which every salesman hopes to manoeuvre – selling where supply is demanded but questions aren't asked. Obviously this happiness is hard to achieve in a less exotic trade than Balkan tobacco. But the transparently simple device of charging enormous, non-negotiable prices and making that fact part of your sales appeal can bring the pleasures of the export-import equation to the High or Main Street.

This particular pitch is the key to the rich speciality shop, the Tiffany or Cartier: the pitchman need only ensure that, like Duveen, he has the best that money can buy. Harry Winston evolved from son of a small New York jeweller to purveyor of million-dollar diamonds to the new aristocracy (the Burtons and such Texans as Mrs. Robert Windfohr) by this well-trodden route. At one point or another he owned the Hope, Jonker and Vargas diamonds; the latter was sold to Mrs. Windfohr, who couldn't even bend her finger with it on. "Harry says," she would remark, "it's the third greatest rock in the world."

The technique reached its most stupendous manifestation, feeding off the gargantuan appetites and incomes of its native state, in Neiman-Marcus, possibly the only general department store in the world which regularly stocks million-dollar bijoux. Long before it found fame by putting His and Her private aeróplanes in a Christmas catalogue, its ambition was only the praiseworthy idea of dressing a whole community beautifully. It was started in 1907 in a two-storey building by Mrs. Carrie Marcus Neiman, and her brother Herbert Marcus; by Christmas 1960 it could afford to lose $5 million, almost entirely in stock, in one fire.

In the process of providing beautiful dressing, the Neiman-Marcus duo discovered that people with an inexhaustible supply of money required an equally endless supply of goods on which to spend it. One vitally important corollary is that the more expensive the goods, the greater the amount of the money supply that can be absorbed. The second corollary is that the more guaranteed the intrinsic virtue of the expensive goods, the less their well-provided purchasers will care about the expense.

As Stanley Marcus once explained to an interviewer, in their start, "many of these millionaires never had the money to buy fine clothes . . . to provide comfortable, gracious decor. . . . But because there was a recognizable authority in the form of a store a hundred miles away, they were able to avoid many of the pitfalls of the rich." It's a selling pitch that never misses. In fact, nobody would regard the Marcus clan, or the lineal descendants of Mr. Fortnum and Mr. Mason, or their equally exclusive counterparts in France, Germany and Italy, as salesmen, as pitchmen; but that they plainly are.

The suave, forceful expertise of purveyors to the rich, however, has had far less effect on the reputation of selling than the slick, aggressive confidence tricks of another important group of salesmen – those who are actually selling an inferior article. Paradoxically, their task is relatively easy: if the sucker doesn't recognize the shoddiness of the goods, he'll fall for anything. By its nature, however, this nefarious branch of the trade is self-liquidating: the shoddy seller runs out of suckers, and must move on to a different pitch.

The inferior breed are unfortunately hard to distinguish from hard sellers in general (since the techniques of persuasion are identical) and from cheap sellers in particular, although the latter are not only respectable, but social benefactors. The sell-it-cheap merchants are the alternative method of cracking the monopoly of established retailers, who, if you give them an inch, will take a mile of profit margin.

The supermarket chains began as price-cutters; the discount stores turned cutting into a religion. Eugene M. Ferkauf, whose very name means "sell", deserves immortality for the concept which created E J Korvette and a personal fortune of $50 million for its boss by the age of forty-one. The idea of a department store without frills, from which the customers carted away their own purchases, made high-speed mileage until it fell foul of two predictable developments. On one hand, the frilly department stores began to compete in price in the area where the discount stores really hurt, on big-ticket appliances; on the other hand, the discounters began to get ideas above their station, and above their management ability.

Ferkauf's management consisted mostly of former high-school friends from Brooklyn, who practised techniques of a certain basic simplicity – like marking up all appliances at $10 over cost, irrespective of that cost. As Korvette spread, so did its administrative problems and costs; it became harder and harder to maintain the low prices.

Much the same thing happened, earlier and more disastrously, to Ferkauf's imitators. Before many of them realized what had happened, they were running full-scale department stores at sub-standard profit-margins. The subsequent spate of setbacks and crashes rubs in the same old lesson: a seller makes his living from the difference between his costs and his prices, and if the prices are low, the pressure on his economics must be high.

The only point at which this rule does not apply is in the type of selling into which, regardless of his basic activity, every salesman is forced. He must sell himself before he can sell his product. In a sense most super-sellers who float their companies do two distinct selling operations: the basic one which creates the business, and the ancillary self-selling, the one which off-loads the business, in part or in whole, on the public, and thus creates the capital wealth.

Nor need these operators be members of the Bernie Cornfeld breed. Wall Street's reputable salesman-practitioners of the hot shot era included none hotter than Gerald M. Tsai, the Chinese-American whose success with the Fidelity funds was a legend of the day. On the strength of name alone, Tsai pulled in $247 million of funds: the investing public was so heavily sold on him that it thereby made it impossible for him to produce the stock market performance which investors fondly imagined they were buying. Tsai's fund hardly performed at all – but still gave Tsai a million-dollar gross income from the very start. He finally sold out for $30 million in the days when mutual fund management companies were still allowed to cash in their chips for their own benefit. The good soft sell always has hard results.

SCENE 3

THE MERIT OF MANUFACTURE

or

Money in the Making

In which we analyse the formula which every great
manufacturer before and after Henry Ford has employed
... and on which the shattering rise of the Japanese since
the Second World War has been based ... to wit, vfm +
cn + dfm = m^2 (the m being short for the biggest money
of all).

Making things is difficult: making them well, that is. The pain
of turning inert materials into articles useful or beautiful or
both is so exquisite that down the centuries the master-
craftsman has always been able to name his own price. But the
Benvenuto Cellinis, the Thomas Sheratons, the Paul Lameries,
only made one artifact at a time. The task of achieving their
standards of excellence over and over again, with each product
identical to and as satisfactory as its twin, triplet, sextuplet and
million-uplet, is of an excrutiatingly hard order.

A mass culture demands mass products, and the great
manufacturing fortunes have gone, as they still go, to the
masters of mass producing not Cellini cups, Sheraton chairs or
Lamerie silverware, but products which, made in the millions,
satisfy the multitude. The greatest fortune ever assembled,
after all, was that of Henry Ford, a mint put together,
appropriately enough, from being the greatest assembler of all
time.

The Ford family, had it played its tax and management
cards right, would still own, directly and indirectly, every lock,
stock and barrel of the Ford Motor Company. Without
counting the immense millions piled up in income over the
years (at the top of the Model A's earning power, Henry
pocketed $13 million in one year and his son Edsel another $8

million) the Ford Motor Company fortune came to $11,634 million in assets and $5,961 million in stockholders' equity, all valued in the market at $8,017 million at the start of 1973.

That aggregation would have left even the Rockefellers in the shade (a rich enough shade, admittedly).

Ford emerged from the welter of competing car firms at the turn of the century, not merely because the Model T offered the best value for money, but because it was designed for mass manufacture by Ford's own mass method. Every manufacturing millionaire has exploited the same basic formula: $vfm + cn + dfm = m^2$, where vfm equals value for money, cn equals consumer need, dfm equals designed for manufacture and m, of course, stands for the inevitable financial reward, even in an industry where, as in cars, the competition is intense and potent.

The product can be widely manufactured by firms in every industrialized state – and still millions are there to be made, simply by making it better. Take the record changer. In Britain workers are supposedly so idle that no local manufacturer can possibly compete with the Germans, the Japanese and the Americans. The record changer, moreover, is an integral part of the post-war boom in recorded music and electronics, in which the above three nationalities have been notably active. Yet the world's largest maker of changers is British.

The company, BSR, was started from scratch by an inventive Scots medico called Dr Daniel McDonald, who founded the business on a design that was simpler and cheaper to make than any of his diabolically clever and hard-working competitors could contrive. Bored with his success, McDonald retired to Switzerland with a cash fortune; getting even more bored with retirement, he started all over again, opposite his old works, with a vacuum cleaner, attacking a market which Hoover has dominated, with apparently efficient production and design, for decades.

The gambit of making cheaper to sell more cheaply, is by no means the only approach: there is also making things more expensively to sell at a higher price. Thus Johnson Wax once proposed to bring out a car polish for sixty-nine cents. It was persuaded by the ad agency that the price was simply too low for so passionately protective an activity as polishing the beloved car. So the company added some expensive ingredients and marketed the wax, with much heavier advertising, at $1.47. The cynics might wonder why the Johnson boys bothered to alter anything about the mix except its price: but there is a curious morality in your true manufacturer. It was after all Henry Ford who promised his customers a cash rebate if sales climbed above three hundred thousand: that cost the old boy $13 million.

The Peugeot business in France, possibly even to the surprise of the Peugeots themselves, became the most profitable car maker in Europe in the early 1970s (not, by the way, a great distinction in those hard times) by the paradoxical device of extravagance. They would spend far more on a component than their US rivals. A Detroit mogul found it all too much to take. "How can you waste money like that?" he demanded after watching Peugeot's pains. "In Detroit we run them all straight through and scrap the defective ones at the end."

Good quality is the most moral gimmick in the world: it accounted for the prime position of Zenith, brain-child of another, differently spelt Macdonald, in a US TV market in which every major electrical company, most backed by far greater resources, was throwing its weight about. The bigger firms suffered from the attendant illness of their healthy bank balances. The latter reflected the edifying cash flow that springs from a multiplicity of businesses: quality, as we have seen, tends to be found in the concentration camps of commerce, where one product or group of products receives the undying attention of every manager.

Those who want to play the quality gambit are ill-advised to toy with diversification. It diverts not only management's attention, but that of the buying public. The customer may accept that the most acoustically refined hi-fi comes from the same stable as the most chromatic colour TV. But you will confuse the poor fellow if you offer him the best jet-engine, toaster and nuclear power station to boot.

Every market usually contains a premium product, commanding a rich extra price, manufactured to better specifications and with more consistent performance than any other: and made by, in most cases, a smaller specialist competing with the gross generalists. It is unfair competition. In theory, the generals, with the big battalions behind them, should win. In practice, the specialist is protected by his special weapon: in an industry where percentage margins or mark-ups are by and large the same, the higher price must yield the higher profit per sale. This law applies not only to the manufacturer (which makes him rich), but to the retailer (who therefore pushes that product to the fore, which makes the manufacturer richer still).

At the retail level, Rolls-Royce has to sell two thousand cars to match the turnover earned on twenty thousand Volkswagen Beetles. Admittedly, there won't be many more than two thousand in any given year who can afford £12,500 for a Rolls: but the Beetle has to go far beyond twenty thousand before it can start to pull ahead: the factory break-even point is numbered in the hundreds of thousands. The enormous weight of capital investment behind a cheap mass-produced item, as VW found to its *angst* when the Beetle got slightly squashed by more up-to-date competition, rapidly turns profit to loss.

The specialist can cover his fixed costs by lower through-put at the price of a higher labour content. It's a far more flexible arrangement, and the equation explains why, in a car industry dominated by dinosaurs, new entrants have continually defied the laws of economics of scale. Contestants as far apart in range as BMW and Lotus have made rapid millions by aiming at a specialized sector in an individualistic way, buying themselves into a high-stake game with cut-price counters.

Colin Chapman, the Lotus leader, even survived a crisis that would have crucified any volume manufacturer: the company went on cheerfully producing cars which nobody had ordered. Chapman pulled out of that spin, and in 1972 made a profit of £1.1 million (taking the market value of the company to £6.9 million), in a year when the Vauxhall subsidiary of General Motors contrived to lose some £4 million.

The specialist has to pick his market sector accurately. He will misfire if the product flops in service – but most specialists (like Chapman or Enzo Ferrari) are more conspicuously fond of their machines than their markets. This old-fangled product orientation is despised by the big corporations, and it's their contempt which makes them unable to compete against the inspired fuddy-duddy. The image of the founder-millionaire wearing overalls, tinkering with some mechanical marvel in work-shop or lab is often reality – that's where Soichiro Honda made his multi-millions, where Ken Olsen of Digital Equipment is happiest.

A born manufacturer loves to have his office at the plant:

it's the professional managers who fly to the skyscraper eyries of the big city where, safe in their nests, they can forget about nuts and bolts. But the plant orientation can work economic miracles fully as startling as those created by the passion for production. Love that plant, and it will grow.

Sir Jules Thorn, though nobody's ideal of the delegating pro of scientific management, exemplified the simple rules. Rule one, the vital factor is cost: if a change will bring down the cost of production, change. Rule two, cost is a function of modernity: if a new machine will improve efficiency and lower cost, buy it. One of Thorn's associates, recalling the early days, said that Sir Jules "did certain things that absolutely shocked me." He bought the key machine on the fluorescent lighting side "before we had the volume to support it."

That leads on to rule three: unless you can get a suitable build-up of sales, expenditure on the latest million-dollar wonder-gadget is the way to bankruptcy. That rule in turn leads to the Vertical Gambit. A big enough market at the far end of the line opens up subsidiary markets all the way back to the raw embryo. This perspective is all the more beguiling to the truly acquisitive tycoon, because going vertical promises to transfer to him all the annoying profits made by his suppliers — profits which he tends to resent.

The true productioneer never believes that anybody else can manufacture a component more cheaply than he can himself. If he doesn't like a supplier's quality or price, he simply makes his own. If the end-market isn't enormous enough to support his ambitions, he buys somebody else's end-market share. Big corporations try the same popular trick: but lacking the entrepreneur's exclusive interest in ultimate profit, they mess up the formula. They are decentralized into product groups and divisions, each with its own target for profit, and each expected to charge prices, even to other divisions in the same group, that will hit the profit bulls-eye on the nose.

At each level of the corporate chain of a production a profit gets taken, which in turn is compounded into the price and profit of the next link of the chain: until at the end of the line, when the product actually escapes into the hands of the customer, the final price carries an accumulated final margin. That compounding chain produces a final price which a truly integrated entrepreneur can knock to hell.

This helps to explain how a textile maverick like Kaye

Metrebian could produce an uncomplicated product like a nylon sheet for 99p when the nearest competition was £1.65. As one of Metrebian's sidekicks remarked of his rivals, "It may be one company, but the yarn is spun in Leigh, woven in Wigan and finished in Glossop. Here, bales come in at one end, and the finished sheets go out at the other".

The aim (as Thorn's Thorn and BSR's McDonald knew well) is to make gadgets more cheaply, so as to lower the price and/or raise the profits on the gadgets into which the gadgets disappear. The true return, the real money, lies in the saving over the lowest available bought-in cost; it's the achieving of lower cost by sub-manufacture, not the notional profit on selling the sub-manufactured part to their own companies, from which the vertical fortunes are made.

Verticalism, moreover, is never found alone. There are always other approaches to the production or marketing mix, unaccountably overlooked by the established entities in the game, even if they have been established since the days of Noah. This dating is roughly true of the furniture industry. Its methods have advanced further since Biblical times than, say, printing has since the age of Caxton. But most furniture makers have not considered their game susceptible to the efficient joys of mass production.

It took an immigrant to prove to the British that the impossible was feasible: an outsider is often needed to cut through tradition. The British furniture industry was changed by a Polish-born shoemaker's son, Chaim Schreiber, who came to England in 1939 and, like many other Jewish émigrés, gravitated to cabinet-making in the East End. By 1969 Schreiber had a well dovetailed turnover of £8 million a year. But his big push, the equivalent of the Ardennes breakthrough, came by abandoning older methods of joining pieces of wood in favour of modern adhesives.

Within four years sales were up to £22 million, as Schreiber exploited his production flow to give rapid delivery. He thus pressed the same button as the Levitz furniture supermarkets in the USA. Precisely what fortunes the Levitz brothers developed from this simple law, not by making, but by marketing furniture straight from stock, has at times been hard even for a number-crushing computer to figure out. The shares in 1972, for example, bounced about like the magic flying rubber dreamed up in the Disney studios. Sales in 1972–73, however, rose by 71% to $326.3 million – which in an industry like furniture, even allowing for the Levitz fraternity's creative ideas about accountancy, demonstrates the force of Schreiber's Law: for the latter, a one-time architecture student, the law meant, at the crest of his wave, a family fortune of around £20 million.

Simple attention to making things, as opposed to marketing them, or flooding the stock market with paper, has distinguished the two most durable economic miracles of the post-war world – those of West Germany and Japan. Millions of customers bought the Beetle (the single most important ingredient of Germany's great recovery, and Adolf Hitler's only lasting claim to fame) not because it was cheaper, smarter, more economical or more comfortable than the opposition (it was none of these things), but because it didn't, unlike competitive cars, fall apart in the driver's hands (even if, in Ralph Nader's hands, it tended to roll over).

The Japanese, possibly because they started by imitating other people's products, founded what are probably the most staggering post-war fortunes by finding better ways to make and design the identical products. They achieved impossible feats, such as making better Leicas than Leitz, before proceeding to advances in design that left Leitz behind. In the dawn of a new genuinely Japanese technology, the insistence on quality and efficient manufacture remained in the risen sun.

The results for such as Konosuke Matsushita have been dazzling to behold – on a par with the creations of wealth in the second American Industrial Revolution, after what Aldous Huxley called the Year of Our Ford. In chalking up his series of world record incomes, Matsushita ran far ahead not only of US salaries, but also of the nearest Japanese; for instance, in 1962, when Matsushita earned £440,000, the runner-up was a £246,000 a year gentleman whose job, obviously a nice number, was baldly described by the taxman as "son of the president of the Kondo Textile Company".

Small wonder that Matsushita is author of a work entitled *The Words of Peace and Happiness Through Prosperity*. His own prosperity stemmed from apprenticeship to a maker of charcoal braziers, which led via meter reading for the Osaka electrical system to starting his own electrical firm in 1917. He made electric lamp sockets in the proverbial one room on two hundred yen of capital.

In 1971 Matsushita controlled the twenty-fourth largest firm outside the USA, with assets of over $2,500 million and sported (which is almost unheard of in Japan) both high profits and a decently sized shareholders' equity. Most Japanese companies are in hock to their eyebrows and only minimally in profit. Matsushita sat in 1971 on over $1,000 million of stockholders' equity and by far the most exalted profits in Japan, at $165.7 million. His personal 5% stake in this combine is one of the east's largest fortunes, a long, long way from two hundred yen.

The company song ends with the stirring anthem "Grow industry, grow, grow, grow! Harmony and sincerity! Matsushita Electric!" This enthusiasm is reflected in the less lyrical fact that one division alone recently had 553 quality control teams, holding, what's more, "many voluntary study sessions". Matsushita, for all his moral fervour, is perhaps the easiest Japanese entrepreneur for a westerner to understand: he even adopted, down to the last form, the Philips' control system, but made it far more effective by applying rigid personal supervision. According to one story, each division had to telephone its results in *every day*, so that Matsushita had them on his desk next morning.

The title of "the oriental Henry Ford I" belongs not to Matsushita but to a blacksmith's son, Soichiro Honda, a man who baffles even Japanese business journalists. "Mr Honda," said one, "is a management executive who always wears red shirts and tells naughty stories when drinking." Honda learnt the importance of efficient production quality when, out of fifty piston rings tested from a batch of thirty thousand, only three passed. That was his first manufacturing venture, which understandably led nowhere.

In 1947 he started to make motorized bicycles, with two-stroke engines adapted to run on pine-root extract. Five years later, however, Honda came of technological age. With the Japanese market in recession, Honda spent £300,000 on German, Swiss and American tools, for the sound reason that they were the best in the world. He then began to take apart the European bikes he was copying – and discovered that their best was not good enough.

European manufacturers believed it was impossible to run motorcycle engines at fifteen thousand rpm, with even faster bursts. Honda not only proved that you could, but started to win Grand Prix races all over the world. Once again, the super-design went with super-efficiency in production engineering. At Honda's motorcycle plants not a single storeroom existed for parts, raw materials or finished machines: deliveries went in at one end, up to one every seven seconds, finished bikes moved straight on to the double-decker trucks at the other.

Building up a billion-dollar company on the pillion of the motorbike is not only a prime economic achievement. It's one that, before Honda demonstrated the technique, would have been disbelieved – especially by the established British companies, bearing once-proud names like Norton, Matchless and BSA. In the Honda era, their decline and fall ended in pathos, with the workers at the once-famous Triumph factory defying the management's efforts to close the works down for ever.

But millions from manufacture, more than most other seven-figure breeds, are closely linked with personalities. It's the aura, drive and design passion of the resident Our Ford which provides the impetus and maintains the edge. Remove that presence, replace it with mere mortal men, and the manufacturing operation runs the risk of losing its inspiration and becoming merely routine. That's when, if the product has been selling on a quality reputation, the public begins to notice that the quality differential no longer exists: and when, if the product has been living off inspired design, the competition begins to overtake in the fast lane.

This process overtook the Beetle – the recalls of bugged VW bugs in the USA marked the end of an era dominated by the personality of the late Heinz Nordhoff. Brilliant manufacture is a highly creative activity: and those who don't make millions at it (or throw them away) fail because they approach this act of creation with all the imaginative flair of a cop testing doorknobs.

SCENE 4

THE FLIGHTS OF FASHION

or

A Taste of Money

> What makes Run Run Shaw run is the same game that
> Hugh Hefner plays ... the exploitation of changing
> popular tastes, in which the tastes and the change are
> always so obvious that the entrepreneur needs only one
> prime attribute to succeed ... possession of the same
> taste.

The mighty corporations devote as much time to future tastes
as to the expensive search for technological novelty. Their
success ratio is equally miserable. A survey in the British
grocery market showed that, out of 3,087 new products
introduced in 1959–66, 63% had disappeared without trace by
1970 – and of the surviving 37%, many must have earned
exiguous profits.

This insensitivity to trends in taste is what distinguishes the
common-or-garden manager from the inspired entrepreneur,
and the mature corporation from its origins. All consumer
goods companies spring from fertile anticipation or understanding of customer desire. Back in time there truly was a Dr
Clarence Birdseye, whose deep-freeze innovation foreran and
facilitated the explosion in convenience foods. Back in these
mists, too, a Dr John H. Kellogg, running a sanatorium in
Battle Creek, Michigan, in 1894 invented the health-faddist's
bread substitute which his Seventh Day Adventist brother,
William K. a dozen years later began turning into a world
cornflakes neo-monopoly.

Ask the successors of John H. and William K. to parade
their own innovations, and the comparison is meagre. The
Kellogg companies are now in their seventh decade of making
millions from a public taste successfully identified while Queen

Victoria was still eating her morning porridge. Public taste changes far more reluctantly than the marketing apostles have persuaded businessmen to believe. Hence the latters' penchant for churning out unwanted new products in the hope that they will create their own demand.

The entrepreneur of true taste rarely makes this error. He recognizes a demand which is apparent or latent. Take the saga of the family which gave its name to yet another invented foodstuff: broccoli.

The inventor created one new taste. He also created a son who invented another – Cubby Broccoli, the collaborator of Harry Salzmann in putting James Bond on film. It took neither genius nor impeccable taste to see that Bond had screen appeal. The vogue for Ian Fleming's books had gathered momentum long before *Dr No* appeared. Broccoli and Salzmann sensed though, how the market should be exploited, which was in the obvious manner. For the laconic style, the exotic gadgetry, the Punch and Judy violence, the sexless sex, the cardboard villains, the artificial luxury – all the ingredients of the Bond package – were clearly visible in other pop entertainments of the TV era. The genius of the film-makers was to glimpse the obvious, to roll all the titillating bits into one professional package, and to continue on an ascending scale of expense, special effects and gimmickry. From *Dr No* via *Goldfinger* to *Diamonds Are Forever* the costs and the take soared upwards in step. By 1973 the combined scores for the Bond epics had topped $600 million.

That's better than broccoli any day. Often in these lucrative satisfactions of taste, the tin has been waiting around for somebody to open. Although the opener needs courage and initiative, he needs above all to share the taste: self-identification usually gives the entrepreneur his instinctive appreciation of the market's hungers – as in the hunger for sublimated sex, for transmogrified cheesecake, which existed in full, nubile glory before Hugh Hefner burst into gate-fold view.

In *Esquire*, the combination of good masculine living, pin-ups, jesting sexual innuendo and sexual frankness, sugared with excellent prose, had worked successfully for decades. But *Esquire*'s come-on girls, originally only painted, had a defect: however langorous their poses, their pudenda and nipples were more or (mostly) less covered. Hefner used the basic *Esquire* formula, plus techniques of nude photography no more advanced than those which naked calendar experts had employed for years, and published wholly nude nudes by the yard. He took *Esquire*'s sexual themes and suggestiveness and handled them with heavy-handed frankness.

Hefner added one special ingredient to this borrowed, improved concoction: an orgiastic, populist philosophy, every man his own Casanova, that bound the soup together. It's useless to argue that no man lives as *Playboy* suggests: Hefner does. With his philosophical outpourings, accessible maid-servants, pluperfect pads, personal Bunnified jet, round bed and millions, Hefner is the Playboy King made manifest.

Just as Henry Luce was the quintessential reader of *Time* and *Life*, so Hefner acts out the role of his own public. His achievement in strictly business terms ranks with Luce's triple hit of *Time*, *Fortune* and *Life*. At a time when publishers like *Life*'s were giving away subscriptions in their forlorn effort to attract advertising, Hefner founded a mass circulation magazine that made money from subscriptions alone, and then proceeded to establish a prime medium among advertisers who would once not have been seen dead in the company of non-breathing nudes.

The magazine cashed in on the sexual Walter Mitty in every man. The Playboy clubs gave middle-class Babbitts the key to a door of private enjoyment which had previously been reserved for the rich. The whole operation is, of course, a tease, another come-on: perfect for customers who fundamentally prefer teasing to reality.

Hefner's dream-world left room to his left for harder-nosed practitioners like Bob Guccione of *Penthouse*, whose customers like to drink their vicarious sex neat, and whose personal lifestyles dutifully reflect that preference. Both men long ago passed the millionaire stage in a magazine market which many had given up for dead. Helen Gurley Brown performed the same sex trick for a publication which was on its death-bed: *Cosmopolitan*.

The necessary skills to syndicate sex probably existed in defunct houses like Curtis Publishing. But the respectable magazine establishment missed, because of its respectability, the blatant information that human beings, male and female, are passionately interested in sex and that, for the best part of two decades, they have become less and less inhibited about expressing that interest, from Hanover to Grand Rapids, and from Oswego to Yokohama.

The obvious, because of their preconditioning, is what establishments miss. George Romney, a semi-failed politician, succeeded as a car manufacturer in the late 1950s by following abundant evidence of a switch in tastes: the $250 million collapse of the Edsel, and the sharp rise in sales of small imported cars, dismissed by Romney's rivals as a passing whim.

Possibly necessity was Romney's virtue, since American Motors had very few shots, and little cash, left in its locker at the time. Nonetheless, his assault, verbal and physical, on the "gas-guzzling dinosaurs" turned out by GM, Ford and Chrysler utterly transformed AMC's market position and Romney's own finances. Had AMC ever produced a series of excellent compact cars, miracles might indeed have happened. As things turned out, Romney's company was precursor rather than beneficiary of a compact, sub-compact and imported revolution that has greatly changed Detroit.

The attack on the gas-guzzlers undoubtedly sprang from deep Mormon convictions in Romney's own healthy-mind-in-healthy-body, up at six to play golf philosophy. In much the same way, the heady cocktail of sex, *schmaltz*, patriotic Americanism, violence, melodrama and wisecracks which poured forth from Hollywood in its golden age mirrored tastes of the mainly Jewish tycoons who gave birth to the industry and presided over its Arabian Nights accumulations of wealth, including their own. In movie mythology, these cold-blooded inhuman monsters ruthlessly plotted the exploitation of mass tastes. Monsters often they were: but the tastes which they exploited were their own. The whole history of mass exploitation revolves around the four ancient appetites — sex, food, drink, escape.

Of the four, drink has probably been the most reliable mint, a staple flood of riches through several family generations, and an easy opening for brand new talent. People need to eat more than they need alcohol. But the price competition in booze is less intense than in food: the need (real or apparent) to generate new products is less pressing and the outlets are happily more various.

Produce a new breakfast cereal, and you are stuck with the supermarkets and their avaricious price-cutting monopoly buyers. In contrast, booze flows in bars, clubs, homes, restaurants, trains, planes – and in consequence it takes a rare genius to go bust in booze. The longevity of Britain's brewing aristocracy or the "beerage", proves the point. It's a source of eternal wonder, given the small evidence of management skill shown by most beerage barons this century. The continuity of their American counterparts suffered severe interruption from Prohibition, although the leading legitimate (so to speak) bootleggers of that era were still up among the leading lights of hard liquor after the Second World War.

Muscling in on these long-running acts is no joke – but not impossible. Two Scotch whiskies cracked the critical US market open, stealing first and second places from the Distillers Company Ltd. (itself an amalgam of old Scotch families), entirely by emphasizing an attribute of taste.

Drinking palates world-wide were moving to lightness and dryness. But nobody had ever thought of blended Scotch whisky as something heavy until some unsung hero started the idea of the "light" Scotch. Whether those who flocked to Cutty Sark and J & B Rare could tell the difference, blindfold or with their eyes open, from any other Scotch is in grave doubt. But the magnificent results make the question and the doubt irrelevant.

The value of a successful brand of the hard stuff can be seen from, say, Arthur Bell, which owns a big whisky seller in Scotland and has made rapid headway in England. In 1972 the company turned in a profit of £3.1 million, which the stock market dutifully magnified into a value of £27 million. That gives some small idea of the wealth created by Cutty Sark for its proprietors, including two families which were selling wine in St. James's two hundred years ago, and by J & B which gets its initials from an equally ancient St. James's establishment, Justerini and Brooks.

The J & B family took the common step long ago of merging into another booze brigade, which merged into yet another, which was merged forcibly into a brewery, which was merged forcibly into a hotel and catering group. A curtailed version of this typical modern commercial saga removed the separateness of another invader of the booze families' secure world. A cider house, Showerings, of some antiquity itself, modernized its profits with a drink, unpleasing to all except its unaccountable millions of purchasers, which filled the gap between beer and spirits for those who wanted a short drink that was neither too strong nor too weak.

This champagne perry, sold as Babycham and advertised with a Disneyesque chamois cavorting amidst the bubbles, suited bar-room tastes so admirably that the Showering family made rapid millions. The personal stakes of three Showerings in Allied Breweries, the giant which originally bought them out, were worth some £8 million at the 1973 peak, with another £3 million in trusts. Purists can seek consolation from a cider firm which stuck to its apples, H. P. Bulmer; the vigorous life within its ancient vats, treated with management revitalization and marketing razzmatazz, lifted Bulmers' 1972 profits to £1.25 million, at which point the family company was worth £10 million.

A profitable clue lies in the renaissance of cider. If thousands, hundreds of thousands or millions of people insist on buying some product, or attending some entertainment – even if, according to the profit and loss account, death is at hand, there must be a fortune lying in that old taste mine waiting to be picked up. For example, the film box office smashes of all time have poured forth black ink at the very moment when the last rites were being uttered over the cinema, and have done so all over the world: in Hong Kong one Run Run Shaw and his brother make eastern Westerns and, says Run Run, "have hundreds of millions. Hong Kong or US Dollars – it doesn't matter."

The products (like *Love Story*) which create mass taste breakthroughs are often mysterious to more sophisticated palates. Sophisticates can't understand the world-wide enthusiasm for a sweetish, fizzy pink wine from Portugal called Mateus Rosé; they deplore the rush to view another saccharine cinematic confection like *The Sound of Music* which cost $7.6 million to make and made $72 million in the USA alone: they shudder at the names of Irving Wallace, Harold Robbins and Arthur Hailey (whose millions, and those of their publishers, have been made from another supposedly unlucrative art-form, the novel).

Possibly this explains why most mass tastes have been created by American men of the people, often from the populist South or Mid-West, in sagas like that of Kentucky Fried Chicken. The secret recipe of Colonel Harland D. Sanders enabled John Y. Brown to turn twenty of his executives into millionaires: his secretary made $3 million: Brown collected $35 million when he sold out, immortalizing his decision in the words "One day I asked myself: 'Is this all you're put on Earth for? To be a chicken man?' " (So, among other things, he promptly became a hamburger man instead.)

Coke, tomato ketchup, corn-flakes, hamburgers, instant coffee, standardized hotels, standardized restaurants, other franchized eating chains like KFC – all these inventions have crossed the USA and then the world on the simple strength of a mass taste simply satisfied on a simple formula with simple economics. But of all these invaluable simplicities, that of down-market taste comes first, and it is desperately hard for the up-market mind to master.

There is no other logical explanation for one major mystery of British commerce: the supermarket conundrum. Would-be millionaires on the right-hand side of the Atlantic have one advantage over the Americans on the left: the Europeans can copy US developments, whereas the Americans have to invent their own gold bricks. Most States-wide manifestations in mass marketing have crossed the ocean in force, none more obviously than the supermarket. Its economics were intrinsically superior to those of the individual grocery store, and the British in particular had been flocking into standardized chain stores of all kinds, from Woolworths downwards, for years.

The supermarket is part of an on-going social revolution which has endless financial ramifications. At first, supermarkets merely supplied staple goods at lower prices; but they rapidly moved on to the trade-up which has been the most basic modern evolution in taste and spending. Even Babycham, with its overtones (or undertones) of champagne, belongs in the game of making luxury tastes, in reality or in appearance, available to a panting public. Trading-up, fed by education and travel, feeds them in turn. Sometimes the elevation is vicarious: humdrum sex-lives trading-up mentally to Hefner's playgirls or Penthouse pets. Sometimes the process is real: the broiler revolution, changing roast and grilled chicken from middle-class treat to everybody's protein.

Old-line money has been among all these golden eggs: the Rockefellers for example, have a big stake in the broiler business. But, as usual, new men have been more tastefully conspicuous. John Eastwood is a perky Briton worth plenty of

301

millions, representing the proceeds of nine hundred thousand broilers a week, plus four-and-a-half million laying hens: he claims that this total makes him the largest producer of protein on two feet, not excluding the beef barons of Texas and the lords of the Argentine pampas.

Those who fail to trade-up, by and large, slip slowly down. A decade ago F. W. Woolworth, whose British chain is the main source of its profits, did a third more turnover than Marks & Spencer. The latter increased its quality, prices and range, and repeated in food the process of integrated retailing and production begun in textiles. In contrast, Woolworths remained solidly, stolidly and stupidly stuck down market. After ten years of this inertia, Woolworth's relative turnover had fallen to two thirds of its British rivals'.

The fact of social change is as obvious as the eternal determinants of taste: trading-up has been as clear as the fact that human beings have a continuing yen for sex. The evidence moreover, is omnipresent, blasted out in the pop culture of the day. And it's from the pop pastures that taste changes are picked up, pocketed and turned into quick cash by the left-hand men and women of all modern business, the advertising agents.

When Mary Wells put Braniff airliners into coats of many colours, she reflected at some removes the fact that people now use colour and notice colour far more freely. The pre-Braniff sameness of air travel reflected not only the similarity of the hardware, the jetliners, but the sameness of the tough, self-made flying men who built the big airlines and stamped their marks all over them – aviation pioneers like C. R. Smith of American Airlines or Juan Trippe of Pan American. In the Mary Wells era, and in her realization, the tastes of these old men, like their management styles, were obsolescent: like so many prop-driven airliners.

When Bill Bernbach, in his campaigns for Volkswagen and Avis, plugged the underdog theme, he consciously or subconsciously reflected another social change: the death of the leadership idea, the realization, in the era of the drop-out, that you don't have to try to be first: it's a matter of choice. The ad-makers have an advantage in spotting trends. They live in a world of words, pictures, music and media, and they automatically pick up its coloration: instantaneously the new images and hard-won visions of artists get stolen for the artwork used in ads; Pop artists, in fact, sometimes seemed to be in a race with their own material.

The sharper pencils on Madison Avenue or its European equivalents are quick enough in all conscience. But the admen are still appreciably slower than those who earn their bread in Pop itself. Every member of the Beatles ranks as a millionaire, not on the strength of past earnings, but from the future income of a group that hasn't performed together since 1969. This calculation doesn't count their loot as individuals, before and since parting.

The possibility of making a Pop mint has waxed exponentially with the international market in records and tapes, which has long since passed $3,000 million a year. The astute singer or promoter need only corner one thousandth of that to be Beatle-rich: a ten thousandth has him or her well on the way. The odds in the Pop stars' favour are actually better than that long shot. One in twenty-five records has a chance of survival: if one out of twenty-five survivors hits some kind of jackpot, the odds become one in 625. Clearly, this is one of those ideal scenes where taste plus initiative can equal a million without the uncomfortable extra ingredient of capital.

Accumulations worthy of a major industrialist have consequently always dignified the Pop scene, from Rudy Vallee via Crosby and Sinatra to Presley. In the mid-1960s Elvis was earning a hot $5 million a year, and sending teenagers into screaming hysteria from pole to pole. In the 1970s, however, the number of Elvis-style fortunes has plainly expanded: expansion was actually inevitable, since pop singers have developed an irresistible tendency to come in multiples.

There have been hit groups before. But the Inkspots and the Andrews Sisters never had it so rich as the Beatles, Stones, Slade or even the wholly synthetic Monkees, and their various, numerous Svengalis. Fragmentation has been facilitated by an enormously enlarged market. Consequently the big music companies, while fat enough by most standards, have lost any advantage over the small man; and the latter has been quick to seize his golden discs.

Lou Adler, former manager of the Mamas and the Papas, who sold one record company to ABC for $3 million, founded another whose assets include an album which made $5 million on a $400,000 investment. Adler also earned from *Time* magazine an oddly uplifting accolade: "Lincolnesque in bearing and probity". Since Adler also had houses in Malibu, Bel Air and Jamaica, Britt Ekland, bell-bottoms and Jesus sandals, things have plainly changed since Abe was a boy.

Another measurable take is that of Ahmet Ertugen, who sold Atlantic Records for $18 million. Ertugen has to his credit Sonny and Cher, Otis Redding, Roberta Flack, Aretha Franklin and all four of the Crosby, Stills, Nash and Young combine. He rejoices in the title of Pop Sultan and, like Abraham Lincoln Adler, collects residences: a Long Island estate and a Manhattan town house, which boasts a floor apiece, no less, for the bedroom and living room respectively.

Society reserves special flavours for those who put cherries in its cocktails. Pop entertainment wins these cash prizes because of the magnitude of its audiences. Each attendee pays a modest fee for his cherry; multiply that fee by the millions and you have a whole orchard, created where nothing grew before. In the higher reaches of faddery, although various priests and priestesses of fashion, from Dior to Quant, have borne plentiful financial fruit, their deployment of taste has lower turnover attached: the mass markets, as Helena Rubinstein knew, make more money from making less tasteful products.

But the same rules apply both high and low. First, follow your own taste: that applies anywhere. Second, choose a soft spot where demand is already heavy or where existing suppliers are panting behind the pace of unmistakable change. Third, always aim for a sector of heavy spending: Wham-O Manufacturing, the hulahoop hot shop, or Botany Industries, which sold $15 million of its Fuzzy Foot fun rugs, needed only a tiny proportion of toy or floor covering expenditure to make fortunes.

But if you are selling golden eagles instead of goldfish, you need the whole world market to make a living: and any such effort shows extremely poor taste – financially speaking.

THE ERROR OF IMITATION

or

Anything You Can Do I Can't Do Better

Containing the doomed efforts of three mightily rich men to make money from an automobile market that belonged securely to other men: and the reason why cobblers who don't stick to their lasts sometimes get cobbled themselves.

The rich man's freedom to move how and where he likes with his loot is snare and delusion as well as opportunity: not least because so many less well equipped mortals importune him to buy a slice of their real or imagined action. Tycoons are as capable as corpocrats of pursuing an inane ambition to the bitter end: and the danger sign, in both cases, often appears in one mantrap – the lust for somebody's else's money-making market.

When this passion takes over, the man's comptroller had etter get used to signing cheques. The phenomenon occurred when Harry Ferguson, the tractor genius, decided that he could build a superior automotive transmission. So he could, but the effort took so many years that Ferguson died before the work was completed: even then, the cost of his system was so high in relation to its benefits that only one luxury car adopted the gadget, and not to much effect, either.

In his tractor system, Ferguson performed some tricks that couldn't be done at all previously, and performed others at much lower cost than the competition. But his automotive devices performed the same stunts only a little better – and far more expensively. That, as his own experience should have taught him, is no way to make money.

The identical phenomenon occurred when Henry J. Kaiser, supreme as a shipbuilder, thought that he could out-do Henry Ford in the self-same automobile market. The Kaiser car is now a historical curiosity, more curious even than Henry Ford II's Edsel. The wisest move which Henry J. made in this connection was to get out before the Henry J. car ruined the family altogether.

Kaiser was quite right about the total market: by 1949 car production in the USA had reached 5.1 million, finally passing the old pre-Crash record of twenty years before. Where the shipbuilder went wrong was in assuming that the American car buyer was as simple and direct in taste as a purchaser of Liberty ships.

Possibly there is some fatal seduction about the automobile, for not only Ferguson and Kaiser succumbed to this lure. Donald Lear got on a faster and happier transportation bandwagon with passenger jets selling at $750,000 or more per throw. Then he poured some of the mint made from executive aircraft into the steam car – a concept that went out while the Model T was enjoying its heyday.

These three men, though rich with the spoils of industries in which they had deployed revolutionary concepts, were not wealthy enough (because no individual could be) to attack successfully the billions in resources and fixed assets of the car makers. Even if they could have designed a supremely better car (which they couldn't, although it doesn't sound too hard) they could not also have financed the mass production and distribution without which a mass market is by definition impossible.

The notion of becoming a second Henry Ford (or, since there is a second, a third) is laughable: in fact, old auto families have been dropping out at a time when nobody much is dropping in. The Rootes males passed on their pains to Chrysler in Britain: Studebaker-Packard vanished from the US scene: on the Continent mergers have radically altered the motor map.

The truly lush pastures for big diversifiers are different in every respect. They don't demand great aggregations of capital: they are not dominated by a handful of well-founded giants: and they don't depend on the build-up of expensive consumer franchises. But the error which leads millionaires to go over such perilous commercial waterfalls in a barrel is the

306

sublime conviction that, whatever the business sport being played, they can do it better.

The key to the car passion is not only that cars bring out the kid in everybody; not even solely the desire to score off a man who gives you as much pain as the Fords gave Ferguson when they pinched his tractor designs. Another factor is that all drivers think, in their heart of hearts, that they could produce a better car — a thought possibly inspired by the irritating defects of their own machines.

But the well-shod individual, like the stacked company, can only reap a wild harvest from a market where the exploitation or the economics are wrong, as in the case of the over-priced deaf aids spotted by Commander McDonald of Zenith. While corporate leviathans have as many defects as leopards have spots, and change them about as often, these faults seldom extend to the basic products from which, over long years, their managers have earned their loaves of bread, jugs of wine and family comforts.

The legendary Canadian financier E. P. Taylor, with interests extending from the Argus giant, owner of juicy stakes in companies like Massey-Ferguson, to succulent personal interests in the Bahamas sun, tackled the British brewers head on by buying up first one small chain of pubs and breweries, then another. Fuddy-duddy though they were, the beer barons could taste a threat: they closed ranks, forced up the prices of independent breweries, mopped up most of them, entered into mergers and trading agreements that would have given the US anti-trust authorities heart failure — and thus saw to it that Taylor, his thirst quickly slaked, in effect sold out and retired from the scene for easier game.

Even the most able of businessmen, sooner or later, finds something that he can't do better than somebody else; that he even does worse. That, in a nutshell is what happened to the conglomerate millionaires. Their collective ability was probably above average: a finer body of men never fiddled an earnings statement. Their collective activity was the enhancement of personal fortunes by the accumulation of corporate interests, and their resale, effectively by issues of stock to the public.

The correct type of accumulation was worth so much to the conglomerate merchants that, after one now notorious instance, ITT's purchase of the abundant millions of Hartford

Fire & Life, it paid the bank of Lazard Frères a million dollar finder's fee. But most of the conglomerators over-bought, or bought bad companies, or took on more than their management abilities (such as they were) could cover.

Not that they recognized the fact. One bravado-rich fellow even stated, after a 38% earnings fall on a 4.3% sales increase, that "our performance last year was a positive answer to those who question the viability of the conglomerate form of business enterprise." That was the unsinkable Charlie Bluhdorn of Gulf + Western.

Martin Stone bought National Screw for his Monogram Industries: both purchase and new parent sank deep into losses. "The problems of modernizing a long-neglected company," admitted Stone, "are almost overpowering, the costs staggering."

Possibly the ghastliest example of all was the effort of Boise Cascade to turn itself into the "General Motors of the timber-products industry". Its executives had freedom to buy practically any operation that bore any relation, however far-fetched, to their traditional wooden business. In the process they popped $600,000 into a construction company for minority housing back in 1967. Aggressive anything-you-can-do-I-can-do-better management rapidly turned that modest investment into a $37 million write-off, which contributed mightily to writing off the entire Boise Cascade effort at magical self-transformation.

The truth is that there is something to be said for one-product, one-market companies: that they are often blazing successes. But however fabulous its past, however staggering its present profitability, the one-product company is always suspect, on the apparently sound theory that it takes only one market to turn sour, or one powerful competitor to muscle in for the hot profits to turn to ashes and the soaring growth to turn to travail.

Yet the one-product-bad, many-markets-good theory is contradicted by the clear fact that the best investments of our time, or anybody else's times, also tend to be one-product. In 1959–69, when the conglomerates were recording their crazy growth patterns, seven mainly single-market sagas made up the rest of the top ten for earnings per share growth taken from *Fortune*'s top five hundred US companies.

The happy seven were Control Data (computers), Xerox,

National Can (containers), American Petrofina (oil), Automation Industries (electronics), even a brewer (Pabst), and Monfort of Colorado: an easy family company, the biggest in beef, Monfort had made its proprietors millionaires thirty times over, although its liberal-minded boss used to take only a $53,000 salary "because that's all I need". As for return on shareholders' equity that year, the top two also fell into the suspect category: Skyline (mobile homes) and Avon Products (door-to-door cosmetics).

Much the same pattern is true of business in Britain and on the Continent, where whopping fortunes have been made by men who strayed little or not at all from lines like chocolate (Ludwig), mail order (Quandt), ball-points (Bich), media (Springer). Of thirty-nine new multi-millionaires counted by *Fortune* in September 1973, and ranging in riches from $50 million to $750 million, only a small handful were in varied lines of business and the variation was mostly into real estate. Otherwise, from the richest (petfood prince Leonard N. Stern) to the poorest (the Tropicana tycoon of orange juice, Anthony T. Rossi) these well-shod winners won big at one principal game.

By and large then, the most successful financial cobblers stick to their lasts and the most ruinous course possible is to ruin the one you have in pursuit of other lasts you don't need. The inviolable maxim applies: never embark on a diversified activity if its prosecution (never mind its possible failure) will harm the existing golden eggs – and Mother Goose, for that matter.

Magnavox was once an enviable one-product company, built over thirty brilliant years of one-market application by Fred Freimann, who died in 1968. But Freimann's successors, heirs to a superb TV distribution system that fed directly into the company's own dealers, were worried, even as the conglomerates cracked asunder, about their own dependence on their single market.

They began to buy – into furniture, mobile home components, musical instruments. They developed new devices in commercial navigation equipment, anti-skid braking, facsimile (the latter lost a million year in year out, culminating in a $3.1 million black eye). But all this time, back at the ranch, Magnavox had made a crucial error in the market from which it was so anxious to get loose. The company didn't reckon that consumers wanted the new-fangled solid state TVs.

Magnavox found itself floundering far behind a field of competitors. In 1972 it contrived to sell 36% fewer sets than it had four years previously, when, in its one-market innocence, the company had earned 29.5% on its stockholders' equity. Ah, yes, Freimann's successors could (and probably do) argue: but, thanks to our inspired policy of diversification, TV now represents only a third of Magnavox sales; think how dreadfully we would have fared if Magnavox were living by TV alone – at least we made a profit in 1972, even if it was the lowest since 1964.

The short answer to such apologia, is that maybe, if Magnavox had kept its eye on the screen, the solid state shambles would never have occurred. If you are simultaneously fussing over home furnishings and looking for other new marbles, there must be less attention to spare for the business in which, by concentrating, you have genuinely been able to do anything anybody else could do – and do it better. And there is surely a moral in the quote from a Magnavox executive, printed in *Business Week*, about Freimann's successor as president – "fundamentally a financial man," who "doesn't pretend to be a marketing man, and certainly not an engineer."

There you have it: the key to business success, as we have seen, is always in feel for the operation on which the attack is based. In the great majority of cases, it takes men who have a basic talent in one market, in one style of operation, sometimes in only one product. These men are often market geniuses: occasionally engineers of brilliance: never (unless money is their product) are they fundamentally financiers.

The Ronson Corporation, like so many others, was founded by an inventor who deployed substantial technical genius. The grandson who led this creation into the humiliation of a takeover bid from some disrespectful Italians was an anything-you-can-do merchant. Faced by expiring patents on Ronson's lighters and by Japanese competition, Louis V. Aronson II put little electric motors on virtually everything in the home, from toothbrushes and carving knives to shavers and blenders. Despite all these efforts, not to mention other ventures which ate more cash than they provided, lighters still remained Ronson's staple: and the new throwaway lighters thus loomed as a serious threat. And alas, Ronson's diversifying caused major stress and slaughter in the executive ranks. Profits had slumped from $7.64 million in 1967 to $1.34 million. Even the Aronson stake, like the family's business ability, had been eroded over time, dropping away to 9%.

Never overestimate your general business powers because you have apparently been a screaming success in one business: and never conclude, either, that, even in that one business, you have all the cards and always play them correctly. The unfair advantage of a Henry Kaiser, Harry Ferguson or Donald Lear, fortunately for them, is that they can afford their foibles. The Mafia, it turned out, ran Las Vegas more efficiently than Howard Hughes. But Hughes has always been fundamentally a hardware man: even his TWA involvement sprang from a technical fascination with aeroplanes.

Las Vegas, in contrast, is nothing but a service industry with no equipment more technical than one-arm bandits and roulette wheels and their technology isn't fascinating to anybody, unless they are being fixed. So, Hughes chose the wrong home for his TWA proceeds. The richer the rake, true, the less likely his progress is to be critical: but, even so, the tragedy is easily avoided by fearless answer to a frank question. What, if anything, makes you/me think you/I can do better?

THE REWARDS OF VIRTUE

or

If You Can't Be Careful, Be Good

A recipe to regain high moral standing which has never been known to fail in the most desperate cases of ill-gotten gains ... and which starts with the recognition that all great gains, by virtue of their greatness alone, are to a true extent gotten ill.

There are no golden rules for achieving the seven-digit nirvana; but there are golden rules, guiding principles, for use on the way up, while on top, and, if the best comes to the worst, on the way down. Like every set of rules compiled since the Ten Commandments, every item isn't relevant on every occasion or to every worshipper: the man or woman who covets his neighbour's ox (or Boeing 727) may have no use whatsoever for adultery.

But the charm of rules is that they can be broken, every single one of them, and the breaker can still win. Making money, after all, is a competitive sport: and success in competition doesn't depend on your observation of precept: it depends on whether you outscore the competition.

It may help to achieve this result by sandbagging the poor fellow, putting anti-pep dope in his tea, taking pep dope yourself, lining his track shoes with lead, tripping him, and so forth. But cheating isn't necessary, even if many millions have been made by cheats. The rich in fact divide into three categories: those who would trample over their grandmothers on any pretext, because that is their horrible nature: those who, faced with the choice of losing money or grandma, would kiss the old lady a tender goodbye: those who would honour their grandmother in any circumstances, no matter what the cost.

The general view of economic history is that most million-aires fit into the middle category: they behave decently, or no more indecently than the mass of mortals, unless pushed, when no holds are barred. A small but significant number are natural grandma-tramplers: and a tiny minority are upright, benevolent and honourable at all times.

Virtue in this sense has nothing to do with good works: all the Rockefeller benefactions can no more wash away the memory of the old boy's sins than the perfume of Araby could cleanse the hands of Lady Macbeth. Many godly religious sects have been handsomely financed by royal flushes of fortune – notably in Texas – but the common assumption is that these benefactions are more often expiations for past offences committed in the service of Mammon, than expressions of great goodness.

It's the same with noble motives: they do not invariably express noble natures. John Spedan Lewis, a second generation genius who transformed his family department store inheritance, handed over control of his business to all the employees under a unique partnership scheme. True, the Lewis family was inordinately rich by this time – but Lewis also gave the staff his Longstock Park mansion, complete with contents, plus a handsome riverside estate for their partnerly recreation.

Those bald facts might imply that Lewis was a saint among men, let alone millionaires. In truth, however, for all his partnership ideals, Lewis was a highly autocratic, high-handed ruler who, after surrendering control, tended to regret the surrender. Admonitions to his successors would appear embarrassingly in the partnership magazine, despatched from his self-styled "burrow in Longstock Park" – and in Lewis' version of partnership it has always been clear that, to paraphrase Orwell, some partners are very much more equal than others. Generosity with material goods is not the same as a generous attitude to power.

Much the same tale can be told of another great social reformer, who was indifferent to personal wealth: Gottlieb Duttweiler, the brave Swiss who spotted that big companies were ganging up on the customer by charging unnecessarily high prices; Dutti undercut the over-chargers by selling first from vans, then from his chain of Migros outlets. Migros was a co-operative, owned by its grateful customers in Switzerland, or so it was supposed by those who had not studied the Migros constitution. The set-up left Dutti and his family a controlling interest, special rights and effective power for as long as they cared to exercise it – which in Dutti's case was until death did him part.

There is the case of the greatest banker ever to bounce a cheque, A. P. Giannini, who steadfastly refused to make his family super-rich from his building of the Bank of America; and there is that of the Tatas in India, whose former wealth is vested in charitable foundations, but who still rule the east's biggest private industrial empire with iron rods.

The cynical view (and cynics have a saving habit of being right) is that capital accumulation in the private sector plays the same role as tax in the public sector – it provides the means by which the mighty and their minions exercise their power. Indeed, the millionaire's millions, no less than the Revenue's riches, represent a tax levied involuntarily from the citizenry.

The citizen contemplating a war in Vietnam knows that the finance came from him and his fellows; contemplating the Bar Harbour estate of the Rockefellers, the sizeable choice acreages of Europe owned by the Rothschilds, or the whopping incomes of the Japanese industrialists, the citizen never thinks that this money came from exactly the same source as the tax dollar: from a percentage of the earnings of the masses. (Not to dwell on the fact that sometimes the private dollars and the tax dollars are one and the same, transferred to the private sector from the public by the beneficence or corruption of the politicians.)

In public life, it was long ago recognized that politicians have to be kept under constant scrutiny and ultimate control if they are not to abuse their power. That process works imperfectly; but the devices for controlling malefactors of great wealth, in Teddy Roosevelt's phrase, are less powerful to start with, are less numerous than the political restraints and work no more effectively.

This fact should intensify the pressure on the financially potent to exercise restraint on themselves – although nobody can expect them to behave in those ways considered normal by people who think themselves normal.

The rich begin by being exceptional, original, unusual, eccentric in varying degrees and styles. Their differences start them on their way, and the rush of power to their purses

314

accentuates their differentiated traits. But to all the rich one law applies: if they have to count the money, pound by pound, dollar by dollar, something is wrong, somewhere – a clerk in the counting house is running away with the loot, or an investment is haemorrhaging or Midas himself has mislaid his touch. And the sensation that something, somewhere is awry must never be ignored – like a pain in the abdomen, it's nature's warning, not to be ignored.

The messages of nature are a millionaire's most valuable communications. Few fortunes could have been created without a successful hunch, a display of divine intuition. Hunch is not luck, however lucky a hunch may seem. Instead, the computer in the skull has run through a whole series of complicated routines, operational research sums, market research equations, multiple regression analyses, discounted cash flow calculations, opportunity costings, decision trees complete with probability factors. All these mathematical marvels have flashed through the brain's maze of electro-chemical circuits with speed so dazzling that the computer's owner himself is unaware of the brilliant series of algebraic assessments which lead him to express a hunch or "gut-feeling".

To ignore this highly sophisticated machine is a folly – akin to that of the owners of a computer, programmed to play the stock market, who refused to believe the thing when it resolutely refused to buy a single stock. "Computer," said they to it, "there must be something you want to buy." It thought again, and still said no. "Computer," they sadly observed, "you must have made a mistake somewhere. We're going to have to override you." The market promptly went into a flat spin, vindicating the computer and mortifying its masters.

The lesson, which applies to millionaires and non-millionaires alike, is to heed your computer: it will even obligingly provide extra warnings, not flashing lights, but physical symptoms (a tightening sensation in the stomach, tingling of the scalp, pulsations in the stomach, commotions in the bowels). These messages from inner space mean that your computer has evaluated whatever asininity you propose to undertake and found it bad.

The warnings seldom come from the conscience. Only the moral have moral qualms – the immoral or amoral, like the denizens of Richard Nixon's White House, believe self-righteously that their ends (self-evidently right) justify their means. There's no argument on this point: the virtuous course (like not stabbing some unsuspecting partner between the clavicles) is always clear, and virtue should always be pursued, even if it costs money. After all, few sensations are more pleasant or enduring than the odour of true sanctity: it's worth every penny.

As a bonus, bear in mind that although virtue is not its own reward, the wages of sin are sometimes death. Grave misdemeanours (as Bernie Cornfeld, *et al*, must have reflected) frequently have grave consequences. For every Rockefeller I who escapes scot-free with his moral crimes, there is a Krupp III who reaps the harvest of his ancestor's misdeeds. Admittedly, finding a fault-free tycoon appears to be only slightly easier than hunting through a haystack for that recalcitrant needle.

Two separate enquiries into the iniquities of wealth (*The Rich and the Super-Rich* and *America, Inc*) each came up with only one candidate for goodness and pelf combined: the same man, T. R. Danforth of Ralston Purina. All that this paucity of saintly candidates implies is that, in making money, as in most areas of achievement, idols have not feet, but entire lower limbs of clay.

Goodness is a private matter. What is known about Danforth is not the whole picture; maybe the entirety would reinforce the good image, maybe not. The good that men do lives after them; the evil is oft interred with their bones. If evil, or quasi-evil, does litter your path, however, the same rule applies as to any other vice: don't carry it to excess. If you must cheat somebody, for instance, don't try to cheat the same man or men again; next time round, they may be ready.

It pays, in any event, to be careful whom you pick to cheat, out-bargain or battle with. Remember the natural law that money flows upwards from the weak to the strong, from the many to the few, from the poor to the rich. It is flying in the face of nature to tangle with a richer tycoon. (A contest with a corporation, as we have seen time and time again, is a different matter. The odds are on David's side because, in all probability, he is both richer and craftier than the paid servants of Goliath.) The plain millionaire who seeks advantage from dealing with a fancy multi-millionaire needs a large insurance policy.

Not only does the richer man have more resources: the chances are that he arrived at his higher status by deploying greater wiliness and garnering greater bargaining skills along his path. Anyway, he has an inherent advantage. By definition, the sum at stake is more important to the smaller man, which makes him more eager to consummate the deal. In that over-eagerness, he is apt to overpay. Far better to stay on the top side.

Keeping the top slice is also highly advisable. Common Millionaires derive their wealth from equity interests. Dilution of that equity – that is, reducing the proportion of profits or assets to which it is entitled – is only justified if compensated for by a nourishing increase in capital worth. But the most tempting form of dilution is rarely justified: and that's the ancient game of sending bad money after good. If a venture blasts off rapidly and then requires further infusion of capital, the sound course is to raise the money from some friendly neighbourhood banker. The return on equity must fall sharply if the millionaire dips into his own resources. Cutting others in on the game is always to be encouraged so long as that first or top slice grows thicker and fatter as a result.

If you are predominantly interested in the money rather than the business, moreover, it makes no sense to maintain any stake higher than respectability demands. You can reduce a controlling interest to 20% before anybody smells either a rat or a sinking ship. A high stock rating should always be cashed in by a cash addict, for the simple reason that what goes up must come down, and always does.

Recognition of that law of financial gravity demands the virtue of humility, which is the essential element in goodness – and one that goes against the driving urge. So the driven man should propel himself to as lofty a height as possible while the propulsion works: he can then more easily withstand a terrible fall. The megalomaniac John H. Patterson of National Cash Register was a loony who insisted on his minions chewing each mouthful thirty-two times, who closed down his Dayton plants entirely to teach the city fathers a lesson, and who absented himself for two years in Europe – all without destroying the cash-generating power of a mighty business. His successors, with not a smidgen of mania between them, did more harm by the mistakes in computery and product development that wiped out NCR's profits in

1972: the moral there is that mad inspiration beats dull honesty every time.

For Patterson was also a notable breaker of laws. It's easier for the rich and powerful to offend against statute, not only because the legal authorities are more reluctant to proceed against plutocrats than pickpockets, but also because the rich, and the rich company, can afford rich lawyers; and because the laws which the wealthy break are often so complex that it takes squads of lawyers several years to work their way through the maze (a tangle made more impenetrable still by the tendency of the rich and their legal eagles to complicate the simplest transactions).

After Calouste Gulbenkian's 5% deal with his partners in Iraq's oilfields had been re-written, one of the lawyers remarked that these contracts could never be the subject of litigation, because nobody would ever be able to understand them. The labyrinth in which financial minotaurs like Bernie Cornfeld lie in wait for their prey similarly appeals to the labyrinthine mind, and is the final defence of the ungodly. But some brave Theseus will wend his way through in the end: and it is a matter of historical fact that, by and large, the criminal millionaire (or for that matter the millionaire criminal) although he may die in luxury, and honours, often does suffer some blow or fate that punishes his sins like a Capone imprisoned for tax evasion and dying of syphilis, or a Buggsy Siegel bullet-holed by his pals.

This Calvinist-sounding truth has morals as well as morality on its side. He who already has millions no longer has any excuse for immorality: even the usual badness. He can afford to be good, which doesn't mean donating wealth to charity, still less to tax-dodging charitable foundations. It means following strict standards of decency — and that demands the hardest self-sacrifice of all, which is for the human leopard to change his spots.

One tycoon, caught in a mess of deceitful accounting by his bright young men, was bewailing his bad luck to a business associate — such a mess had entangled him before, he moaned, referring to a well-known incident a few years back in which he had been widely castigated as a crook. His version of the old story utterly convinced his hearer: as the tycoon reasonably argued, he was over sixty and very rich — why on earth would he have engaged in any personal skulduggery?

The true answer was simple: he did, just because he didn't need to. The honest crook, so to speak, lies and cheats because he must, and at the time (let alone in hindsight) can't tell the difference between fact and fiction. In this case, not only had the tycoon in the first place been guilty as charged (or not charged – the police stayed clear) but was re-enacting a very similar scenario at the time of his apologia.

Many leopards need a professional spot-changer or watcher in their employ. As a generalization, a master is only as good as his best servant: the quality of a man's nearest and dearest associate is an excellent guide to his own true stature. If the deputy, partner or sidekick is made of clay, so, more often than not, are the master's feet.

This is an uncommonly useful fact; so long as the master can maintain objectivity about those around him, he can, by applying this test, derive an objective judgement about himself. Unfortunately, the self-deceptive mechanism comes into play. Surrounded by ninnies, the maestro convinces himself that his staff are made up of every genius known to the business world. They naturally demonstrate that true and fine talent by hanging on to his every word and behest.

The ultra-rich can be excused for living in a dream world, since so much of their life story is in itself of dreamlike quality. The billionaire H. L. Hunt once said that "there are times when I wish I would wake up stone-broke. It would be a great adventure to see how good I was, to see if I could create lots of wealth again." This, of course, was wishful thinking of the woolliest kind: the process which took him from fifty bucks in 1921 to a couple of billion three decades later proved nothing about his "goodness" in any context other than oil.

But the story, like all get-rich tales, is a true adventure, and a true-life one. You could excuse the old cuss for saying, in effect, that he wanted to live so rewarding a life all over again. And, in his use of the word good, he put his oil-stained finger on a vital clue: that, in addition to human decency, the rich can afford high professional standards.

By and large, the millionaire has some professional talent which is incomparably superior to that of his fellows. This talent is the horse he rides to the winning post. To develop this star talent fully, and surround it with the most able supporting cast money can buy, is a relatively dignified pastime: and one which has the concomitant virtue of defending a man's fortune. It's not asking much to demand that the man be good at his job and insist that others be equally proficient at theirs.

In this he will differ from one not untypical monster who, in addition to forcing an audience of 140 to listen to a two-day masterly monologue, would sabotage anybody else's ideas as soon as he heard about them – in order to prove that he was indispensable. Very few fortune-makers are: but even those who are possessed of rare genius must recognize that, if man doesn't dispense with them, God certainly will – at least from this earth.

Until that event, certain moral precepts will guide the feet more safely to their destination, material as well as spiritual. If you are happy being private, count your blessings: not your hypothetical unmade public millions. If you can't manage by yourself, buy somebody who can. If you've made money by fooling all of the people, stop it before some of them find out. If you're telling lies to others, tell the truth to yourself. If you succeed by doing less badly than others, don't kid yourself that you've triumphed by doing much better. If you must buy other businesses, run the many as carefully as the few or the one. If you maintain a complex structure, for tax, divorce or other reasons, make sure that at least you understand it. If you diversify, keep your eye on the real ball and the main chance. If you must bet, pick certainties. If you back others, don't pick a simulacrum of your younger self, or anybody else, if your choice is not governed by expertise and experience.

If you borrow, borrow big – and with security. If you lend, lend proportionately small – and with double security. If you work for a company, remember that feathering the corporate nest is the honest way of feathering your own. If dealing, don't steal. If you start small, preserve your little virtues. If you put your hand in the public purse, do so legitimately: graft is criminal. If you are lucky, light a candle. If you are dealing with a fat corporation, light two candles.

If you are paying too much tax, change your tax adviser. If you have an invention, sell it reluctantly – and dearly. If you are selling, don't cheat. If you can make things better, go on doing it. If you know what people want, give it to them. If your personal life is complex, put plenty in the piggybank: two Humble Oil beneficiaries, Mrs. Cecil Blaffer Hudson and Bobo Rockefeller, collected nearly $13 million between them as they competed for the world record divorce settlement.

320

All these are laws of the obvious. But making gigantic fortunes is mostly nothing but the exploitation of the obvious – an obvious so glaring that nobody else has noticed, or known how to exploit. The discovery must be obvious because, unless the truth is large, it will never yield the gains which will add up to a net worth of suitable size. Countless big fortunes have arisen through standing self-evident propositions, received truths, on their heads – including the ancient saw, "if your idea's so good, why isn't anybody else doing it?"

The answer is that one reason why the idea is so good is exactly because nobody else has caught on. What the financially-blind use as an excuse for their lack of vision, the long-sighted employ as a radio telescope. There are, true, examples of fortunes made by indulging in some general, obvious passion. All that proves is that making money proves nothing.

The fact adds to the questions asked down the centuries by religious leaders and philosophers, by political thinkers like Veblen and, above all, Marx: questions that will never go away, because they have no answer. To put them at their simplest, these permanent doubts, partly moral, partly rational, partly egalitarian, can be expressed in one huge query: why does one man possess so much, while another has so little?

Because the unanswerable questions of ownership, inheritance, control, accountability and so on are never tackled (and perhaps never can be), society is uneasily divided between fascination by fortunes and guilty resentment of the rich. But any student of the wealthy, and of the means by which they acquired their wealth, must conclude that there is no rational relationship between their riches and their achievement: the one is wildly disproportionate to the other. This statement of fact carries inevitable connotations of disapproval. It is also the reason (as a few of the rich have had the grace to recognize) behind the powerful truth that "from him to whom much is given, much shall be required". For it is equally true that, to him to whom much is given, too much is given.

BIBLIOGRAPHY

It would not have been possible to write this book without many sources, including several publications: notably the *Financial Times*, *Time*, *Fortune*, the *Wall Street Journal*, *Management Today*, *Business Week*. But the following books, to whose authors I am eternally grateful, are indispensable to anybody wishing to research the history of wealth in our times.

For the United States, past and present:
America, Inc., Morton Mintz and Jerry S. Cohen, Dial Press
The American Idea of Success, Richard M. Huber, McGraw Hill
History of the Great American Fortunes, Gustavus Myers, Modern Library
The Robber Barons, Matthew Josephson, Eyre & Spottiswoode
Only Yesterday, Frederick Lewis Allen, Harper
The Rich and the Super-Rich, Ferdinand Lundberg, Lyle Stuart

For the glories of recent British capitalism:
Bid for Power, George Bull and Anthony Vice, Elek
Men and Money, Paul Ferris, Penguin
The Property Boom, Oliver Marriott, Hamish Hamilton

For the inside story on scandals:
Do You Sincerely Want to Be Rich?, Raw, Page and Hodgson, André Deutsch
The Great Salad Oil Swindle, Norman C. Miller, Gollancz
Insull, Forrest McDonald, Child

For insight into Wall Street:
The Seven Fat Years, John Brooks, Gollancz
The Great Crash, J. K. Galbraith, Hamish Hamilton
The Money Game, Adam Smith, Michael Joseph
Supermoney, Adam Smith, Michael Joseph

For tales of the rich:
The Rothschilds, Frederick Morton, Secker & Warburg
Duveen, S. N. Behrman, Gollancz
Onassis, Willi Frischauer, Bodley Head
The Proud Possessors, Aline B. Saarinen, Weidenfeld & Nicolson
Ford, Booton Herndon, Cassell
The Super-Americans, John Bainbridge, Gollancz

Pantaraxia, Nubar Gulbenkian, Hutchinson
Think, William Rodgers, Weidenfeld & Nicolson

For hints on the disposal of loot:
Gambling, Alan Wykes, Spring Books
The Big Spenders, Lucius Beebe, Hutchinson

For general enlightenment:
How to Be a Successful Executive, J. Paul Getty, W. H. Allen
The Gnomes of Zurich, T. R. Feltenbach, Leslie Frewin
The Sources of Invention, Jewkes, Sawers, Stillerman, Macmillan
Up the Organization, Robert Townsend, Michael Joseph

INDEX

326

328

331